Contemporary Issues in International Business and Entrepreneurship

Contemporary Issues in International Business and Entrepreneurship

Edited by

Lasse Torkkeli

Cambridge Scholars
Publishing

Contemporary Issues in International Business and Entrepreneurship

Edited by Lasse Torkkeli

This book first published 2021

Cambridge Scholars Publishing

Lady Stephenson Library, Newcastle upon Tyne, NE6 2PA, UK

British Library Cataloguing in Publication Data
A catalogue record for this book is available from the British Library

ISBN (10): 1-5275-6980-2
ISBN (13): 978-1-5275-6980-5

TABLE OF CONTENTS

International Business and Entrepreneurship in the 21st Century

Lasse Torkkeli

Adjunct Professor of International Business at Turku School of Economics at University of Turku

The first two decades of the 21st century have seen international business and entrepreneurship around the world grapple with global developments from the terror attacks to financial crises, from Brexit to the policies of Donald Trump as the president of the United States. Long-term global challenges such as those presented by the changing climate have been complemented with technological progress from sustainable technologies to digitalization of products and services. The latest major global development at the time of this writing in early 2021 is the ongoing COVID-19 pandemic which has, according to United Nations Conference on Trade and Development (UNCTAD, 2021) over the past year resulted in a decrease of over 40% in global foreign direct investment (FDI). The pandemic and its accompanying restrictions on global trade and on entrepreneurs has already had a major impact for research in international business (Caligiuri et al., 2020; Verbeke & Yuan, 2021) and in entrepreneurship (Shepherd, 2020; Zahra, 2020).

Indeed, the world of contemporary international business and entrepreneurship is dynamic and ever-changing, impacted by digitalization of societies and businesses, by the rise of environmental entrepreneurship and international business practices in response to climate change, and by the increasing volume of immigrant entrepreneurship due to increasing global migration, just to name a few of the key long-term phenomena. Research on international business and international entrepreneurship has done its best to keep up with these changing realities, but much remains to be done. For instance, we have not had a clear picture on how new emerging technologies, such as the internet of things, artificial intelligence or blockchain will impact the ways in which multinational enterprises and international entrepreneurs will do business through the 21st century. We similarly have not had clear explanations for the dynamics of industry emergence or individual sensemaking in the domains of international business and entrepreneurship.

Bringing together contributions from some of the brightest young minds in international business and entrepreneurship research today, this volume ventures into these timely domains. We shed light on timely phenomena such as digitalization and digital platforms, cleantech, internet of things, migrant entrepreneurs, and the nature of global trade in this new reality, among other timely topics.

This book is structured in three main sections as follows: The first part of the book focuses on the impact that digitalization is having on research and practice in international business and entrepreneurship. Valtteri Kaartemo starts off our exploration by asking the very contemporary question of, "How will advances in technology and computer science, i.e. artificial intelligence, blockchain technology, and augmented reality, change international business?", and reports a Delphi study where both scholars and practitioners of international business and entrepreneurship weigh in on the question. His findings indicate that there are differences of opinions between practitioners and researchers on which technologies will be more impactful to international business and entrepreneurship. The results of this study will enable future efforts to focus more clearly on the technologies that are likely to have the biggest impact on both research and practice.

Elisa Aro and Eini Haaja continue from there with their study on digital platform providers. International business and entrepreneurship research have been surprisingly slow to take on this topic, considering the fact that digital platforms enable rapid internationalization, can disrupt entire industries, and tend to result in new types business models for entrepreneurs and businesses in general. The chapter examines a joint digital platform development project by a group of SMEs, explaining how sensemaking in a joint digital platform development works. In addition, the chapter provides an illustration of a "failure case" in collective opportunity development in the entrepreneurship domain, making it an important complement to international entrepreneurship studies which have tended to focus almost solely on entrepreneurial successes and avoided discussing failures (Nummela et al., 2016). The first part of the book concludes with the chapter by Luke Treves, who assesses another contemporary issue that international business and entrepreneurship scholars have tended to overlook: the role of internet of things (IoT) in business model innovation in the digital age we are living in today. Discussion on digital transformation as a larger societal phenomenon leads into outlining the main implications of business model innovation for IoT-related entrepreneurship in general.

The second part of the book illustrates some of the main macro-level issues in international business and entrepreneurship today. The chapter by Arti Yadav and Badar Alam Iqbal describes the role of FDI in today's era of increasing digital and environmental sustainability. As they point out, the impact of FDI on the environment can be both positive and negative, it has a vital role in progress towards digitalization-based economy and in ensuring that global trade is based on both economic and sustainable goals. The second chapter in this part, by Hamza El Guili, Lasse Torkkeli and Anisur R. Faroque, develops a framework for understanding how SMEs trying to manage their exports during a global crisis should approach export promotion. Practical and policy recommendations arising from this framework underline the importance of setting up and updating modern communication channels to ensure effective interaction between those institutions and organizations providing export support, and those firms receiving it. This part of the book is concluded by the study of Igor Laine and Lasse Torkkeli, who take on a sector of industry whose rise is increasingly important in 21st century international business and entrepreneurship: the cleantech sector. The study applies the perspective of organizational ecology to explain how cleantech industry in a country perspective, here Finland, emerges, develops and internationalizes.

The third and final part of the book closes in from the macro-level to focus on the microfoundations of international business and entrepreneurship. The role of the individual has often been neglected in traditional international business research - which has tended to focus on the firm-level, that is on multinational enterprises – and in international entrepreneurship, where the focus has often similarly been on the firm-level, especially on rapidly internationalizing international new ventures (McDougall & Oviatt, 1994) and born globals (Rennie, 1993; Knight & Cavusgil, 2004). However, the beginning of the 21st century has since seen the development of the "gig economy" platforms such as Uber and Wolt, rise of individualism and the value of intrapreneurial behavior in international business (e.g., Halme et al., 2012), as well as the emergence of a new generation of millennial entrepreneurs (Liu et al., 2019). Therefore, shedding light on the individual entrepreneurs and employees in multinational enterprises is both important and timely. To this effect, the chapter by Agnes Asemokha and Satu Vesin describes how entrepreneurs make sense of and change their business models as they perceive international opportunities. Business model change in general has received less attention in international entrepreneurship research, considering the fact that the business model is argued to determine entrepreneurial internationalization (Hennart, 2014) to begin with. The chapter by Jie Chen illustrates the role of the individual in an important research topic in international business, Chinese state-owned enterprises. They have a major role in the global economy and investment landscape, yet there has been very little research on how Chinese state-owned enterprises are managed internally. The chapter sheds light on that, while clarifying how relationships between the Chinese expatriate managers in foreign subsidiaries and the local assembly line workers function. In doing so, the study provides a view into the individual in the Chinese multinational context. Last but not least, the chapter by Maria Ivanova-Gongne and Olga Dziubaniuk highlights a topic that will be one of the key global developments in international business and entrepreneurship in the 21st century: immigrant entrepreneurship. The study explains the role that bicultural identity of migrant entrepreneurs has when they try to develop their enterprises in their new home country. Applying the sensemaking perspective, the chapter describes dynamics of culture frame switching in international entrepreneurship and its role in contemporary international business and entrepreneurship.

With these words, we welcome you the reader to join us on this journey to the world of contemporary international business and entrepreneurship here in the 21st century.

References

Caligiuri, P., De Cieri, H., Minbaeva, D., Verbeke, A., & Zimmermann, A. (2020). International HRM insights for navigating the COVID-19 pandemic: Implications for future re-search and practice. *Journal of International Business Studies,* Jun 2, 1–17.

Halme, M., Lindeman, S., & Linna, P. (2012). Innovation for inclusive business: Intrapreneurial bricolage in multinational corporations. *Journal of Management Studies*, *49*(4), 743-784.

Hennart, J. F. (2014). The accidental internationalists: a theory of born globals. *Entrepreneurship Theory and Practice, 38*(1), 117-135.

Knight, G. & Cavusgil, S. T. (2004). Innovation, organizational capabilities, and the born-global firm. *Journal of International Business Studies*, *35*(2), 124-141.

Liu, J., Zhu, Y., Serapio, M. G., & Cavusgil, S. T. (2019). The new generation of millennial entrepreneurs: A review and call for research. *International Business Review*, *28*(5), 101581.

McDougall, P. P., Shane, S., & Oviatt, B. M. (1994). Explaining the formation of international new ventures: The limits of theories from international business research. *Journal of business venturing*, *9*(6), 469-487.

Nummela, N., Saarenketo, S., & Loane, S. (2016). The dynamics of failure in international new ventures: A case study of Finnish and Irish software companies. *International Small Business Journal*, *34*(1), 51-69.

Rennie, M. W. (1993). Born global. *The McKinsey Quarterly,* (4), 45-53.

Shepherd, D. A. (2020). COVID 19 and entrepreneurship: Time to pivot?. *Journal of Management Studies*, *57*(8), 1750-1753.

UNCTAD (2021). Global Investment Trend Monitor, No. 38. Available: https://unctad.org/system/files/official-document/diaeiainf2021d1_en.pdf

Verbeke, A., & Yuan, W. (2021). A Few Implications of the COVID-19 Pandemic for International Business Strategy Research. *Journal of Management Studies*.

Zahra, S. A. (2020). International entrepreneurship in the post Covid world. *Journal of World Business*, 101143.

PART 1:

DIGITAL INTERNATIONAL BUSINESS AND ENTREPRENEURSHIP

THE IMPACT OF FUTURE TECHNOLOGIES ON INTERNATIONAL BUSINESS

VALTTERI KAARTEMO

Postdoctoral Researcher at Turku School of Economics at University of Turku

1. Introduction

There has been more interest in technology in international business research. Discussion around the Fourth Industrial Revolution predicts that advances in technologies, such as sensors, robots, additive manufacturing, augmented reality, and artificial intelligence, impact offshoring and backshoring decisions, making local value chains more competitive and challenging the hegemony of global value chains (Dachs et al. 2019; Mees-Buss et al. 2019; Sinkovics & Sinkovics 2020). Liu et al. (2019) suggest that business ventures building on the Internet of Things, blockchain, and artificial intelligence are drastically changing the world. However, little is known about the impact of future technologies on international business practices. Fortunately, Monaghan et al. (2020, p. 20) call for interdisciplinary insights, asking, "how will advances in technology and computer science, i.e. artificial intelligence, blockchain technology, and augmented reality, change international business?" It is important to answer this question as this insight has not only business implications but can also help us define the future's strategic industries that will carry both economic and geopolitical importance. For instance, Petricevic and Teece (2019) suggest that artificial intelligence, advanced manufacturing, quantum information science, and 5G may become strategic industries in the future.

The purpose of this book chapter is to envision the impact of future technologies on international business. The study reveals the most impactful technologies and their associated changes to international business practice. The empirical data build on a Delphi study that was conducted in summer 2020. The expert panels consisted of both scholars and practitioners of international business and entrepreneurship.

In the following chapter, I describe the research method in detail. Next, I present the findings of the Delphi study. I also briefly discuss the current state-of-the-art in international business research around the technologies. As a result, I am able to highlight the novel findings of the study and suggest how they contribute to international business literature.

2. Methods

To answer the research question, I employed a structured Delphi study (Dalkey & Helmer, 1963) to gain insight from a diverse group of experts. As it is difficult to know in advance what technologies may be considered to have the most impact on international business practices, the Delphi method allows wider discussion than quantitative studies (Winkler et al., 2015), and it is especially suitable for studying rapid environmental changes (Hayes, 2007). The Delphi method enables the experts to contribute ideas, provide feedback, revise initial assumptions, and assess the findings collectively but anonymously (Mitroff & Turoff, 1975).

In addition, multiple rounds of data collection and feedback enable the experts to revise their initial assumptions and opinions and contribute to group consensus in an interactive way (Dalkey & Helmer, 1963). The insight developed throughout the study gives the individuals an opportunity to modify their judgments against the collective views of the panel (Mitroff & Turoff, 1975). Therefore, it is important to keep the same informants throughout the study.

The Delphi process started with expert selection. I felt it was important to include both international business practitioners and scholars in the expert panel. I invited people from different continents.

Experts from both subpanels (the 5G network and the healthcare market) were formally invited to participate in the study by e-mail in May 2020. As Delphi does not seek to establish explanatory power from statistical variance, the number of respondents is usually small, with approximately 10–18 experts in a group (Okoli & Pawlowski, 2004). I aimed to receive a commitment from around 15 experts. I knew that not everyone would be able to commit to a relatively long research process over the summer. Therefore, I aimed for a 50% response rate and invited 15 international business scholars and 15 international business practitioners to the panel.

The final panel comprised 16 experts (response rate 53.3%): 8 international business scholars and 8 international business practitioners. Both male and female experts (7 men and 9 women) were included. All respondents represented different organizations and held different positions (e.g., CEO, professor, international business director). Each participant also remained active and provided their insight throughout the process.

3. Data collection and analysis

I collected and analyzed the data in four rounds (see Figure 1) from May 2020 to September 2020.

Figure 1 Data collection and analysis

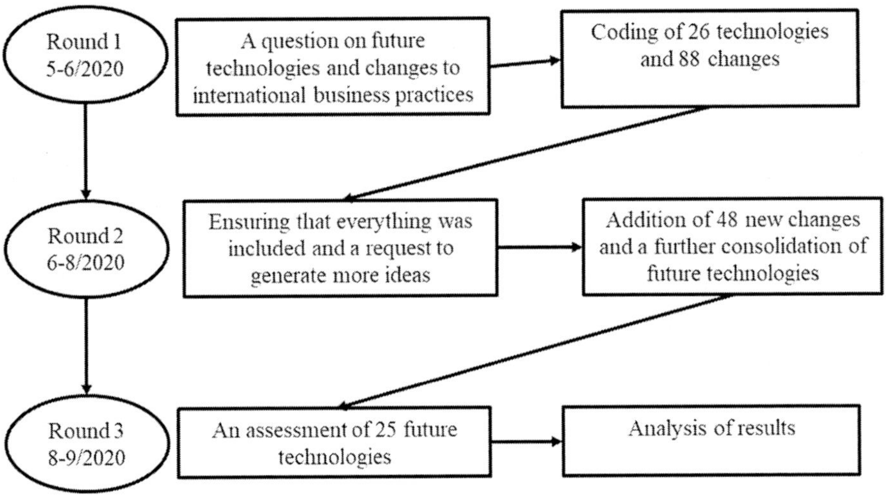

In Round 1, I gave the experts two tasks: "Name 5 technologies that are going to change international business in 5–10 years," and "Envision the changes in international business that each of these technologies is triggering. Please link your answer to the 5 technologies above." I summarized Round 1 answers around technologies. As part of that process, I needed to combine some technologies and changes to make the findings more accessible to the panel. Altogether, there were 26 technologies and 1–20 envisioned changes in international businesses linked with each technology.

In Round 2, I gave the experts an opportunity to review what the other experts came up with in the previous round. I presented a summary of the first-round results so the experts were able to ensure that their insight was accounted for and to generate new ideas for technologies or changes that were not present. The experts suggested 48 changes and additions to the original list of important technologies and the changes that the technologies were envisioned to trigger. Based on these responses, I revised the list and consolidated some technologies and changes further. As a result, the final list covered 25 technologies and related changes to international business practices.

In Round 3, I asked the experts to highlight the top 10 technologies that will have the biggest impact on international business practices in 5–10 years. As a result, I was able to identify technologies that most (50% or more) of the experts considered to be among the most impactful. Moreover, I was able to compare the results of each subpanel: scholars and practitioners.

4. Experts' view on the most impactful future technologies and the envisioned changes on international business practices:

I was able to identify 10 technologies that international business scholars and practitioners perceive as creating the biggest impact on international business practices in the next 5–10 years. Of note, the changes to international business were not ranked in terms of importance; the envisioned changes may be very subjective, and therefore, readers of this chapter can browse through the list and consider which changes they find most meaningful. Interestingly, all experts listed artificial intelligence among the top 10 technologies. It also gained the most envisioned changes during the first two rounds of the Delphi process. Other impactful technologies are 5G, blockchain, communication-related technologies, digital platform and online sales technology, fintech (incl. cryptocurrencies), food technology (incl. synthetic food and vertical farming), renewable energy technology (incl. Battery technology and electric vehicles), augmented reality, and robotics. A detailed list of the envisioned changes to international business practices is available as an appendix. Here, in the following, I describe the main changes from my subjective view.

Artificial intelligence is expected to change international business practices by improving analytics, resulting in more accurate and optimized production and delivery and overall efficiency of international trade. Importantly, it is possible to have a better understanding of local taste, habits, and trends by analyzing data. Many technology companies are already doing this, and a wider spread of AI technology may make this more common.

Communication-related technologies are expected to make international communication faster and more efficient than before. This is interesting because, while there have been media for cross-border communications for a long time, technology is expected to further decrease the need for the movement of people. While this may make communication faster and more efficient and could positively impact processes within and across organizations, it may also have unintended negative consequences. The experts are concerned about a lack of target market understanding when managers learn about the foreign market remotely.

Digital platform and online sales technology carry a similar impact to communication-related technologies in that they reduce the need for international travel. There is less need for facilities, and fewer people need to relocate. The experts view this development fairly positively, as it provides new opportunities for companies around the world. It also changes how people and companies buy goods and services. In other words, the country of origin partly loses its importance. Yet, one might consider the lack of localization as a negative aspect when standardized products are distributed around the globe.

All other digital, internet-based technologies and services will be mediated, in part, by the impact of 5G technology. It will partly support the spread of AI- and IoT-based solutions. The experts expect that it will enable a more stable and efficient infrastructure for international trade and communication. Yet, there are also concerns about security, as companies and services become more and more reliant on the internet.

Blockchain technology and fintech (incl. cryptocurrencies) are expected to disrupt industries. Important changes are expected in international business in logistics when the movement of goods can be traced better and more reliably. This improves security and lowers costs in many areas of business. Through the introduction of cryptocurrencies, the transfer of large sums of money around the world is faster and more affordable than ever before. While blockchain technology enables more effective collaboration and increases the security and transparency of business transactions, there are also concerns around geopolitics. Cryptocurrencies, in particular, are expected to cause economic deviation and instability.

The experts also envisioned important changes through food technology, as it makes food production less bound to the land. Synthetic food and vertical farming can bring food production closer to where people live and consume the food products, which brings new global opportunities for food production and increases food security. By fighting against hunger, food technology can have a wider societal impact and a bigger indirect influence on international business.

In line with food technology, renewable energy technology enables the development of more sustainable products for international markets. It also makes international travel more sustainable. The experts are aware that a more drastic change from fossil fuels to renewable energy may cause political tensions and may thus have an indirect impact on international business practices.

Augmented reality introduces new opportunities for virtual meetings, sales, maintenance, and customer service. It is expected to improve the productivity of humans and increase the perceived value of customers. It may also bring new opportunities to provide localized service across borders. But, as mentioned above regarding new communication technologies, augmented reality may reduce the personal understanding of a market if managers rely too much on augmented reality.

Last, experts envisioned that robotics brings production from low-cost markets closer to the home country. Robots help with increased automation in customer service, data automation, and operations. As robots are expected to replace humans, experts envision that the increased use of robots will reduce the number of employees in emerging markets. This may create some conflict, while also shifting people from dangerous jobs to a safer work environment.

While the two expert panels (scholars and practitioners) mostly listed the same future technologies as being the most impactful, five technologies were voted into the top 10 by a majority of either a panel of scholars or a panel of practitioners, but not both.

A majority of international business scholars voted global reliable internet (4/8 votes) as being among the most impactful future technologies, as it drives massive adoption in underserved communities, opens new markets, provides educational international resources to remote and previously digitally excluded communities, and democratizes all aspects of international business and the ability of all nations to participate in buying and selling.

Unlike international business scholars, a majority of practitioners voted Cybersecurity technology (5/8 votes), Autonomous driving / Autonomous logistics (incl. Drone technology) (4/8 votes), IoT (incl. Telematics) (4/8 votes), and Quantum computing (4/8 votes) as being among the top 10 most impactful future technologies. Cybersecurity technology is envisioned to provide safe internet-based businesses and to create sophisticated internet-based jobs. Autonomous driving / Autonomous logistics was considered to make logistics more efficient and reliable, reduce labor costs and take away jobs in logistics, increase labor costs in programming and correcting algorithms, decrease or increase accidents, and enable faster delivery of goods. Thus, the experts suggested both positive and negative impacts on various business actors. IoT is envisioned to change international business using humans to using nonhuman personnel, increase global efficiency of logistics and supply chain management, and facilitate offerings in a new way on a global level. Quantum computing was similarly seen as important for international business practices as it dramatically influences the use of other technologies, making them either obsolete or better.

5. Discussion

This study highlights the impact of future technologies on international business in a way that is unique to the literature. While there have been some suggestions on how future technologies, in general, might impact international business, this is the first study that takes a closer look at what the most impactful future technologies are and reveals the potential changes to international business practices. In the following, I show what has been discussed around the most impactful technologies in the prior literature. This helps to link the findings to the ongoing scholarly debate in international business and highlights the contribution of this study vis-à-vis leading IB technology articles.

5G. It is interesting that there are no studies that focus on the impact of 5G on international business. For instance, the study by Kaartemo and Nyström (2021) is limited to overall market changes. The lack of interest in 5G in international business literature is surprising given that 5G enables more stable, high-speed, and efficient digital infrastructure for international trade solutions. It acts as a platform for other technological solutions, such as artificial intelligence and the Internet of Things, which may, in turn, have a great impact on international business. AI, for instance, is expected to enable better and more optimized service across borders. For time-reliant activities, it is important that operations are supported by fast and stable internet connections, which 5G enables. While it can have a great positive impact by democratizing international communication, there is also a threat that 5G triggers international political debate and disruption regarding security concerns. As a result, the emergence of 5G may make countries more inward-looking, in part changing the tradition of free trade development that many international companies depend on.

Artificial intelligence. Except for a recent study by Deng et al. (2020) on the potential impact of artificial intelligence on shopping channel choices, the technology has remained as a side note in various technology-related studies. Hence, the envisioned changes to international business practices remain unheard of in leading international business journals. While individual scholars have mentioned the technology, there is no thorough empirical research on the implications of artificial intelligence for any aspects of international business. This is shocking, given that there are already plenty of different real-world applications utilizing artificial intelligence. One might even question labeling it as “a future technology.” Nevertheless, artificial intelligence is expected to grow in importance, and the experts unanimously agree that AI will have an impact on international business practices within 5–10 years.

Blockchain. Nambisan et al. (2019) note that “blockchain technology can enhance the extent of information shared and processed by foreign partners.” Otherwise, the impact of blockchain technology on international business practices remains implicit. Although I included cryptocurrencies among fintech in this study, even cryptocurrencies as a special application of blockchain technology are not discussed in international business literature.

Communication-related technologies. This is the most abstract technology among the future technologies. In principle, communications technologies have attracted attention from IB scholars since the turn of the millennium (Rao 2001; Santangelo 2001). But this does not mean that we only discuss past technologies. As I collected the empirical data during the COVID-19 pandemic, it is no wonder that the experts started to consider how the need for moving people and the biological risk of human physical interactions will decrease in the future. Interestingly, the experts also raised a dark side of this development: managers may start losing their personal understandings of the market when they operate overseas remotely.

Digital platform and online sales technology. Digital platforms have gained more interest from international business scholars than most other future technologies combined. As noted by Ojala et al. (2018), digital platforms enable companies to serve multi-sided markets and rapidly scale globally. This raises questions about some of the basic assumptions in the traditional Uppsala model and its more revised versions (Chen et al. 2019). Jean et al.

(2020) discuss the antecedents and outcomes of digital platform risk for international new ventures' internationalization. Their findings reveal that digital platform risk tends to reduce the internationalization scope of international new ventures. Altogether, these studies question some earlier theories and models and extend them, as digital platforms and online sales technologies enable startups to internationalize in a way that was previously impossible. This interest in digital platforms has even led to the development of the framework of digital platform internationalization (Li et al. 2019).

Fintech (incl. Cryptocurrencies). In this study, cryptocurrencies were considered a part of fintech, while they could be also seen as a part of blockchain technology (also among the most impactful technologies). In general, the impact of cryptocurrencies on international business practices remains unknown, although they provide new opportunities for borderless trade and frictionless movement of capital. Top international business journals lack mentions of bitcoin or any altcoins. As an exception, Ajouz et al. (2020) studied the acceptance of Sharīʿah-compliant precious metal–backed cryptocurrency as an alternative currency. Fintech is also relatively untouched territory; there is no discussion on how it can provide emerging economy customers better access to international goods or how it may cause economic deviation and instability. While Hammerschlag et al. (2020) interviewed 14 African fintech firms to understand their intra-African expansion, fintech is mostly just an industry context for these companies. As a result, there is basically no study that would discuss the impact of fintech on international business practices.

Food technology (incl. synthetic food and vertical farming). Given that food technology introduces a potential for revolutionizing one of the biggest industries in the world, it is surprising that it remains a novel era for international business research. It provides interesting insight for bringing food production back home and may represent interesting network effects from global value chains to the role of international new ventures in the traditional market.

Renewable energy technology (incl. Battery technology and electric vehicles). Recently, Kaartemo and Gonzalez-Perez (2020) noted that renewable energy is relatively rarely studied in international business. This is unfortunate, given that the development and adoption of renewable energy relates to the most important social and environmental challenges on a global scale. While a recent special issue on critical perspectives on international business featured a handful of articles laying the groundwork for the theme (Alarcón 2020; Asemokha et al. 2020; Frutos-Bencze et al. 2020; Rialp-Crialdo et al. 2020), there is still a need for further studies linking renewable energy with international business.

Augmented reality. As noted by Sinkovics and Sinkovics (2020), international business studies on augmented reality remain wide open for substantive research. It is surprising that there has not been any interest in the impact of augmented reality on international business. After all, it provides new opportunities for communications and generally drives several changes there, such as diminishing the need for traveling. Importantly, it can change sensitive experiences and may thus be important for changing international tourism, which is one of the biggest industries in the world.

Robotics. As part of the discussion on megatrends that are changing the business ecosystem, Esposito and Tse (2018) noted the importance of robotics in raising new opportunities just like the Internet revolution in the past. Yet, the impact of robotics on international business practices remains understudied. Sinkovics and Sinkovics (2020) propose that robotics along with additive manufacturing can provide promising, lively, and impactful research avenues for international marketing.

6. Concluding remarks

This study reveals the most impactful future technologies from the perspective of international business. As a result, the findings enable researchers to focus on technologies that are going to have the biggest impact. Moreover, the study illuminates the changes that experts associate with these technologies. Hence, international business scholars may use envisioned changes as a starting point for future studies. Interestingly, the study hints that practitioners perceive some technologies to be more impactful on international business than researchers do. This can provide insight to guide research efforts around these technologies and around changes that might otherwise remain overlooked. In addition to some positive changes that the technologies may bring to international business, there is also the potential for negative consequences, or the "dark side" of future technologies.

Building on Delphi methodology, this paper provides a method for international business and entrepreneurship scholars to identify the most impactful technologies. It is encouraged that similar studies be conducted in different geographic regions, with different time horizons, specifically focusing on certain industries to get more detailed insight.

Acknowledgments

This research is funded by the Academy of Finland (315604) and the Niilo Helander Foundation.

References

Ajouz, M., Abdullah, A., & Kassim, S. (2020). Acceptance of Sharīʿah-compliant precious metal-backed cryptocurrency as an alternative currency: An empirical validation of adoption of innovation theory. *Thunderbird International Business Review*, *62*(2), 171-181.

Alarcón, C. (2019), "Transforming wood energy in Sweden and Chile: Climate change, environmental communication and a critical political ecology of international forestry companies", *critical perspectives on international business*, Vol. 16 No. 4, pp. 361-377. https://doi.org/10.1108/cpoib-05-2018-0039

Asemokha, A., Ahi, A., Torkkeli, L. and Saarenketo, S. (2019), "Renewable energy market SMEs: antecedents of internationalization", *critical perspectives on international business*, Vol. 16 No. 4, pp. 407-447. https://doi.org/10.1108/cpoib-05-2018-0043

Chen, L., Shaheer, N., Yi, J., & Li, S. (2019). The international penetration of ibusiness firms: Network effects, liabilities of outsidership and country clout. *Journal of International Business Studies*, *50*(2), 172-192.

Dachs, B., Kinkel, S., & Jäger, A. (2019). Bringing it all back home? Backshoring of manufacturing activities and the adoption of Industry 4.0 technologies. *Journal of World Business*, *54*(6), 101017.

Dalkey, N. and Helmer, O. (1963), "An experimental application of the Delphi method to the use of experts", *Management Science*, Vol. 9, pp. 458–467.

Deng, G., Zhang, J., Ye, N., & Chi, R. (2020). Consumers' human nature and their shopping channel choices in the emerging artificial intelligence era: based on Xunzi's humanity hypothesis. *International Marketing Review*.

Frutos-Bencze, D., Avdiu, K. and Unger, S. (2019), "The effect of trade and monetary policy indicators on the development of renewable energy in Latin America", *critical perspectives on international business*, Vol. 16 No. 4, pp. 337-359. https://doi.org/10.1108/cpoib-04-2018-0037

Hammerschlag, Z., Bick, G., & Luiz, J. M. (2020). The internationalization of African fintech firms: marketing strategies for successful intra-Africa expansion. *International Marketing Review*.

Hayes, T. (2007), “Delphi study of the future of marketing of higher education”, *Journal of Business Research*, Vol. 60 No 9, pp. 927–931.

Kaartemo, V. and Gonzalez-Perez, M.A. (2020), "Renewable energy in international business", *critical perspectives on international business*, Vol. 16 No. 4, pp. 325-336. https://doi.org/10.1108/cpoib-08-2019-0062

Kaartemo, V. and Nyström, A.G. (2021), “Emerging technology as a platform for market shaping and innovation”, *Journal of Business Research*, Vol. 124, pp. 458–468.

Kim, D., & Cavusgil, E. (2020). Antecedents and outcomes of digital platform risk for international new ventures’ internationalization. *Journal of World Business*, *55*(1), 101021.

Li, J., Chen, L., Yi, J., Mao, J., & Liao, J. (2019). Ecosystem-specific advantages in international digital commerce. *Journal of International Business Studies*, *50*(9), 1448-1463.

Mees-Buss, J., Welch, C., & Westney, D. E. (2019). What happened to the transnational? The emergence of the neo-global corporation. *Journal of International Business Studies*, *50*(9), 1513-1543.

Mitroff, I. and Turoff, M. (1975), “Philosophical and methodological foundations of Delphi”. In: H. Linstone & M. Turoff (Eds.), *The Delphi Method: Techniques and Applications*, Addison-Wesley, Reading, Mass.

Monaghan, S., Tippmann, E., & Coviello, N. (2020). Born digitals: Thoughts on their internationalization and a research agenda. *Journal of International Business Studies*, *51*(1), 11-22.

Nambisan, S., Zahra, S. A., & Luo, Y. (2019). Global platforms and ecosystems: Implications for international business theories. *Journal of International Business Studies*, *50*(9), 1464-1486.

Ojala, A., Evers, N., & Rialp, A. (2018). Extending the international new venture phenomenon to digital platform providers: A longitudinal case study. *Journal of World Business*, *53*(5), 725-739.

Okoli, C. and Pawlowski, S. (2004), “The Delphi method as a research tool: An example, design considerations and applications”, *Information & Management*, Vol. 42, pp. 15–29.

Petricevic, O., & Teece, D. J. (2019). The structural reshaping of globalization: Implications for strategic sectors, profiting from innovation, and the multinational enterprise. *Journal of International Business Studies*, *50*(9), 1487-1512.

Rao, P. M. (2001). The ICT revolution, internationalization of technological activity, and the emerging economies: implications for global marketing. *International Business Review*, *10*(5), 571-596.

Rialp-Criado, A., Zolfaghari Ejlal Manesh, S.M. and Moen, Ø. (2019), "Home (not so) sweet home: Domestic political uncertainty driving early internationalisation in the Spanish renewable energy context", *critical perspectives on international business*, Vol. 16 No. 4, pp. 379-406. https://doi.org/10.1108/cpoib-03-2018-0031

Santangelo, G. D. (2001). The impact of the information and communications technology revolution on the internationalisation of corporate technology. *International Business Review*, *10*(6), 701-726.

Sinkovics, R. R., & Sinkovics, N. (2020). The Internet and international marketing–from trigger technology to platforms and new markets. *International Marketing Review*.

Winkler, J., Kuklinski, C.P.J.W. and Moser, R. (2015), "Decision making in emerging markets: The Delphi approach's contribution to coping with uncertainty and equivocality", *Journal of Business Research*, Vol. 68 No. 5, pp. 1118–1126.

Appendix 1
Top 10 technologies that are going to have the biggest impact on international business practices in 5–10 years

1) Artificial intelligence (16/16)

- improves customer experience across countries and cultures
- enables digital food labeling
- enables the more accurate reaction to local demands
- enables the more accurate and efficient production and delivery of products and services
- changes international business from humans to nonhumans, which alters the nature of business network relationships and thus conflict, negotiation, trust, etc
- increases efficiency of global trade
- enables a better development and identification of international opportunities
- enables new business models
- improves the personalization of products and services
- enables a better understanding of customer preferences, including latent/non-expressed preferences
- enables a better understanding of market trends
- enables a better understanding of technological change
- enables a better understanding of population shifts
- disrupts social interaction
- optimizes routes for both local and international logistics
- improves relationships with the customer in digital channels
- improves the competitiveness of Western factories against the Asian factories
- enables more cost-effective, secure, and fast production
- enhances market intelligence and data-backed strategic decision-making
- makes services and products based on AI the norm
- automates boring jobs humans used to do and puts people out of work
- posits challenges to developing and underdeveloped countries that won't be financially able to catch up with the technological upgrade
- decreases cultural and institutional knowledge for managers regarding international markets (no live personal experience)
- helps identify fake information or messaging

2) Communication-related technologies (11/16)

- makes participation from diverse corners faster and more efficient
- changes organizational forms, processes, and operations
- decreases the need for movement of people
- provides incentives for developing more human intuitive communication software and hardware
- reduces the biological risk of human physical interactions
- reduces the international managers' live, personal understanding of a market

3) Digital platform and online sales technology (11/16)

- reduces the need for facilities, production, and employees located around the world
- allows individuals and small businesses to find one another and trade goods or services
- creates centralized consumers goods and services markets
- reduces the biological risk of human physical interactions
- changes buying patterns
- enables borderless buying options
- improves the ability of local firms to serve global markets
- provides a way for non-digital firms to learn how to digitalize aspects of their business.
- democratizes innovation and entrepreneurship around the world

4) 5G (9/16)

- enables more stable, high speed and efficient digital infrastructure for international trade solutions
- enables AI- and IoT-based solutions
- activates trade of more sophisticated internet-based services
- triggers international political debate and disruption regarding security concerns.
- democratizes international communication

5) Blockchain (9/16)

- disrupts rules in certain industries
- brings up geopolitical issues
- enables more effective collaboration
- enables new business models
- facilitates all information and financial flows for all aspects of international trade

- increases the transparency of business transactions
- improves the tracking of movement of goods and tracing them to suppliers in different countries
- changes global distribution and global trade
- improves the security of supply chains
- lowers financing cost for all supply chain parties
- increases carbon footprint for business and users
- increases incentives for higher-skilled hackers
- reduces the need for personally attending notary services

6) Fintech (incl. Cryptocurrencies) (9/16)

- causes economic deviation and instability
- reduces the cost of international trade and remittance
- improves the ability of emerging economy customers to pay for international goods
- enables the transfer of large sums of money from anywhere to anywhere in the world

7) Food technology (incl. synthetic food and vertical farming) (9/16)

- makes food production unbound to the land
- enables global sales possibilities for food
- increases food security and it could support the fight against hunger

8) Renewable energy technology (incl. Battery technology and electric vehicles) (9/16)

- makes the global delivery of products more sustainable
- makes traveling more sustainable
- provides market incentives for sustainable mining and circular economy
- disrupts reliance on traditional energy supplies thus creating political tension

9) Augmented reality (8/16)

- introduces new possibilities for distanced virtual meetings
- introduces new opportunities for visualizing solutions pre-purchase
- introduces new opportunities for maintenance/repair
- allows humans to possess computer-like abilities
- allows computers to possess human-like abilities and in terms of IB, adapt easily across cultures in terms of cultural and institutional knowledge, speaking the appropriate language, etc.

- improves the productivity of the human labor force
- increases the value of perceived sensitive experience
- reduces the international managers' live, personal understanding of a market

10) Robotics (8/16)

- brings production from low-cost economies back to the home country
- reduces jobs in emerging markets
- displaces humans in various operations
- increases automation with customer service, data automation & operational speed
- provides alternatives to dangerous jobs previously performing by humans (mining, health care of highly contagious diseases)

DEVELOPING A DIGITAL PLATFORM IN INTER-FIRM COLLABORATION: CHALLENGES OF MATERIALISING A COLLECTIVE OPPORTUNITY[1]

ELISA ARO[1] AND EINI HAAJA[2]

[1]Research Manager, Pan-European Institute at University of Turku

[2]Research Manager, Pan-European Institute at University of Turku

1. Introduction

Digital transformation has affected the way companies generate value for local and foreign customers (Ojala, Evers and Rialp 2018). A specific phenomenon in this respect is the emergence of new types of firms, termed digital platform providers, which change current business models and disrupt industries (ibid.). A digital platform refers to 'a shared, common set of services and architecture that serves to host complementary offerings' (Nambisan 2017, 1032). Digital platforms constitute a highly contemporary phenomenon as they are rapidly spreading to different industries with increasingly complex architectures (de Reuver, Sørensen and Basole 2018). In particular, trade wars and the COVID-19 pandemic have quickly led to the need to restructure global supply chains, which has considerably increased the value (economic and also political) of accessing and utilising digital platforms (Zahra 2021).

Scholars in different fields are now striving to understand digital platforms and their impact on industries and business (de Reuver, Sørensen and Basole 2018). One of the burning questions is how digital platforms emerge in the first place (ibid.). This requires looking into the processes of the entrepreneurs and firms that create digital platforms. The number of digital

[1] The authors express their gratitude to Business Finland for its financial support (Grant 2587/31/2016).

platform providers is increasing, and they often aim at scaling their offerings to international markets rapidly (Yoo, Boland, Lyytinen and Majchrzak 2012; Ojala, Evers and Rialp 2018). However, the creation, let alone the global scaling, of digital platforms rarely builds on the capabilities of individual firms but on intensive collaboration within multiple firms. In fact, digital platform development concerns developing highly complex systems in which fluent inter-firm collaboration is essential. Moreover, it can be a lengthy process, during which partners must have a shared understanding of the opportunity they aim to exploit and together overcome challenges that may emerge during the materialisation of this opportunity.

While much research has investigated the processes related to R&D, studies on inter-firm collaboration remain rather limited in this respect. In particular, it is widely acknowledged that several collaborative innovation initiatives fail, but much remains to be explored regarding why this happens (Keupp, Palmié and Gassmann 2012). Prior research tends to build on successful cases, and more research is needed on the hazards and challenges of innovative collaboration and on how firms react to them (ibid.). In particular, the entrepreneurial perspective of the processes whereby multiple entrepreneurs recognise collective opportunities, and manage to maintain a shared view of them over time, is in need of further research (Andresen, Lundberg and Wincent 2014; Mainela, Puhakka and Servais 2014; Haaja and Nummela 2020). Few studies have explored digital development initiatives that never lead to commercialisation and international scaling even though such research would provide valuable insight into how digitalisation can be increasingly supported.

This study analyses how a digital platform development project among a group of small and medium-sized enterprises (SMEs) operating in the maritime industry failed in its attempt to create a joint digital platform. We build on the prior literature on collective opportunity recognition as well as collective and fragmented sensemaking and on an analysis of empirical data comprising interviews and meeting observations from 2016 to 2018. We show how the sensemaking and views of opportunity among the collaborators fragmented along the project and identify four modes of sensemaking through which the fragmentation manifested over time. The study contributes to the entrepreneurship literature by offering an enhanced understanding on the dynamics of collective opportunity recognition and to the literature on sensemaking through the identification of specific managerial modes in the collaborative product development context. In conclusion, we present managerial implications and avenues for further research.

2. Theoretical framework

2.1 The recognition of collective opportunities

Entrepreneurship research focuses on the concept of opportunity and, in particular, on the individual-opportunity nexus (Shane and Venkataraman 2000; Short, Ketchen, Shook and Ireland 2010; Davidsson 2015). This refers to entrepreneurs' recognition of opportunities, which appears before entrepreneurial processes. Opportunities can be made as well as found (Venkataraman, Sarasvathy, Dew and Forster 2012) as entrepreneurs sense elements of the real world and try to materialise opportunities through enactment (Ramoglou and Tsang 2016). The process of opportunity recognition is highly subjective and context-specific as past opportunity considerations, for example, affect the recognition of new ones (Wood, Williams and Drover 2017).

Relationships between entrepreneurs also affect opportunity recognition (Ellis 2011). While entrepreneurship often involves collaboration and the co-exploitation of opportunities, the processes by which multiple individuals jointly identify, form and exploit opportunities are also important (Andresen, Lundberg and Wincent 2014). Here, the collective recognition of opportunities is essential; several entrepreneurs must recognise an opportunity in the same setting in order to find it worth acting upon in collaboration (Haaja 2020). All partners recognise the opportunity based on their own interests, whereby the view of opportunity is not exactly the same but largely shared (Ciabuschi, Perna and Snehota 2012). On this basis, collective opportunities emerge when several individuals interact and recombine resources (Mainela 2012).

Collective opportunity recognition is required to start a collaboration project, and it is crucial to the successful exploitation of a targeted collective opportunity (Haaja and Nummela 2020) even when sudden changes appear. Indeed, collective opportunity recognition as well as its continuation depend on how the involved entrepreneurs make sense of their changing environment.

2.2 Sensemaking in opportunity recognition

Sensemaking is a process by which individuals structure unknown situations and decide how to act in the face of unexpected events that change their environment (Weick 1995). Sudden changes can be highly confusing, but, in the entrepreneurial context, they may also be interpreted as opportunities (Zahra, Korri and Yu 2005). Mental images act as frameworks in sensemaking, allowing the individual to notice the change, label it, predict what is to follow and act 'thinkingly' (Weick, Sutcliffe and Obstfeld 2005). Mental images refer to subjective, context-specific information structures which comprise information about the actor's actions and progress in the setting (Beach and Mitchell 1987; Mitchell and Beach 1990). Based on the mental images of a specific opportunity context, sensemaking concerning changes in that setting can be auspicious, whereby the context is viewed as favourable and fruitful or, alternatively, ominous, by which the context is considered harmful and unattractive (Haaja and Nummela 2020).

When multiple people make sense of a situation together, they generate a shared meaning of it (Maitlis and Christianson 2014). The shared meaning entails multiple understandings that bear resemblance to each other so that coordinated action is achieved (ibid.). Another important phenomenon is sensegiving as individuals try to influence other people's sensemaking so that they would view the organisation's circumstances in a specific way (Gioia and Chittipeddi 1991). On this basis, organisational sensemaking varies in terms of control by the sensegiving of leaders and animation by the sensegiving of stakeholders (Maitlis 2005). Consequently, organisational sensemaking can be defined as 'guided', 'fragmented', 'restricted' or 'minimal' (ibid.). Collective opportunity recognition among multiple individuals builds on well-guided collective and auspicious sensemaking concerning changes in a context, whereas fragmented and even partly ominous sensemaking is expected to prevent the recognition of shared opportunities (Haaja and Nummela 2020). Overall, collective opportunity recognition and sensemaking at the individual and inter-personal level allow us to study the progress of inter-firm collaboration in detail.

3. Methodology

3.1 Research design

We employ the qualitative case study approach as it is recommended for obtaining an in-depth understanding of a case in focus (Merriam 2009) and for investigating dynamic business networks settings with both contextual and process elements (Halinen and Törnroos 2005). Moreover, we conduct a processual case study with longitudinal data as this enables connecting the process, its context and its outcomes (Pettigrew 2012).

Our case, a collaborative digital platform development, took place as an R&D project for which the involved firms received public financial support together with university partners. We as researchers followed the progress of the project in an involved university, and while providing academic insight in the project, we collected data on the progress of collaboration. We collected our primary data through interviewing the firm representatives – this was considered the best way to capture changes in their mental images and thereby sensemaking along the process. Utilising the point-mapping technique presented by Halinen, Medlin and Törnroos (2012), the interviews were conducted as snapshots approximately every six months. The interviewees work at the executive level and were involved in the platform development project. The project lasted for 2.5 years, and each representative was interviewed four to five times between September 2016 and December 2018, with the interviews lasting from 15 to 90 minutes.

Additionally, we collected observational data to explore inter-firm sensemaking in the group. This resulted in recordings and notes from 11 group meetings. The meetings included official project board meetings and unofficial workshops in which the firm representatives discussed the work progress. This observational group-level data eventually played a secondary role due to the limited amount of truly interactive discussion yet allowed us to evaluate how the partners' interaction and joint sensemaking evolved.

3.2 Data analysis

To analyse this complex data from a process in a business network, we employed the meta-framework and narrative research techniques by Makkonen, Aarikka-Stenroos and Olkkonen (2012). To begin, we used the mental image concept to look for factors that influenced the sensemaking processes and opportunity recognition of the studied firm representatives. Following the study by Haaja and Nummela (2020) on collective opportunity recognition in the business internationalisation context, the data from each interview were coded using a mental image framework involving past experiences, contextual attractiveness and strategies and resources on both the personal and firm levels. This way, we visualised the mental images of each informant at time points, concerning both the collaboration of the partnership and the creation of the digital platform. The image contents were further characterised to involve either positive or negative connotations, which helped to determine whether the mental images regarding collaboration and the digital platform were inclined more towards auspicious or ominous sensemaking. Altogether, 17 mental images were illustrated.

As a process concerns events and actions occurring gradually in a context (Pettigrew 1997), we continued the analysis by identifying event trajectories with macro-, meso- and micro-level events that influenced the informants' sensemaking. Macro-level events refer to phenomena occurring in the macro environment of firms, while meso-level events result from the network dynamics, and micro-level events concern events within the individual firms (Makkonen, Aarikka-Stenroos and Olkkonen 2012). We compared the events against the managers' mental images, allowing us to see how each one made sense of the events, auspiciously or ominously. Thereafter, the individual-level sensemaking of each informant was compared with that of the others in the group to identify collective and fragmented sensemaking. Additionally, group meeting memos and discussions were reviewed to analyse how the group jointly made sense of unexpected events and whether collective or fragmented sensemaking could be observed. As a final step, we compiled a macro story of the case, involving four successive phases. This allowed us to compare differing ways of sensemaking and to see how sensemaking at the inter-firm level became fragmented, and the shared view of the collective opportunity faded. Finally, member checks were carried out by sending the study results to the firm representatives (Lincoln and Guba 1985).

4. The case of collaborative digital platform development

4.1 Phase 1: Full steam ahead

The studied group of SMEs comprised four firms. Firm A supplies complex turnkey projects to its maritime customers and had an essential role in the project as the group was to pilot the platform with its end customer. The other firms acted as suppliers by developing elements of the platform. Firm B operates as a logistics supplier for A, and its role in the project was to develop a logistics service tool for the platform. Firm C supplies IT solutions for several industries, and its task was to provide the IT services required in building the digital platform. Firm D, in turn, develops concepts to improve process efficiency in project-based industries through digital solutions. With existing relationships to firms A and C and having common customers with firm B, it was the lead partner in setting up the project, and its role was to provide service elements that would form an essential part of the digital platform. In practice, the jointly developed digital platform was to be validated with a true customer case during the project (see Figure 1) and later commercialised and scaled up internationally and beyond the maritime industry.

All project partners had high expectations for the project in the beginning, and their sensemaking was auspicious both in terms of digital platform development and collaboration. The need for the platform was clear, they all expected high benefits and/or sales potential for it and each partner had a role in supplying specific expertise in the project. The project also received public financial support, and the work could start concretely. However, three out of four managers expected challenges to be encountered during the project, such as concerning how to find a common ground in the collaboration. Nevertheless, the whole group shared the view of a collective opportunity in both the pictured digital platform and the collaboration group, and collective sensemaking took place regarding the start of the project.

Figure 1. Group of SMEs participating in the digital platform development

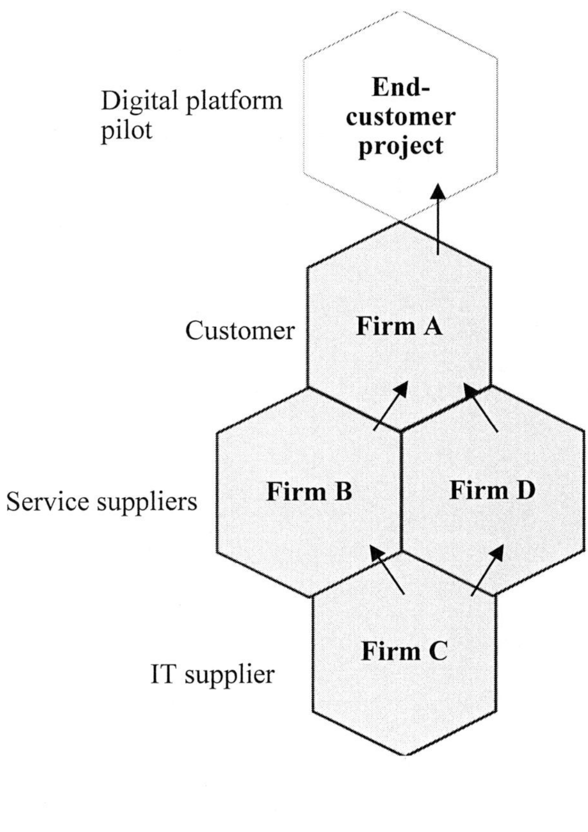

4.2 Phase 2: Stormy waters

After the project had been running for a couple of months, the group encountered its first setbacks as a hurricane cancelled the project of firm A's end customer in which the digital platform was to be piloted. In addition, a busy period in business operations and emerging confusion related to some still rather abstract service features led firm A to gradually lose the need for the platform. Collaboration between firms A and D did not progress, but firm D was eager to continue searching for a new angle for the work to continue. Nevertheless, it felt natural for the managers of firm A to progress with the development of the logistics part planned by firm B. As another unexpected event, the partners were informed of a restriction related to the use of their publicly funded project capital in mutual purchases within the partnership, which they did not know about when planning the project. This restriction had severe effects as some initially set purchases needed to be cancelled between several partners, and instead external firms were contacted. Additionally, since the start of the project, two of the firms had noticed some overlap in the operative models and project activities and also faced some challenges in terms of timetables, budgets and defining the interface. For these reasons, external firms were contracted to carry out part of the tasks.

These sudden incidences changed the collaborative setting, and the sensemaking of the group started to diverge. Respondents from firms B and D continued to perceive the digital platform and collaboration auspiciously – despite of the setbacks, they saw great benefits in the digital development and still considered the team adequate for the planned task. Managers in firms A and C viewed the collaboration more ominously. However, firm A's sensemaking towards digital platform development was still auspicious and, according to this firm representative, the upcoming solution would provide several benefits for the firm. In contrast, the sensemaking regarding digital platform development had turned ominous for firm C; the need for the digital solution was not yet clear for this firm, and, according to the firm representative, the fact that the project partners could not purchase services from each other with the subsidised money meant that the risk the development work involved for the firm could no longer be shared.

Thus, the sensemaking regarding collaboration within the group was fragmented at this point in time even though the individual sensemaking processes of two firm representatives were still auspicious. The confusion about how to act together next was also visible in the group discussions in which the partners described their own activities and plans instead of discussing joint steps.

4.3 Phase 3: Fog in front

At this point, several partners felt that they could not create a digital platform together but rather several different solutions individually. Some bilateral development had already taken place, and several firms had sought new external partnerships to create their own solutions. Due to these modified ideas of what the digital product would be, all four firm representatives viewed the development of digital solutions auspiciously.

However, the sensemaking of several managers had become ominous regarding collaboration, resulting in a fragmented view on what was to follow with the group. Firm A acknowledged that if they had known about the funding rule on mutual purchases earlier, they would probably have not taken part in the collaboration. Moreover, their main customer segment had changed recently, whereby the original project setting was not that attractive anymore, and firm A was no longer in need of the services of firm D. Collaboration between firms A and B continued, including as a part of their natural business operations.

Firm B continued auspicious sensemaking both concerning the digital solution and the partner group. The restriction on mutual purchases and some overlapping of activities decreased part of collaboration, but piloting activities were planned to take place with firm A in a new end-customer project. In relation to this, firm B indicated that digital service features could not be integrated into customers' systems before the services were sufficiently advanced, which created challenges in terms of delivering concrete results to customers before implementation.

Firm C, in turn, had at this point gained a better understanding of its own goals in terms of digital solution development, but the collaboration context seemed less attractive. Firm D continued to see the digital solution as a great opportunity, proceeded with its own development work and carried out test pilotings outside the project partnership. However, managers from firms C and D were willing to collaborate with the others in the future.

Thus, even though some activities still took place between individual firms, sensemaking was fragmented, and most representatives no longer saw a collective opportunity in the joint platform development. In the meetings, they presented their progress separately, as if they had multiple projects instead of a joint one. However, the possibility of integrating separate solutions in the near future was still brought up in one of the meetings.

4.4 Phase 4: Running aground

At the end of the project, collaboration had not materialised between the partnering firms, not even the piloting between firms A and B. It had been a long time since the partners had even attempted to reach a joint objective. However, the three firms that had a supplier role in the project had either piloted their solutions or were planning to pilot them outside this partnership in other customer cases, thus continuing to view the digital solution development auspiciously. In contrast, firm A had concluded that they had not gained concrete results from the project because of the challenges that had arisen, and at the same time they focused their effort on ordinary business operations instead of the joint project.

The collaboration ceased before it had even properly started, but three firms saw that they had reached the expected goals individually, which is why all the managers were eventually not disappointed in the fragmented collaboration. Some of them reflected that such a complex collaboration should have started more rapidly and dynamically although sometimes conditions change to the extent that the work cannot be forced. Most partners voiced that the project had still resulted in valuable knowledge, network connections and project experience. As a result, the group could not update their project plan collectively and develop the planned common digital platform, let alone try to commercialise it, but left the project with some lessons learned for the future.

5. Discussion

5.1 The fragmentation of views on opportunity in joint digital platform development

In the collaborative digital platform development case explored in this study, the group of partners confronted surprising micro-, meso- and macro-level events that changed the conditions for pursuing their original goal. Inter-firm-level sensemaking about what is going on takes place through interaction. In mutual discussions, the partners mostly wanted to keep up the view that the project was progressing well. However, as events changed the circumstances, the partners' views of the collective opportunity dispersed. Still, the partners did not voice this clearly in the observed group discussions; instead, they focused mostly on aspects that were progressing well even though in individual interviews they expressed some critical views. The firms did not find ways to engage in deep discussion on difficulties, on how the course of the joint work could be changed and what that would require from each partner. Consequently, even though collective sensemaking clearly took place at the start of the project, it soon turned fragmented as challenging events started to emerge.

The fragmentation of inter-firm sensemaking takes us to individual-level sensemaking processes. These are based on individuals' subjective mental images regarding the collective opportunity context, which we conceptualised here as concerning the product development context (digital platform) and the collaboration context (group of partners). As regards the first, we found that the majority of the partners rather easily modified their views of the targeted opportunity in terms of the digital solution and started to create individual digital tools separately. The characteristics of the digital platform and the joint steps for creating it had not been defined clearly together at the beginning of the project. Thus, as the product dimension of the collective opportunity was highly imaginary, each partner saw it in a new light amidst the events and evolving mental images of the opportunity context. On that basis, many of them still saw the customer need for the digital solution and considered its development as an opportunity for their own firms and even proceeded to seek out new partners and customer pilots. Therefore, most firm representatives' sensemaking concerning the digital solution remained auspicious throughout the project.

In contrast, it appears that the partners were not that agile in renewing their views of the collaboration group. The group of partners with its characteristics was real instead of an imaginary digital platform idea, and changing the roles of the other partners would have required efforts from all. Due to the lack of clear roles, a common customer case and dynamic project leadership, the confusion and problems that resulted from the events generated ominous sensemaking for the partners one by one. Ominous sensemaking caused them to prioritise other engagements instead of engaging in deep discussions to analyse and update the project's joint objective. Consequently, even though they had viewed the digital platform development auspiciously even in the midst of changes, the ominous sensemaking concerning the group in the changing circumstances led the majority of the partners to modify their views of the product development opportunity subjectively and to pursue those ideas separately instead of together adjusting their goals and plans in materialising a collective opportunity. Thus, the inter-firm-level sensemaking fragmented, and the view of the collective opportunity vanished. This process is illustrated in Figure 2.

Figure 2. The fragmentation of the collaborative digital platform development process

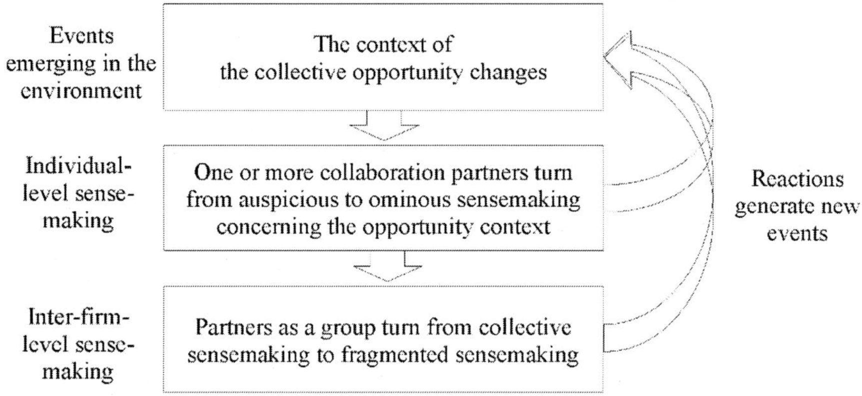

We may conclude that the partners' individual-level sensemaking concerning the collaborative digital platform development dispersed when it came to the product development context as well as the collaboration group context. Thus, individual-level sensemaking seems decisive in the fragmentation of inter-firm sensemaking and in the vanishing of the view of a collective opportunity.

5.2 Modes of sensemaking in joint digital platform development

Our findings indicate that fragmented sensemaking manifests through the simultaneous appearance of more than one of four managerial modes of sensemaking (see Table 1) which were identified in the thinking of the firm representatives along the investigation period. 'Collaborative innovator' views both the digital platform development and inter-firm collaboration contexts in an auspicious manner. 'Independent innovator' considers the digital platform development context useful for the firm, but inter-firm collaboration is unattractive. The 'consorter' mode represents the opposite for that mode, meaning that the firm representative views the digital platform development context ominously, while she/he perceives the inter-firm collaboration context auspiciously. The 'stagnant' mode means that neither contexts are attractive for the firm.

Table 1. Managerial modes of sensemaking identified along the joint digital platform development process

		INTER-FIRM COLLABORATION CONTEXT	
		AUSPICIOUS SENSEMAKING	OMINOUS SENSEMAKING
DIGITAL PLATFORM DEVELOPMENT CONTEXT	AUSPICIOUS SENSEMAKING	'Collaborative innovator'	'Independent innovator'
	OMINOUS SENSEMAKING	'Consorter'	'Stagnant'

When all partners are in the 'collaborative innovator' mode, collaboration works fluently, and the firms are willing to invest in collective sensemaking and thereby solving emerging challenges both in terms of product development and collaboration. The collaboration is most likely to succeed when all are in this mode. All the four managers employed this mode of sensemaking at the beginning of the project, being open to solving all problems possibly emerging either in the collaboration or in the digital platform development. However, over time, the sensemaking of some of the involved managers changed to a different mode, whereby the collective sensemaking became fragmented. As a result, the views of the managers regarding the collective opportunity failed to coalesce.

Indeed, irrespective of what the modes are, the inter-firm sensemaking becomes fragmented if partners employ different modes, thus challenging the progress of collaborative product development. 'Independent innovators' have a high risk of pursuing development work independently since sensemaking in regard to the digital platform development context is auspicious within individual firm contexts but not within the overall group. In contrast, if a manager in the 'consorter' mode represents a firm that has a crucial role in a collaborative development project, the whole development project may be jeopardised if the digital platform context is not changed. Partners undergoing the 'stagnant' mode of sensemaking can be most harmful for the joint initiative as they have no interest in it at all. Thus, when managers within a group are in different modes simultaneously, their roles in the development project may play a key role in how the joint work proceeds and which corrective actions are needed in order to reach the targeted outcome.

If all partners employ the same mode and engage in collective sensemaking, but the mode is other than 'collaborative innovator', the joint work might also be at risk. A group of 'independent innovators' is likely to have challenges in finding ways to collaborate openly, and they easily split up, whereas 'consorters' are keen to work together but the digital development context needs to somehow change in order for the project to proceed. A group of 'stagnant' managers hardly constitutes a group. All in all, the best setup for a complex collaborative digital platform development project is a group of partners that all manage to maintain the 'collaborative innovator' mode and actively engage in collective sensemaking in front of challenging events, whereas other combinations of managerial modes have more challenging preconditions for the fruitful progress of collaboration.

6. Conclusions

6.1 Theoretical contribution

Digital platforms are rapidly shaping industries and business. They have transformed services in fields including finance, media, mobility and payments and are spreading to different industrial contexts (de Reuver, Sørensen and Basole 2018). In the midst of trying to understand what digital platforms are and how they can be applied in different sectors, one of the underlying questions is how platforms actually emerge (de Reuver, Sørensen and Basole 2018). Uncovering these dynamics is a highly contemporary issue for entrepreneurs as some of them are (or might be in the future) involved in creating digital platforms, and, nevertheless, platforms may shape the business environment globally in any industry. Our study addresses this urgent research need by analysing the creation of a digital platform in a multi-actor setting and illustrates the challenges of collaborative digital technology development.

In particular, the study adds new insight to the literature on entrepreneurship and sensemaking. Firstly, the study contributes to prior research in entrepreneurship by providing an understanding of the dynamics of collective opportunity recognition, an understudied phenomenon in entrepreneurship (Andresen, Lundberg and Wincent 2014; Mainela, Puhakka and Servais 2014), in a collaborative digital platform development context. Illustrating the process through which managers make sense of unexpected events individually and collectively, and react to them accordingly, allows us to see how critical it is for the progress of collaboration that all partners invest in collective sensemaking and in maintaining the view of the targeted collective opportunity even if it is changed along the way. If the partners' sensemaking of the digital platform development – in terms of the partner group and/or the platform itself – becomes fragmented over time, whereby some of the partners start to view the development context ominously, they no longer share the view of an opportunity worth working on, and the success of the project is at great risk. External events can jeopardise the original objective, but it is up to the partners to recognise a new opportunity for collaboration in the changed circumstances.

Secondly, the study provides insights into the literature on sensemaking by proposing four managerial modes in a collaborative product development context. Based on the ominous and auspicious sensemaking that can take place in regard to the developed digital platform and the group of partners in a changed situation, the four modes represent the views held by the involved managers at each point in time. At the beginning of the project, all partners are likely to view the setting through the 'collaborative innovator' mode, but challenging events may turn the views to 'independent innovator', 'consorter' or even 'stagnant' mode. If partners employ different modes in their individual-level sensemaking, the inter-firm level sensemaking about the collaborative platform development becomes fragmented, generating confusion about the next steps and goals and possibly demolishing the overall collective opportunity that depends on the efforts of all partners. If the collaborative platform development faces challenging events, the identification of these modes allows the group to conceptualise whether the views of the partners are starting to diverge because of ominous sensemaking towards the product or the partner group.

By visualising how the process of collaborative digital platform development involves objective external events as well as sensemaking at both the individual and inter-firm levels, this study allows us to understand how complex and fragile the joint development of digital technology can be. The emergence of unexpected external events cannot be controlled, but the insight gained from this study provides a way to conceptualise, and hence possibly support as well as further investigate, the processual dynamics of such projects.

6.2 Managerial implications

This study allows us to draw a number of managerial implications. First, the findings indicate that the group of SMEs did not have a clear understanding of how to reach the common goal in the development project let alone how to overcome emerging bumps in the road. Therefore, similar collaboration projects should place particular effort into enhancing collective sensemaking.

To support this, the common goal and roles of each partner should be voiced and revised regularly and with particular care if sudden changes take place. This supports keeping up the 'collaborative innovator' mode and collective opportunity recognition even in light of sudden changes, whereby partners are more likely to continue to share the view that the joint initiative is worth the effort. And if they no longer do, that should also be openly discussed to clarify whether the problems concern the group or the product.

As regards partner roles, this study also shows that keeping up collective sensemaking in the midst of challenges requires proactive leadership from the project coordinator. The coordinator should clarify relevant technical rules and procedures to all partners and, even more importantly, organise regular discussions among the partners to support collective sensemaking and the updating of the shared workplan in changing circumstances. In addition, it would be important to hold regular one-on-one discussions to follow how the views of each partner are evolving and whether the employed managerial modes are starting to change. Likewise, it is crucial that the partners themselves are willing to invest their time in these discussions, share information and communicate openly. These ways allow the group to prevent the fragmentation of views and efforts or, in the face of insurmountable changes, to see that it is most fruitful to go separate ways in mutual agreement.

6.3 Limitations and suggestions for further research

While this study is based on rich interview data, it is mostly based on individual-level discussions with the collaboration partners as they did not engage in deeper interaction in inter-firm discussions. We look forward to seeing future studies explore our findings in light of data which involve more inter-firm interaction. In particular, it would be interesting to see how different managerial modes are visible in partners' mutual discussions and how that possibly shows in sensegiving (Maitlis 2005) as well as sensereceiving (Hoyte, Noke, Mosey and Marlow 2019), whereby partners respectively try to influence each other's sensemaking and internalise that influence.

In addition, our study explores digital platform development in a business-to-business industry context and among partners of which some were new to each other and others already had an existing business relationship. We suggest that collective versus fragmented sensemaking manifests through four managerial modes of sensemaking concerning joint digital platform development and that in order to obtain more empirical findings on the proposed four modes, further studies should test the modes in different empirical settings. For example, would the dynamics of individual sensemaking somehow differ if all partners were more familiar with each other? Or, how would the modes look in digital platform development in a business-to-consumer context? Through all these avenues of further research, we can gain more information to support successful collaboration between SMEs and the efficient development of complex digital solutions.

References

Andresen Edith, Lundberg Heléne, and Wincent Joakim. 2014. "Processes in collaborative entrepreneurship: a longitudinal case study of how multiple actors exploit a radically new opportunity". *International Entrepreneurship and Management Journal*. Vol. 10. No. 4. 713–726.

Beach Lee Roy, and Mitchell Terence R. 1987. "Image theory: Principles, goals, and plans in decision making". *Acta Psychologica*. Vol. 66. No 3. 201–220.

Ciabuschi Francesco, Perna Andrea, and Snehota Ivan. 2012. "Assembling resources when forming a new business". *Journal of Business Research*. Vol. 65. No. 2. 220–229.

Davidsson Per. 2015. "Entrepreneurial opportunities and the entrepreneurship nexus: A re-conceptualization". *Journal of Business Venturing*. Vol. 30. No. 5. 674–695.

de Reuver Mark, Sørensen Carsten, and Basole Rahul C. 2018. "The digital platform: a research agenda". *Journal of Information Technology*. Vol. 33. No. 2. 124–135.

Ellis Paul D. 2011. "Social ties and international entrepreneurship: Opportunities and constraints affecting firm internationalization". *Journal of International Business Studies*. Vol. 42, No. 1. 99–127.

Gioia Dennis A., and Chittipeddi Kumar. 1991. "Sensemaking and Sensegiving in Strategic Change Initiation". *Strategic Management Journal*. Vol. 12. No 6. 433–448.

Haaja Eini. 2020. "Why do some SMEs engage in joint internationalisation and others do not? Exploring the role of mental images in collective international opportunity recognition". *Journal of International Entrepreneurship*. Vol. 18. 15–43.

Haaja Eini, and Nummela Niina. 2020. "The flourish, failure and future phases of joint internationalisation: A longitudinal case study on collective international opportunity recognition". *European Journal of International Management*, forthcoming.

Halinen Aino, and Törnroos Jan-Åke. 2005. "Using case methods in the study of contemporary business networks". *Journal of Business Research*. Vol. 58. 1285-1297.

Halinen Aino, Medlin Christopher J., and Törnroos Jan-Åke. 2012. "Time and process in business network research". *Industrial Marketing Management*. Vol. 41. No. 2. 215–223.

Hoyte Cherisse, Noke Hannah, Mosey Simon, and Marlow Susan. 2019. "From venture idea to venture formation: The role of sensemaking, sensegiving and sense receiving". *International Small Business Journal: Researching Entrepreneurship.* Vol. 37, No. 3. 1–21.

Keupp Marcus Matthias, Palmié Maximilian, and Gassmann Oliver. 2012. "The Strategic Management of Innovation: A Systematic Review and Paths for Future Research". *International Journal of Management Reviews*. Vol. 14. 367–390.

Lincoln Yvonna S., and Guba Egon G. 1985. *Naturalistic inquiry*. Newbury Park, CA: Sage.

Mainela Tuija. 2012. "From internal resources to collective opportunities". *Journal of Business Research*. Vol. 65, No. 2. 230–231.

Mainela Tuija, Puhakka Vesa, and Servais Per. 2014. "The Concept of International Opportunity in International Entrepreneurship: A Review and Research Agenda". *International Journal of Management Reviews*. Vol. 16, No. 1, 105–129.

Maitlis Sally. 2005. "The social processes of organizational sensemaking". *Academy of Management Journal*. Vol. 48, No. 1. 21–49.

Maitlis Sally, and Christianson Marlys. 2014. "Sensemaking in Organisations: Taking Stock and Moving Forward". *The Academy of Management Annals*. Vol. 8, No. 1. 57–125.

Makkonen Hannu, Aarikka-Stenroos Leena, and Olkkonen Rami. 2012. "Narrative approach in business network process research – Implications for theory and methodology". *Industrial Marketing Management.* Vol. 41. No. 2. 287–299.

Merriam Sharan B. 2009. *Qualitative Research, A Guide to Design and Implementation, Revised and Expanded from Qualitative Research and Case Study Applications in Education*. San Francisco: John Wiley & Sons.

Mitchell Terence R., and Beach Lee Roy. 1990. "… Do i love thee? Let me count …" toward an understanding of intuitive and automatic decision making. *Organizational Behavior and Human Decision Processes.* Vol. 47. No 1. 1–20.

Nambisan Satish. 2017. "Digital Entrepreneurship: Toward a Digital Technology Perspective of Entrepreneurship". *Entrepreneurship Theory and Practice*. Vol. 41. No. 6. 1029–1055.

Ojala Arto, Evers Natasha, and Rialp Alex. 2018. "Extending the international new venture phenomenon to digital platform providers: A longitudinal case study". *Journal of World Business*. Vol. 53. 725–739.

Pettigrew Andrew M. 1997. "What is processual analysis?". *Scandinavian Journal of Management*. Vol. 13, No. 4. 337– 48.

Pettigrew Andrew M. 2012. "Context and action in the transformation of the firm: a reprise". *Journal of Management Studies*. Vol. 49, No. 7. 1304–1328.

Ramoglou Stratos, and Tsang Eric W. K. 2016. "A Realist Perspective of Entrepreneurship: Opportunities as Propensities". *Academy of Management Review*. Vol. 41. No. 3. 410–434.

Shane Scott, and Venkataraman S. 2000. "The Promise of Entrepreneurship as a Field of Research". *Academy of Management Review*. Vol. 25. No 1. 217–226.

Short Jeremy C., Ketchen Jr. David J., Shook Christopher L., and Ireland R. Duane. 2010. "The Concept of "Opportunity" in Entrepreneurship Research: Past Accomplishments and Future Challenges". *Journal of Management*. Vol. 36. No 1. 40–65.

Weick Karl E. 1995. *Sensemaking in Organizations*. Thousand Oaks, CA: Sage.

Weick Karl E., Sutcliffe Kathleen M., and Obstfeld David. 2005. "Organizing and the Process of Sensemaking". *Organization Science*. Vol. 16. No. 4. 409–421.

Venkataraman Sankaran, Sarasvathy Saras, Dew Nicholas, and Forster William R. 2012. "Reflections on the 2010 AMR decade award: Whither the promise? Moving forward with entrepreneurship as a science of the artificial". *Academy of Management Review*. Vol. 37. No. 1. 21–33.

Wood Matthew S., Williams David W., and Drover Will. 2017. "Past as prologue: Entrepreneurial inaction decisions and subsequent action judgments". *Journal of Business Venturing*. Vol. 32. No. 1. 107–127.

Yoo Youngjin, Boland Jr. Richard J., Lyytinen Kalle, and Majchrzak Ann. 2012. "Organizing for Innovation in the Digitized World". *Organization Science*. Vol. 23, No. 5. 1398–1408.

Zahra Shaker A., Korri Juha Santeri, and Yu JiFeng. 2005. "Cognition and international entrepreneurship: implications for research on international opportunity recognition and exploitation". *International Business Review*. Vol. 14. No. 2. 129–146.

Zahra Shaker A. 2021. "International entrepreneurship in the post Covid world". *Journal of World Business*. Vol. 56. No. 1. 101143.

BUSINESS MODEL INNOVATION IN THE DIGITAL AGE: THE INTERNET OF THINGS

LUKE TREVES

Junior Researcher at LUT School of Business and Management

1. Introduction

We are living in what is commonly referred to as the "digital age," which is distinguished by an overlapping ecosystem of digital technologies – each one building on those before and catalysing those to come. This process often referred to as 'digital transformation (DT),' is not only changing nearly every aspect of our personal and communal lives, but also the dynamics of companies and organisations of every size, and in every industrial sector. It is requiring them to realign their products, services, processes, and business models to the conditions of an increasingly digital world (Kreutzer et al., 2017, p. 1). It is also rewriting the rules of customer engagement, competition, data utility, innovation, and value. If companies do not find an appropriate response to these changes, they run the risk of going out of business. Consequently, responding to them requires more than a piecemeal approach; it calls for a total integrated effort – a process of holistic DT within companies, other types of organisations, and whole economies more generally. A key element in this DT will be a company's ability to adapt its business models (BM) to take advantage of and meet the challenges these technologies create. History has demonstrated that many prominent firms that have previously been known for their innovative products, suddenly lose their competitive advantage due to a combination of blinkered mindsets, inflexibility to adapt, or an inability to recognise the threats that new technologies or start-ups pose to their existing BM(s). Strong players such as AEG, Blockbuster, Grundig, Nixdorf Computers, Triumph, Brockhaus, Agfa, Kodak, Quelle, Otto, and Schlecker are vanishing from the business landscape one after the other due to their failure to adapt their BMs and strategies to the changing environment before it was too late (Gassmann et al., 2014).

Peter Drucker, often considered the father of modern management, observes that: *"Today's competition between enterprises is not the competition between products, but the competition between business models."* Building upon this idea Matt Atkinson Chief Marketing Officer at Tesco PLC provides a succinct and insightful overview of the modern economy and organisational landscape in the Foreword of the academic book "The 10 Principles of Open Business: Building Success in Today's Economy" (Cushman & Burke, 2016). Atkinson reflects, "*The world is in a state of transition, where technology, customers and economics are driving change* (no longer products and the producing company). *At the centre of which is the ongoing demand from customers, for transparency and collaboration. The connected nature of these technologies, and the shift in these technologies are creating new businesses, and new business strategies and models. It is essential that businesses are reactive to these changes and adopts appropriate tactics.*" Subsequently, the "BM" concept has become extremely influential over the past 20 years.

A BM can generally be defined as a unit of analysis to describe how a company works. More specifically, the BM is often depicted as an overarching concept that takes notice of the different components a business is constituted of and puts them together as a whole (Osterwalder & Pigneur, 2010). This concept has been more prevalent in the communication of businesspeople and in the business press than in the management research literature, but the latter literature has witnessed a significant increase in interest over the past decade. Likewise, business model innovation (BMI) has been increasingly promoted as a necessary reaction to strategic discontinuities and disruptions, and is shifting bases of competition, increasing the importance placed on innovation and knowledge as value-creating attributes, and is leading to the emergence of new forms of competition through the development of new BMs based on DT. Added to this mix the digitisation of society and the economy, founded on technologies such as the Internet of Things (IoT); is transforming the value propositions and BMs of companies, organisations, and vendors, by enabling them to adapt existing or introduce new BM constructs that allow them to remain relevant and derive value for all of their stakeholders. For example, "servitization" models that involve companies developing digital capabilities to provide services and solutions to their customers, which supplement their traditional product offerings, are becoming increasingly popular. This type of BM creates new revenue streams by allowing the manufacturers and service providers to monetise the data they collect as part of the process and enhance existing offerings with new service level agreements (SLA).

These attractive new opportunities are resulting in true organisational and cultural transformation as much as a technological advancement. This demands what Kranz (2017) refers to as an "architectural approach to IoT deployment," which follows standard deployment patterns and the making of small modifications based on a situation and the specifics of the problem being addressed. The evolution of business perspectives of the IoT can be seen to be driven by two underlying trends: i) the change of focus from viewing the IoT primarily as a technology platform to viewing it as a business ecosystem/network; and ii) the shift from focusing on the BM of a company to designing ecosystem/network BMs (Leminen et al. 2012). Adopting an ecosystem/network approach enables companies to break down internal and external silos and requires a more a holistic view of the enterprise. In this context, companies are required to look at BMs beyond a firm-centric lens and respond to changing business dynamics as part of an ecosystem/network of partner stakeholders e.g. other companies, Government agencies and customers. In other word's an agile and integrated approach to BMI is essential for companies to survive and excel in the digital age. This is critical in the case of so-called 'Digital' or 'IoT' entrepreneurs whose ventures and transformation of existing businesses through the creation of novel digital technologies and/or novel usage of such technologies; and are considered by many countries as a critical pillar for DT and resulting digital economic development. This idea is explored in more detail in the remainder of this chapter.

2. Digital Transformation

DT of industries and society is a key element for growth, entrepreneurship, job creation, and welfare. DT enables speeding up the development of innovative responses not only to local economic and societal challenges, but for reaching sustainable development goals (Business Finland, 2018). Despite the apparent promise and significance of DT, there is not a commonly accepted definition for the term. Moreover, the terms digitalisation and digitisation are often used interchangeably leading to some confusion. Schallmo et al. (2018) propose a comprehensive definition of digital research based on previous research on the subject relevant to our focus, which is as follows:

> *"The DT framework includes the networking of actors such as businesses and customers across all value-added chain segments, and the application of new technologies. As such, DT requires skills that involve the extraction and exchange of data as well as the analysis and conversion of that data into actionable information. This information should be used to calculate and*

> *evaluate options, in order to enable decisions and/or initiate activities. In order to increase the performance and reach of a company, DT involves companies, business models, processes, relationships, products, etc."*

In short, DT describes the use of digital technologies (such as ubiquitous broadband, cloud storage, mobile technologies, data analytics, machine learning/ artificial intelligence, and emerging production technologies such as additive manufacturing) and the data they produce to connect companies/ organisations, people, physical assets, and processes to generate better business outcomes, including capitalising on customer needs, realising efficiencies and productivity growth, improving the effectiveness of decision making across the company/organisation, and enabling new BMs (Hao et al., 2020). DT is thus distinct from digitisation, which refers to adding digital elements to existing processes, BMs, and strategies. In this sense, DT affects all sectors of society, particularly economies. It opens new networking possibilities and enables cooperation between different actors, who, for example, exchange data and thus initiate processes. In this context, the DT of BMs plays an essential role because BM's individual elements can be digitally transformed.

While DT offers the potential for new, innovative BMs, companies that are exploring DT may find that their previously used technologies still yield better cost benefit ratios than new, yet expensive, technologies that remain untested in the market (Arnold et al., 2020). For these reasons, companies that face relentless changes in the technological environment need to balance their decisions between an orientation towards the present and one towards the future. For this, companies rely upon their absorptive capacity - the ability of a firm to recognise the value of new, external information, assimilate it, and apply it to commercial ends - before designing their innovation strategy and eventually innovating their BM (Müller et al., 2020). To address these issues, we focus on one of the DT 'base technologies' – those that support and provide connectivity and intelligence for smart systems in an integrated way (Frank et al., 2019) - the IoT. We choose this emphasis due to the DT's reliance on the creation of networks and interconnectivity among existing assets enabled by the IoT (Frank et al., 2019), and the significant influence IoT is forecast to have on the nature of future dynamics of companies and their offerings (Atzori et al., 2010).

3. BMI in the context of The Internet of Things (IoT)

The IoT

The term "IoT'' – also called the Internet of Everything or the Industrial Internet – is a relatively new and potentially disruptive computer paradigm that is likely to change business processes, strategies, and competencies across many industries (Lee & Lee, 2015). From a technological perspective, IoT is used as an umbrella keyword covering various aspects related to the extension of the Internet and the Web into the physical realm, by means of the widespread deployment of spatially distributed devices with embedded identification, sensing and/or actuation capabilities (Miorandi et al., 2012). More specifically, it is: "A technological paradigm in which devices, machines, and humans interconnect with each other in order to create data-based services to support day-to-day living" i.e. smart homes, human activity monitoring (Lee & Lee 2015). In this context:

- **"The things"** refer to tags, sensors, and smartphones, etc., which are applied to collect measurement data from and share processes information to end-user locations.
- **Wireless sensor networks and radio-frequency identification** are the technical tools used to transmit the data from one point to another.
- **Applications** are the tools through which a user can access and manipulate the gathered data.

Value is subsequently realised by complementing smart, networked assets with contemporary technologies including scalable computing, information analytics, and mobility; and presenting it in a way that is useful to a user (Frank et al., 2019). In this sense, IoT envisions a future in which digital and physical entities can be linked, utilising appropriate information and communication technologies, to enable a whole new class of applications and services (Miorandi et al., 2012). This is achieved through (i) the resulting global network interconnecting smart objects using extended internet technologies, (ii) the set of supporting technologies necessary to realise such a vision (including, e.g., RFIDs, sensor/actuators, machine-to-machine communication devices, etc.) and (iii) the ensemble of applications and services leveraging such technologies to open new business and market opportunities (Atzori et al 2010). Affordable sensors and fast connections have radically increased the amount and type of data available and altered the way companies collect and use it. More importantly, they have changed the way many companies conduct their business, and are challenging some of the oldest brands to rethink their identities (Schimek, 2016).

Consequently, IoT is an important enabling technology, which is being increasingly implemented by companies and organisations of all sizes and represents one of the top strategic technology trends to shape future business opportunities. From a business perspective, companies can use IoT to connect products and devices, which allows them to tap new areas of business and to offer their customers entirely new product and services. Additionally, direct lines of communication with customers provide realistic insights into how they use connected products and services and allow companies to tailor their offerings accordingly based on accurate, descriptive, and real-time data. Companies will enjoy a clear competitive advantage if they realise it is imperative to connect their products and devices through IoT in an integrative way, but those who only focus on the technological aspects of an IoT project have already lost the race. Additionally, companies who devote their full attention to customer benefits are the most likely to enjoy long-term success. It is therefore essential to identify and innovate promising BMs and supporting tactics before embarking on an IoT project. Such models should establish and maintain long-term relations with business ecosystem/network partners and customers, by offering them new digital experiences and added value. Examples of this include new or improved services, higher efficiency, or better quality (Bosch Software Innovations, 2017). Before examining the impact of IoT on BMs and BMI it is important to establish what is meant by these terms.

3.1 The Business Model (BM)

A BM refers to the logic through which companies design the architecture and mechanisms they use to create, deliver and capture value for their stakeholders through their activities (Foss & Saebi, 2016; Jørgensen et al., 2018; Osterwalder & Pigneur, 2010; Reim et al., 2014; Teece, 2010). More specifically, the BM concept takes notice of the different functions a company is constituted of and puts them together as a whole (Osterwalder & Pigneur, 2010). These functions typically include a value proposition, target market(s), value chain, revenue mechanisms, value network or ecosystem, and competitive strategy (Chesbrough, 2007). Accordingly, each company is implicitly based on a BM, even though it is not always explicitly presented. A BM can add to the competitiveness of a company by offering a logical and consistent approach to the (innovative) design and execution of the business. In other words, a BM describes how the magic of a company works based on its individual bits and pieces.

3.2 Business Model Innovation (BMI)

In the past 50 years, the average BMs lifespan has fallen from about 15 years to less than five. As a result, BMI is now an essential capability for companies seeking to drive breakout growth, reinvigorate a lagging core, or defend against industry disruption or decline. The BM is therefore gaining in importance as a starting point for BMI and transformation. BMI describes a holistic approach to new BM design or existing BM reconfiguration, which sees a deliberate change of one or more key element of a BM and its respective interrelations. This normally leads to a qualitatively new BM, which differs distinctively from the previous one. The resulting BM can range from an incremental improvement to a radical new way of doing business (Bucherer & Uckelmann, 2011).

In this sense, BMI is the art of enhancing advantage and value creation by making simultaneous—and mutually supportive—changes both to a company value proposition to its customers and its underlying operating model. BMI is important to companies as it usually has a stronger impact on profit margins than product and service innovations and it can disrupt established industries. BMI can, therefore, be viewed as an attempt to develop or identify new BM strategies by "searching for new logics of the company and new ways to create and capture value for its stakeholders. It focuses primarily on finding new ways to generate revenues and define value propositions for customers, suppliers, and partners (Foss & Saebi, 2015, pp. 169)."

4. BMI in the Digital Age: An IoT perspective

As has been described, BMI acts as a means of enhancing advantage and value creation by enabling better informed, simultaneous, and mutually supportive changes, both to company's' value proposition to customers and its underlying operating model. At the value proposition level, these changes can address a company's choice on target market segment(s), its product and/or service offering(s), and revenue model(s) (Deimler & Kachaner, 2020). As companies become increasingly reliant on digital technologies in all their activities, BMI should also serve as means to align technology development and economic value creation and ensure they remain competitive in times of rapid change fuelled by technological innovations, including IoT. Porter and Heppelmann (2014, 2015) underline the importance of this approach by maintaining that connectivity offered by up-to-date technologies, including IoT, are driving the development of new products and processes, and new BMs, with strong implications on the organisation of the company. Companies must leverage the possibility of "servitizing" their businesses through difficult-to-imitate services, differentiating themselves not only from competitors, but also downstream players that are empowered by the digitalisation process (Vendrell-Herrero et al. 2017). Despite this, IoT has often been portrayed primarily as a technical-implementation challenge, with the drive for adoption spearheaded by specialists in the Chief Information Officer (CIO) function. Yet real business gains from IoT require changes to business processes. Connecting production equipment to the internet, for example, will allow a company to manage its usage more effectively and predict when maintenance is needed. However, if the supporting BMs are not appropriately innovated and optimised, then the value will not be maximised and at worst not realised at all. It is, therefore, important for companies to understand the impact IoT is having and will have on their BM and subsequent BMI (Kraijak & Tuwanut, 2015).

The overarching principle of an IoT BM is to focus on customer needs and capture and deliver value through the exploitation of its pervasive nature, and the rapid improvement of IoT-enabled technologies that allow different innovative activities and differentiated customer offerings (Atzori et al., 2010; Lu et al., 2018). As previously mentioned, the real upheaval IoT will create is through its ability to enable companies to evolve from product producers to service providers, a process commonly referred to as servitization. These services are typically supplied to customers through customised Product-Service System (PSS), which are described as a marketable set of products and services capable of jointly fulfilling a user's needs (Mont, 2002). Most PSS offerings are categorised into three BM types: product-oriented (PO), use-oriented (UO), and result-oriented (RO) BMs, as these continue to be the most prevalent types of product/service BMs (Reim et al., 2015; Rosa et al., 2019; Tukker, 2004). Whilst these models have been around for several decades, IoT can enhance them through its ability to pool resources into systems in real-time, that include multiple linked systems, meaning that there are endless ways to use the information and to innovate IoT BMs, which can create, deliver and capture value in different ways (Leminen et al., 2012). For example, for a tool manufacturing company that intends to make a PO offering (e.g., tool optimisation software), activities that surround creating, delivering, and capturing value will continue to be linked primarily to products but with an added service function. In contrast, using a RO model (e.g., total care solution) the PSS provider takes full responsibility for providing the promised results by intimately combining products and services. The transition of traditional pure products BMs to IoT PSS-based forms allows for the creation of value through services in different parts of the system (Osako et al., 2019). However, the selection of the BM depends to a large extent on the company's resources, capabilities, and user needs (Leminen et al., 2012), which can ultimately create strategic and competitive benefits for companies adopting these forms of BMI (Frank et al., 2019; Tukker, 2015, 2004).

5. IoT BMI implications for entrepreneurship

A change can be observed within the entrepreneurial landscape where entrepreneurs are increasingly transitioning from an internet context to an IoT context, with the use of many IoT systems and technologies (Atzori et al., 2010). From an IoT perspective, the term 'entrepreneur' can be applied in a broad sense. First, it includes private entrepreneurs who establish new ventures related to the IoT. Second, the term includes business leaders of existing private and public organisations who engage in innovation and experimentation with different elements of IoT to improve existing business processes or offer new value propositions to customers (Krotov, 2017). Currently, many countries consider the advancement of IoT and digital entrepreneurship as an essential pillar for future economic development. The IoT is therefore moving from a technology of the future to a present must have tool, which creates significant commercial opportunities accessible to any type of company no matter its size, age, or access to finance. The transition towards IoT entrepreneurship is therefore of critical importance.

The rapid proliferation of digital technologies enabled by the IoT is profoundly changing operating environments, reshaping traditional business models and processes (Bharadwaj *et al.*, 2012). These technologies are also giving rise to new ways of collaboration, leveraging resources, and reshaping the mentality of entrepreneurs, and hence affect their decision-making processes (Shen et al., 2018). This is resulting in BMI driven by factors, such as new and potential streams of revenue generation, competitive edge, satisfying customer demand, and customer stickiness. To achieve these objectives, entrepreneurs - besides companies of all sizes and maturity levels - are developing BMs that hinge on new relationships with customers and a host of other stakeholders. These BMs expand from the transactional (product sale and, in many cases, after-market parts and service) to those that offer IoT generated data, and the services, insights, and solutions that can be derived from that data (PWC, 2017). In this context, the overarching principle of an IoT BM is to focus on the customer, the capture and delivery of value through the exploitation of the IoT's pervasive nature and the rapid improvement of IoT-enabled technologies to facilitate different innovative activities and differentiated customer offerings and applications (Atzori et al., 2010; Lu et al., 2018). IoT offerings and applications are also increasingly built upon an integrated cloud/internet-based platform (Gubbi *et al.*, 2013), which can provide seamless integration of physical devices, data storage and data analytics to various IoT applications. These integrated systems can allow for such capabilities as virtualisation (also called platform as a service or PaaS) of computing resources and delivering end-user IoT applications in software as a service (SaaS) manner (Krotov, 2017). These IoT offerings and applications typically fall within two BM strategy categories:

(1) Bottom-up or sustaining BM strategies - whereby entrepreneurship strategies use IoT to enhance existing products or services. This requires analysing the properties of existing BM's and devising new ways for improving existing processes or transactions; or
(2) Visionary or disruptive BM strategies – whereby entrepreneurs create a new BM based on the vision of a world in which every object is part of a global, ubiquitous network. Requiring them to question themselves, 'if this vision becomes a reality, what kind of new transactions or business models will be possible?'

In both scenario's, IoT is predominantly viewed as a collection of human and nonhuman objects embedded within a physical environment, connected via a ubiquitous, wireless network (Krotov, 2017). This has resulted in the emergence of three prevalent IoT/digital BMI types: (1) Product-orientated; (2) Use-orientated; and (3) Results-orientated (Table 1) (Reim et al., 2015).

	Product-orientated	Use-orientated	Result-orientated
Value creation	Provider takes responsibility for the contracted services	Provider is responsible for the usability of the product or service.	Provider is responsible for delivering results.
Value delivery	Provider sells and services the product sale and service (e.g. maintenance or recycling).	Provider assures the usability of the physical product along with service.	Provider is responsible for delivering results.
Value capturing	Customer pays for physical product and for the performed services.	Customer can make continuous payments over time (e.g., leasing).	Customer payments are based on outcome units; that is, they pay for the result.

Table 1. Comparison of IoT orientated BM categories in terms of value creation, value delivery and value capturing (Reim et al., 2015).

The real upheaval that the IoT will create is through its ability to enable entrepreneurial businesses to evolve from 'product' producers to 'service' providers - 'servitization,' which create a new set of rules that entrepreneurs, particularly internet-entrepreneurs should be aware of (Yu *et al.*, 2017). By collecting and analysing large amounts of unique data from all their customers using IoT-enabled technologies, entrepreneurs can offer additional service-oriented BMs that foster continuous innovation, improved design and quality and customised goods, rather than the production of large volumes of standardised products. This is done using adaptable open and online platform systems, which allow system members to access resources and capabilities from a network of partners and/or platform systems. Enabling them to develop a diverse range of customer focused IoT service solutions (Westerlund et al., 2014), which has previously been mainly within the domain of large companies equipped with abundant resources and capabilities to overcome previous technology development issues independently.

Table 2 provides an overview of some of the types of IoT BMs, which companies are designing or have developed, to best align IoT in a way that best supports their overall business strategy and customer base. It also provides examples of potential monetisation streams of these models. For entrepreneurs, this move towards more customer-focused and service-orientated BMIs is imperative for their business, as it can generate positive word-of-mouth about their company amongst existing and potential customers. Subsequently, creating more opportunities to expand more quickly, and in some cases, generate more innovation for the entrepreneur(s). This innovation stems from acquiring new knowledge from varying IoT channels, such as those arising from interaction via social media, which can be a unique source of competitive advantage. This can enable them to effectively implement and develop their IoT BMI as part of an ongoing process.

Business Model Type	Description	Potential Monetisation
Product performance monitoring	Customer accesses data from connected asset independently for real-time, periodic "check-ups" on an asset's performance and efficiency of use and signals for predictive maintenance.	Charge a separate premium for apps or web-based tools, cybersecurity, data storage, software updates, or charge an upfront premium for the IoT-enabled asset at the point of sale.
Data analysis/diagnostics from manufacturer	Manufacturer (or third-party vendor) provides predictive maintenance alerts and prescriptive insights, including push alerts on service/ maintenance, security alerts, and software upgrades. Manufacturer owns and remotely manages the data.	Charge, on a subscription basis, for some, or a complete suite of these products and services. Alternatively, can charge on an outcome basis (e.g., improvements in asset uptime or unplanned downtime) and can include bonus incentive or a penalty, based on the outcome. Or, a hybrid of the two.

IoT-driven field services	Manufacturer extends service by offering enterprise-wide solutions, leveraging an asset's product performance data and analysis via alerts to the customer of needed actions/insights (e.g., identifying the part required to prevent a malfunction, identifying the most qualified field technician, or determining a software update to address an issue, manufacturer owns and remotely manages data.	Charge, a subscription basis, or a complete suite of, IoT products and services. Alternatively, can charge on an outcome basis (e.g., improvements in asset uptime or unplanned downtime) and can include bonus incentive or a penalty, based on the outcome. Or, a hybrid of the two.
"The Pay-Per" model	Just as some manufacturers are already charging on an asset usage basis, or on the service that an asset is providing (e.g., Asset Pay-Per), IoT enabled products also lend themselves to similar "pay-per" offerings, including pay-per hour of output, pay-per-alert, pay-per-insight, pay-per-warning, and pay-per-solution, which can be described as IoT Software Pay-Per. Manufacturer owns and remotely manages data.	Manufacturer charges only when a customer uses products, and only when it receives insight or warnings on performance, maintenance, or insights on gaining efficiencies such as power consumption.

Table 2. Overview of common IoT Business Models (adapted from: PWC, 2017)

Several 'second-order' BM value propositions can also be developed, which support the current IoT infrastructure. These are defined second order as they are not immediately related to what appears to be the essence of IoT- the interaction between human and non-human objects and their environments. Instead, these BMs support elements of IoT. A prime example of this is the promising area of creating new business propositions from the 'big data' generated by the devices and sensors that make up IoT (Krotov, 2017).

Whilst, this movement towards IoT BMI, particularly 'servitization' orientated BMs is opening a wealth of new opportunities for entrepreneurs, there are also several concerns they should be aware of. For example, it is increasingly critical for entrepreneurs operating in an IoT environment to monitor more systematically, both the interaction with customers and the sharing of information amongst customers (Yu *et al.*, 2017). Privacy and security, and overreliance on IoT technologies in making business decisions; are also critical issues. The entrepreneur's active participation therefore remains an essential element in final the decision making on IoT BMI changes. Critically, entrepreneurs who have either just launched, or are preparing to launch, their own business must realise the potential IoT has for their solution(s), how that solution(s) is packaged and fits within existing IoT ecosystems, and is subsequently taken to market. Entrepreneurs, therefore, need a strong business case from the outset – for an IoT solution based on actually required business outcomes (for example, compliance), not just an application – with a proof of concept that is unfaltering in its ability to demonstrate value, consider cost, and prove Return-on-Investment.

Despite the early promise of IoT BM implementations and an increasing number of entrepreneurs using IoT-enabled technologies to pursue new business opportunities, there continue to be substantial discrepancies in how advanced different economic sectors are in integrating it into their BMs. For example, significant traction has been made in the logistics, transportation, and smart cities but remains in the early stages of integration in healthcare and agriculture. Research also suggests, fewer than one in ten companies has achieved "extensive" IoT implementation, for both external and internal operations (Westerlund et al., 2014). According to a 2017 PWC survey on the monetisation of the Industrial Internet of Things, it was found that about half of the manufacturers (47%) currently offering IoT products and services are selling customer-managed IoT platforms (i.e., selling a bundling of product and IoT service, related data gathering and analysis technology and software). Yet 30% of manufacturers have gone beyond that, selling IoT product-as-a-service offerings (e.g., the manufacturer remotely captures customer IoT data and sells data analytics and services, including alerts on performance and maintenance needs). Just 4% of manufacturers are selling fully integrated multi-sourced IoT platforms. Wide-scale adoption of IoT can also be particularly challenging for incumbent companies, who are often concerned with the threat of tech-start-up firms who have no legacy systems/cultures.

The choice of IoT BM can be a complex process for entrepreneurs, particularly as many of them are at an early stage of their DT and IoT journey. As in other technology markets, such as personal computers and the Internet itself, there can be three evolutionary phases:

1. "Arms suppliers" succeed by providing the building blocks of the infrastructure.
2. Companies build broadly scaled applications, such as online searches on the Internet.
3. Companies build adjacent businesses, such as e-commerce on the Web (Manyika *et al.*, 2015).

At the current stage in the evolution of the IoT industry, the complexity of IoT systems, the limited capabilities of many customers to implement them, and the need for interoperability and customisation provide opportunities for hardware, software, and service providers of "end-to-end" IoT solutions to meet specific needs. For IoT technology suppliers, the base of the competition will likely include distinctive technology, distinctive data, software platforms, and the ability to provide complete solutions (ibid).

Looking forward it will be increasingly important for entrepreneurs to integrate the capabilities IoT offers into their user/consumer offerings and supporting online channels and communities. At the same time, they will need to define their digital vision and translate it into a set of clear targets and performance indicators that create accountability and serve as guideposts for progress (Sousa & Rocha, 2019). Key issues that result from this include, (1) the need to ensure the exchange of win-win data between IoT-enabled technologies and ecosystem/network members. (2) Effective integration and management of a diverse range of relatively immature objects/innovations across internal and external boundaries, and (3) becoming more comfortable working within and as part of unstructured ecosystems/networks. This requires a movement away from the dominant company-centric view of conceiving BM(s), wherein the BM is the undivided "property of the firm." To more generic level descriptions of BMs that are supportive in capturing the specific value from IoT for ecosystems/networks.

6. Conclusion

Digital transformation and the IoT is an Unavoidable Fact of Life and is rapidly emerging as a significant business transformation driver that can disrupt competitors, both known and unknown. Entrepreneurs play a critical role in the development of the IoT (or any other technology). Driven by their desire for self-gain, self-actualization, or contribution to their communities, these entrepreneurs use their technical knowledge, business experience, and intuition to create new BMs in the realm of the IoT. Bringing these business ideas to fruition often requires addressing existing technical, managerial, and legal issues by developing new technologies, new business processes, and connecting the dots to IoT in numerous other ways. Entrepreneurs collectively set various vectors for further development of the IoT (Krotov, 2017). DT and IoT require entrepreneurs from across all industrial sectors to rethink their businesses from the ground up. Although this will not happen overnight, companies need to start contemplating and envisioning the possibilities now. IoT is a learning experience, and not all ideas will work. Not every new BM or go-to-market strategy will prove to be a winner or disruptive force, but some will. Additionally, these changes will not be a one-time occurrence and will require constant alterations as business, operations, and customers demand evolve in rapidly developing business environments. IoT is already and will further change competition dynamics, drive BMI and lead to new BM types for user and supplier companies.

A good starting point on this journey would be to review how similar change issues were handled in the past and apply and adapt the lessons learned. An awareness and thoughtfulness to how many new variables an entrepreneur, established company, or organisation is planning to introduce in an IoT BM and stage its integration carefully. A business justification for integrating IoT solutions into a BM also needs to be developed. If this cannot be identified immediately, an entrepreneur should continue to learn, experiment, and benchmark their results against those of their peers'. At some point, they should identify a compelling ROI for their first IoT project and start their journey. Other key takeaways are:

- Entrepreneurs – as well as all types of organisation - should start their IoT journey by "thinking big but starting small." This means that you need to be realistic about implementing IoT BM solutions and taking a stepped approach i.e. IoT should not be implemented in one go. Start by targeting low-risk projects that have clear business benefits, then become increasingly more ambitious as expertise and support grow. This approach is likely to have a better success rate and bring more stakeholders on-board.

- Interactivity and engagement between entrepreneurs, companies, and/or types of organisation and the customer is the key to successful IoT-driven BMI.
- Cooperation and working in partnership with other companies, organisations, and the end-customer – the so-called "co-economy"; who have complementary products, services, processes, etc., is essential to succeeding with the IoT and in the digital economy. Doing it alone, no matter a company's size or resources is unlikely to lead to success with IoT. Companies and organisations must start assembling ecosystems/networks of partners from inside and outside the company and make sure they can work together well.
- The challenge of legacy integration must not be underestimated.
- Companies must resist the temptation to develop custom solutions, but instead insist upon open platforms that can be adopted by the industry and networks they operate in, and flexible enough to allow entry into new markets at a rapid pace.
- Communication along all channels of a business ecosystem/network is critical for IoT and BMI success. As well as taking advantage of the power of established relationships to instigate the adoption of IoT throughout these ecosystems/networks.

This can all appear a daunting and overwhelming challenge. However, there are numerous reasons for entrepreneurs embracing DT and IoT including, (i) strategic advantages gained through reinventing their business through BMI, (ii) attracting and retaining the best and brightest employees, and (iii) innovative go-to-market strategies to attract and retain customers. Finally, new, or reengineered BMs, leveraging digital technologies can create new business and revenue opportunities, unachievable in the past and open new doors to business growth.

References

Annarelli, A., Battistella, C. and Nonino, F. (2016) 'Product service system: A conceptual framework from Annarelli, A., Battistella, C. and Nonino, F. (2016) 'Product service system: A conceptual framework from a systematic review', *Journal of Cleaner Production*. Elsevier Ltd, 139, pp. 1011–1032. https://doi.org/10.1016/j.jclepro.2016.08.061.

Arnold, C., Kiel, D., and Voigt, K. I. (2020). Innovative business models for the industrial internet of things. *26th International Association for*

Management of Technology Conference, IAMOT 2017, 26 1379–1396.
Atzori, L., Iera, A. and Morabito, G. (2010) 'The Internet of Things : A survey', *Computer Networks*. Elsevier B.V., 54(15), pp. 2787–2805. https://doi.org/10.1016/j.comnet.2010.05.010.
Benamar, L., Balagué, C., and Zhong, Z. (2019). Internet of Things devices appropriation process: The Dynamic Interactions Value Appropriation (DIVA) framework. ***Technovation***, 89, 102082. https://doi.org/10.1016/j.technovation.2019.06.001.
Bharadwaj, A., El Sawy, O.A, Pavlou, P.A. and Vekatraman, N. . (2012) 'Digital Business Strategy: Toward A Next Generation Of Insights', *MIS Quarterly*, 37, pp. 471–482. https://doi.org/10.25300/MISQ/2013/37:2.3
Bosch Software Innovations (2017). 5 steps to successful IoT solutions. *Innovations, B. S.*, available at: https://futureiot.tech/wp-content/uploads/2018/11/Bosch_5-steps-to-successful-IoT-solutions_wp.pdf
Bucherer, E. and Uckelmann, D. (2011) 'Business Models for the Internet of Things', *Architecting the Internet of Things*, pp. 253–277. https://doi.org/10.1007/978-3-642-19157-2_10.
Business Finland (2018) Digital Finland Framework, *Business Finland*, available at: https://www.businessfinland.fi/globalassets/julkaisut/digital-finland-framework.pdf
Chesbrough, H. (2007) 'Business model innovation: It's not just about technology anymore', *Strategy and Leadership*, 35(6), pp. 12–17. https://doi.org/10.1108/10878570710833714.
Cushman, D. and Burke, J. (2014) *The 10 Principles of Open Business: Building Success in Today's Open Economy.* Palgrave MacMillan.
Deimler, M. and Kachaner, N. (2020). Business Model Innovation Delivers Competitive Advantage. *Boston Consultancy Group,* available at: https://www.bcg.com/en-nor/capabilities/innovation-strategy-delivery/business-model-innovation
Foss, N. and Saebi, T. (2015) *Business Model Innovation the organizational dimension.* OUP Oxford.
Frank, A. G., Dalenogare, L. S. and Ayala, N. F. (2019) 'Industry 4.0 technologies: Implementation patterns in manufacturing companies', *International Journal of Production Economics*. Elsevier B.V., 210(January), pp. 15–26. https://doi.org/10.1016/j.ijpe.2019.01.004.
Gassmann, O., Frankenberger, K. and Csik, M. (2014) 'The St . Gallen Business Model Navigator', *University of St. Gallen.*
Gubbi, J., Buyya, R., Marusic, S. and Palaniswami, M. (2013) 'Internet of Things (IoT): A vision , architectural elements , and future directions',

Future Generation Computer Systems. Elsevier B.V., 29(7), pp. 1645–1660. https://doi.org/10.1016/j.future.2013.01.010.

Jørgensen, S., Jacob, L. and Pedersen, T. (2017). *Restart Sustainable Business Model Innovation Palgrave Studies in Sustainable Business*, available at: http://www.palgrave.com/gp/series/15667.

Kreutzer, R. T., Neugebauer, T. and Pattloch, A. (2017) *Digital Business Leadership, Digital Business Leadership*. Springer, Germany. https://doi.org/10.1007/978-3-658-11914-0.

Kraijak, S. and Tuwanut, P. (2015). A survey on Internet of Things architecture , protocols , possible applications , security , privacy , real-world implementation and future trends. *Conference: 2015 IEEE 16th International Conference on Communication Technology (ICCT)*, 26–31. https://doi.org/10.1109/ICCT.2015.7399787

Kranz, M. (2016) *Building the Internet of Things: Implement New Business Models, Disrupt Competitors, Transform Your Industry*. John Wiley and Sons.

Krotov, V. (2017) 'The Internet of Things and new business opportunities', *Business Horizons*. 'Kelley School of Business, Indiana University', 60(6), pp. 831–841. doi: 10.1016/j.bushor.2017.07.009.

Lee, I. and Lee, K. (2015) 'The Internet of Things (IoT): Applications, investments, and challenges for enterprises', *Business Horizons*. 'Kelley School of Business, Indiana University', 58(4), pp. 431–440. https://doi.org/10.1016/j.bushor.2015.03.008.

Leminen, S., Westerlund, M., Rajahonka, M., and Siuruainen, R. (2012). Towards IOT Ecosystems and Business Models. *In: Andreev S., Balandin S., Koucheryavy Y. (eds) Internet of Things, Smart Spaces, and Next Generation Networking.* ruSMART 2012, NEW2AN 2012. Lecture Notes in Computer Science, vol 7469. Springer, Berlin, Heidelberg. https://doi.org/10.1007/978-3-642-32686-8_2

Lu, Y., Papagiannidis, S., and Alamanos, E. (2018). Internet of things: A systematic review of the business literature from the user and organisational perspectives. *Technological Forecasting and Social Change*, 136, 285–297. https://doi.org/10.1016/j.techfore.2018.01.022

Manyika, J., Chui, M., Bisson, P., Woetzel, J., Dobbs, R., Bughin, J., and Aharon, D. (2015). The Internet of Things: Mapping the value beyond the hype. *McKinsey Global Institute*, (June), 144.

Miorandi, D., Sicari, S., De Pellegrini, F. and Chlamtac, I. (2012). Internet of things: Vision, applications and research challenges. *Ad Hoc Networks*, *10*(7), 1497–1516. https://doi.org/10.1016/j.adhoc.2012.02.016

Mont, O. K. (2002). Clarifying the concept of product – service system. *Journal of Cleaner Production, 10(3)*, 237–245. https://doi.org/10.1016/S0959-6526(01)00039-7

Müller, J. M., Buliga, O. and Voigt, K. I. (2020). The role of absorptive capacity and innovation strategy in the design of industry 4.0 business Models-A comparison between SMEs and large enterprises. *European Management Journal*, (In Press), 1–11. https://doi.org/10.1016/j.emj.2020.01.002

Osako, L. F., Matsubayashi, M. O., Takey, S. M. and Cauchick-Miguel, P. A., (2019). Cost evaluation evaluation challenges for Internet Internet of Things (IoT) based Product / Service-Systems (PSS): *Procedia CIRP*, 84:302, 302–306. https://doi.org/10.1016/j.procir.2019.04.187

Osterwalder, A. and Pigneur, Y. (2010) *Business Model Generation: A Handbook for Visionaries, Game Changers, and Challengers.* John Wiley and Sons, United States.

Porter, M. E., and Heppelmann, J. E. (2014). How smart, connected products are transforming competition. *Harvard Business Review*, 92(11), 64–88.

Porter, M. E., and Heppelmann, J. E. (2015). How smart, connected products are transforming competition. Harvard Business Review, 93(10), 96–114.

PWC. (2017). Monetizing the Industrial Internet of Things. Industrial Internet of Things. *Pricewaterhouse Coopers*. Available at: https://www.pwc.com/us/en/industrial-products/publications/assets/pwc-monetizing-the-industrial-internet-of-things.pdf

Reim, W., Parida, V., and Örtqvist, D. (2015). Product-Service Systems (PSS) business models and tactics - A systematic literature review. *Journal of Cleaner Production*, *97*, 61–75. https://doi.org/10.1016/j.jclepro.2014.07.003

Rosa, P., Sassanelli, C. and Terzi, S. (2019). Towards Circular Business Models: A systematic literature review on classification frameworks and archetypes. *Journal of Cleaner Production*, *236*, 117696. https://doi.org/10.1016/j.jclepro.2019.117696

Schallmo, D., Williams, C. A. and Boardman, L. (2017). Digital transformation of business models-best practice, enablers, and roadmap. *International Journal of Innovation Management*, 21(8): 1–17. https://doi.org/10.1142/S136391961740014X

Schimek, R. S. (2016). IoT Case Studies: Companies Leading the Connected Economy. *American International Group (AIG)*, 1–16. Available at: https://www.aig.co.uk/content/dam/aig/emea/united-kingdom/documents/Insights/iot-case-studies-companies-leading-the-

connected-economy-digital.pdf
Shen, K. N., Lindsay, V. and Xu, Y. (2018) ‘Digital entrepreneurship’, *Information Systems Journal*, 28(6), pp. 1125–1128. https://doi.org/10.1111/isj.12219.
Sousa, M. J. and Rocha, Á. (2019) ‘Skills for disruptive digital business’, *Journal of Business Research*. Elsevier, 94, pp. 257–263. doi: 10.1016/j.jbusres.2017.12.051.
Teece, D.J. (2010). Business models, business strategy and innovation. *Long Range Planning*, 43 (2–3), 172–194. https://doi.org/10.1016/j.lrp.2009.07.003
Tukker, A. (2004). Eight Types of Product Service Systems. *Business Strategy and the Environment*, 13(4), 246–260. https://doi.org/10.1002/bse.414
Tukker, A. (2015). Product services for a resource-efficient and circular economy - A review. *Journal of Cleaner Production*, Elsevier Ltd, Vol. 97, pp. 76–91. https://doi.org/10.1016/j.jclepro.2013.11.049
Vendrell-Herrero, F., Bustinza, O.F., Parry, G. and Georgantzis, N. (2017), Servitization, digitization and supply chain interdependency. *Industrial Marketing Management*, 60, 69–81. https://doi.org/10.1016/j.indmarman.2016.06.013
Westerlund, M., Leminen, S., Rajahonka, M. and Ferber, S. (2014). Designing Business Models for the Internet of Things. *Technology Innovation Management Review*, 5–14.
Yu, X., Roy, S.K., Quazi, A., Nguyen, B. and Han, Y. (2017) ‘Internet entrepreneurship and “the sharing of information” in an Internet-of-Things context: The role of interactivity, stickiness, e-satisfaction and word-of-mouth in online SMEs’ websites’, *Internet Research*, 27(1), pp. 74–96. https://doi.org/10.1108/IntR-02-2015-0060.

PART 2:

MACRO-LEVEL INTERNATIONAL BUSINESS AND ENTREPRENEURSHIP

FOREIGN DIRECT INVESTMENT IN THE ERA OF DIGITALIZATION AND ENVIRONMENTAL SUSTAINABILITY

ARTI YADAV

Post-Doctoral Fellow, Indian Council of Social Science Research, Department of Commerce, Aligarh Muslim University, Aligarh, India.

AND BADAR ALAM IQBAL

Emeritus Professor and Professor Extraordinarius; School of Transdisciplinary Research and Graduate Studies [STRGS) University of South Africa; Pretoria (South Africa)

1. Introduction

Globally, digitalization has transformed the way to do business and it has a significant role in defining the present pattern and trend of foreign direct investment. In the present scenario, the role of digital transformation is highly visible through its high level of involvement in the manufacturing and service sector of economies around the world, which also paved the way to discuss its impact on the sustainability of the environment (IEA, 2017; Global e-Sustainability Initiative, 2020). The economic growth of economies is driven by the pattern of consumption, production and the most important one is the cautiousness towards the environment. The economic scenario today is changing, driven by progression in consumption, production pattern, and environmental cautiousness. The inception of the digital era and increased awareness about climate change has led to various changes that have a significant impact on society (UNEP, 2015). Digitalization is more like a necessity, as it is needed in various aspects such as online shopping, social networking, financial and non-financial transactions, cloud computing, big data, and mobile technology (Iqbal & Yadav, 2019; Iqbal & Yadav, 2021). Advancement in the level of digitalization has significantly enhanced the quality and processing speed in terms of lower information costs and other transaction costs (OECD,

2018). Digitalization is changing the way in terms of participants, ways to do business across borders, and economic gains as well (Wautelet, 2017; Press, 2015). The effect of digitalization can also be seen in the international production of multinationals (MNEs). In recent years, there has been a rapid rise in the number of technological multinationals as in UNCTAD's top 100 MNEs, the number of technological MNEs has been doubled during 2010-2015. They come out as active players as, during that particular time period, there has been an increase of 65 percent in the assets, and an increase by 30 percent has been recorded in operating revenues and employees (UNCTAD, 2017a; UNCTAD, 2017$_b$).

Today, environmental pollution is becoming a serious issue. It is the contamination of the physical and biological components of the atmosphere of Earth, causing an adverse effect on the normal environment. Pollution of air, land, and water occurs because of excessive use of nature's capacity or excessive use of natural resources (Muralikrishna and Manickam, 2017). In its production process, an industry uses finite environmental resources. The rapid growth of industrialization at the national and international level has led to the generation of various issues around the world and environmental pollution is one of them (Das, 2016). The environmental crisis can reduce the quality of life for both the present as well as the future generation. The influence of FDI (Foreign Direct Investment) on the environment can be both ways, positive or negative, and leads to the generation of interest in the concept of environmental sustainability in relation to FDI. Therefore, this chapter contributes to the literature by synthesizing the role of FDI in the era of the digital economy and its responsibility towards environmental sustainability.

2. Review of Literature

In the era of globalization for both developed and developing economies the dawn of Information Communication and Technology has led towards social and economic transformations related to benefits (Quibria and Tschang 2001; Quibria, Ahmad, Tschang and Macasaquit, 2002). Digital platforms and infrastructure lead to the evolution of globalization through the exchange of data and information across markets in foreign economies. It is resizing businesses and developing virtual market spaces (Manyika et al., 2016; Baldegger 2019). With the help of digitalization, multinationals can easily sell digital services and can have patents leading to affect location and investment decisions (Elkjaer and Damgaard, 2018). The digital economy has changed the way to do business around the world and it has significant repercussions for FDI. The study found that compared to traditional multinationals, the highly digitalized industries see less FDI. Further, digitalized industries deliberately have their establishment in developed economies. Financial and fiscal motives mainly define their patterns for investment (Casella and Formenti, 2018). Sinha, Keshari, Chaudhury and Sengupta (2019) found that the digitalization process can act as a positive step through spillover effects in FDI and employment linkage. Also, if the FDI inflow is in advanced technology-based or non-labour intensive industries, there will be economic growth, however, it is jobless. Digitalization can indirectly affect the inflow of FDI as advanced digital infrastructure enhances the attractiveness of export-oriented flows of FDI in economies. Further, the use of digitalization can bring transparency in various activities of the hosting economy paving way for less corruption and a decrease in other issues associated with FDI inflow (Mote, Pawar and Dani, 2016; Sinha, Chaudhury and Sengupta, 2020).

Not only in developed economies but also in developing economies, pollution of the environment is a critical issue. Environment pollution occurs when the effect of harmful by-products of human activities has significant damage over the system and it cannot be deactivated easily (Folnovic, 2020). The beginning of the industrial revolution has lead to an increase in pollution levels around the world. In the growth of environmental pollution, the main factors which lead to the invariably use of natural resources are the advancement of technology, urbanization, and growth of the population (Muralikrishna and Manickam, 2017). Various measures have been taken by industrialized economies to protect the environment. It has been found that there are measures that can help in the total prevention of ecological issues, however, they are costly (Clarke et. al., 1994; Kumar and Kumar, 2016). In the process of economic growth, environmental pollution is a significant problem on the quality of human life in terms of its survival. Moreover, environment corrosion has a direct effect. According to the study, one of the reasons for environmental degradation is Foreign Direct Investment. Further, there are various advantages associated with FDI for economies in extracting and utilizing resources, but for sustainability to prevail, there should be laws and regulations to protect the environment (Mabey and McNally, 1999; Hitam and Borhan, 2012).

Bildirici (2020) examines the relationship between FDI inflow, CO_2 releases, terrorist attacks, energy use, and economic growth for China, India, Israel, and Turkey. The study found that FDI inflows in the selected economies cause a rise in environmental pollution as well as it is a positive source of real GDP contribution. To, Ha, Nguyen and Vo (2019) studied the issues related to FDI leading to degradation of the environment and the validity of the Kuznets curve related to the environment in selected markets of the Asian region. The study applied panel dynamic ordinary least square and fully modified ordinary least square. The findings of the study show that foreign direct investment has a strong and significant impact on the environment and oil consumption is a major input source affecting emission. It signifies that an improvement in the quality of the environment can be observed if there is a reduction in the level of oil consumption. The study suggests that the priority of policymakers should be on economic growth, however with a reduction in the level of oil consumption and degradation of the environment. Further, there should be application growth policies which have long term effect for economic growth and development without any negative effect on the environment (Everett, Ishwaran, Ansaloni and Rubin, 2010). Various studies have signified the potential negative consequence of FDI on the environment, however, the study by Demena and Afesorgbor (2020) found that the prospective environmental cost because of an increased level of emission may weaken the gains to an economy achieved through the increased level of FDI inflows, but there is a chance that FDI can also lead to a cleaner environment with the introduction of green technologies. The effect of FDI can be negative as well as positive (Sasana, Sugiharti and Setyaningsih, 2018; Li, Dong, Huang and Failler, 2019).

Some studies have shown a positive impact of FDI or mixed impact on the environment, for instance, Jugurnath and Emrith (2018) investigated the impact of FDI on environment degradation and found that FDI and CO_2 are not positively and significantly related. In other words, the impact of FDI is not always negative on the environment as it is also expected as the key source of cleaner advanced technology and sustainable modes of production for small island developing states. Ashraf, Doytch and Uctum, (2020) studied the effect of greenfield foreign direct investment and mergers and acquisitions on the environment, specific to CO_2 emission sector-wise. The result signifies that greenfield foreign direct investment increases pollution in poorer countries, while mergers and acquisitions decrease pollution mainly in industrialized countries. In the case of developed economies, Greenfield FDI decreases pollution in the transport industry, but it increases pollution in poorer countries. Further, it found that mergers and acquisitions type of FDI is less harmful to the environment in developed economies. It suggests that for environmental conservation alongside economic development, FDI must be regulated and scrutinized for developed and poorer nations.

3. FDI and Digitalization

Information Communication Technology (ICT) or digitalization is a general term signifying technologies that are used for accumulating, storing, editing, and corresponding information in various forms (Kundishora, 2008). Globally, ICT has a vast reach in terms of enormity, commonness, and efficacy because of its features like low cost, high processing speed, and capability to communicate (Zekos, 2005, Trucano, 2010). Digitalization can also add value to the national GDP of an economy and can enhance the competitiveness of an economy's products and services in the home as well as foreign markets (Kvochko, 2013). Figure 1 shows the global ICT developments for mobile, telephone, internet, fixed broadband, and active mobile broadband users.

Figure 1: Global ICT developments (2001-2009*)

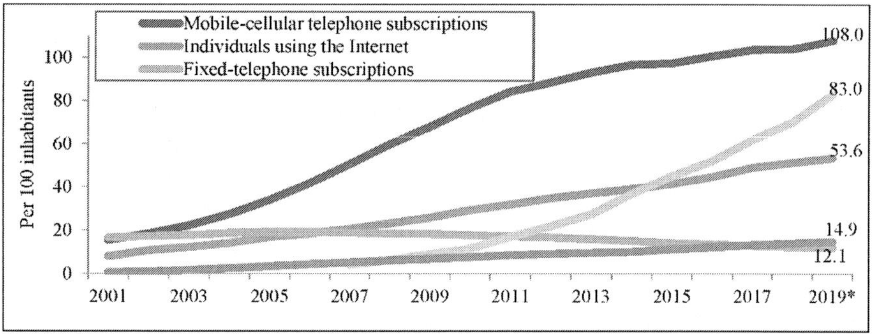

Note: *Estimate, Source: ITU World Telecommunication /ICT Indicators database

Figure 2 shows the global numbers of individuals using the internet. Digitalization can effectively support economic integration at the international level, constricted the digital divide, enhance the standard of living, and can help in the management and utilization of biodiversity (Souter and MacLean, 2012). Restructuring of institutions, society, and economies come under the process of digital transformation (Unruh and Kiron, 2017). The economic benefits of digitalization are expected to be 3 times of broadband. Further, it also contributes to the employment level by reducing the level of employment by 0.84 percent for every 10 percent increase in digitalization (Strategy&, 2012).

Figure 2: Global numbers of individuals using the internet, total and per 100 inhabitants (2002 to 2019*)

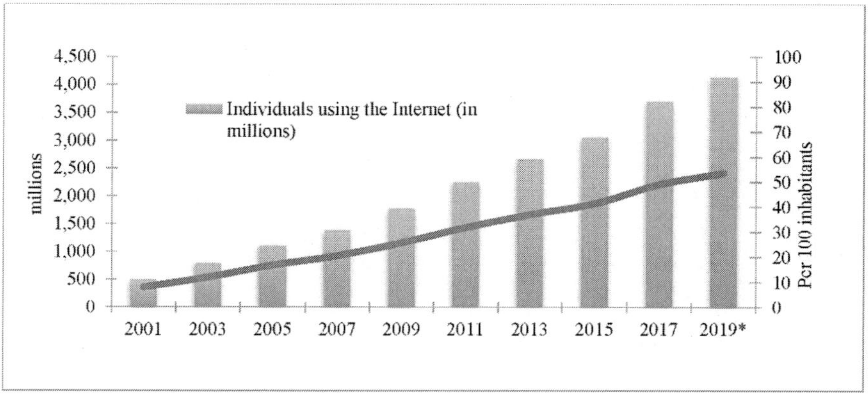

Note: * Estimate, Source: ITU World Telecommunication /ICT Indicators database

The growth of the digitalization culture is not even in economies around the world. Compared to 2008, now (2019) the shares of developing economies in terms of individuals using the internet are more than that of developed economies (Figure 3) (ITU World Telecommunication, 2019). The Asian region has the highest share (50 percent) of internet users followed by Europe (16 percent), Africa (11 percent), and other regions. A Higher degree of creativity and innovation has been found in economies that have adopted digitalization. Digitalization also helps in trade internationally subject to regulations at the domestic level (UNCTAD, 2019). Investment in the high level of ICT education, in terms of skilled human capital, is required to achieve the probable benefits of digitalization.

Figure 3: Internet Users Distribution in the World

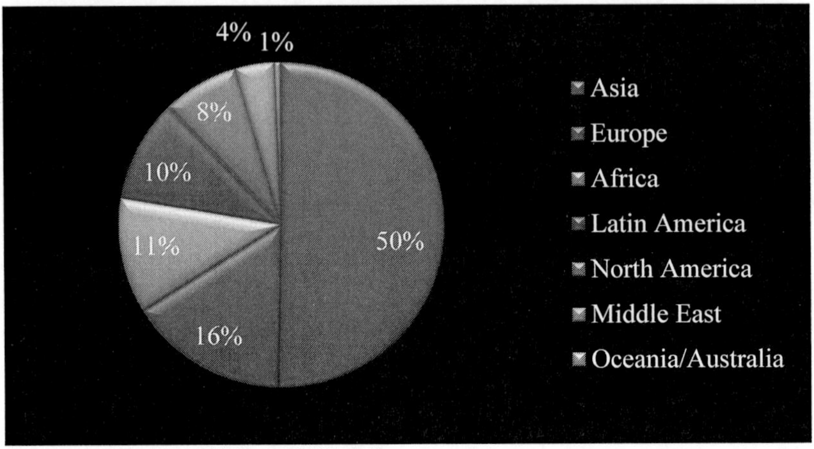

Source: Internet World Stats (2020 Q1),
https://www.internetworldstats.com/stats.htm

Investment by multinationals in terms of Foreign Direct Investment is not only the source for foreign currency but also leads to the generation of advanced technology, employment, technical proficiency, competitive efficiency, and effectiveness (UNCTAD, 2004). Figure 4 and Figure 5 show the global FDI inflows and outflows around the world, developed economies, and developing economies. The share of FDI globally is falling. It falls by around 13 percent in the year 2018 when compared with 2017. The flow of FDI is declined in developed economies, however, it remains stable for developing economies and also shows a rise of 2 percent. Further, the investment from developed economies abroad is reduced by 40 percent and from developing economies fall by 10 percent in 2018 (UNCTAD, 2019).

Figure 4: Global FDI Inflows (1990-2018) (million US$)

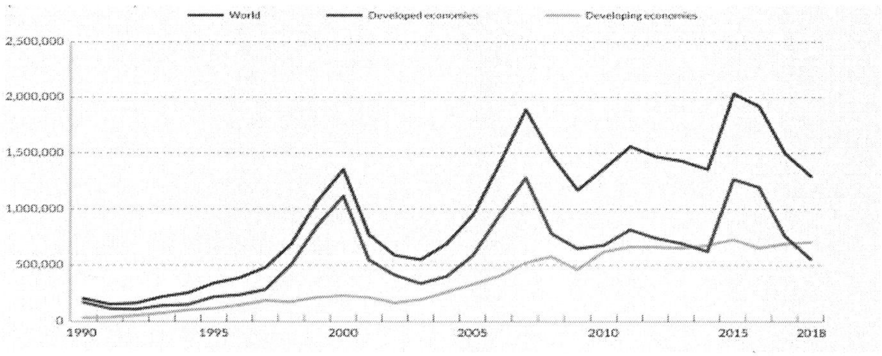

Source: UNCTAD (2019)

Digitalization has a great significance for foreign investors in terms of process simplification and paperless transactions devoid of any bias or error. Various transactions related to banks, bills payment, or financial transactions can be done from anywhere at any time. Further, innovations like artificial intelligence or Robo-advisory is possible only because of Digitalization (Jain, 2018). Digital infrastructure should be strong and properly regulated in terms of measures and policy initiatives to encourage investment to be beneficial for both domestic companies as well as foreign firms (Stephenson and Sen, 2020). Digitalization in FDI can lead to the sustainable development of economies through less use of traditional mechanisms and acceleration of the innovation process leading to more transparent and good governance globally.

Figure 5: Global FDI Outflows (1990-2018) (million US$)

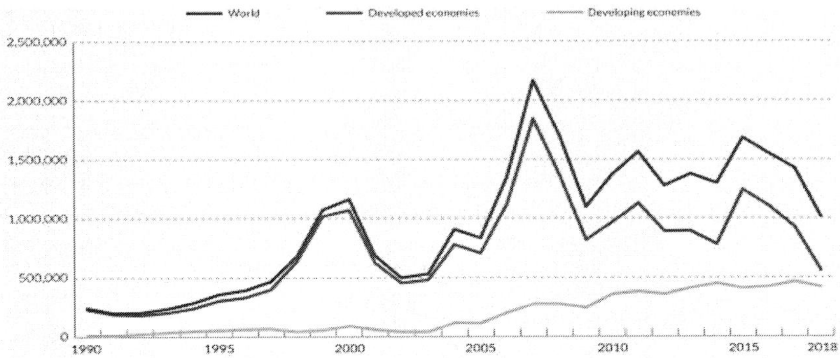

Source: UNCTAD (2019)

Internationalization strategies of multinational organizations also have an impact on digitalization, as now physical presence is not necessary to engage or operate in a global market. The impact of digitalization can be partially seen on market-seeking and resource-seeking FDI and fully on knowledge-seeking FDI (Eden, 2016; Bruno and Lorenzo, 2018). Information, Communication & Technology has become one of the significant determinants of FDI inflows directly (as a global linking channel) as well as indirectly (through directly affecting other determinants like entrepreneurship and innovation) (Sinha and Sengupta, 2019).

Digitalization in FDI can sometimes be considered in negative terms as most of the ICT products are carbon-intensive. Continuous development of digitalization and its use in various investors' projects can lead to the generation of issues like toxic waste, carbon dioxide, and other greenhouse gas emissions, and the disposal of electronic waste. The ICT sector is expected to contribute around 15 percent of total emissions by 2020 (UNCC, 2016). Destruction of the environment is mostly associated with economic activities and FDI has a significant role in it. Figure 6 shows the direct and indirect ways through which industrial digitalization can have an impact on the environment and FDI can also be part of such industries. Therefore, the role of investment is critical for the sustainability of human existence (Mabey and McNally, 1999; Hitam and Borhan, 2012).

Figure 6: Effect of Industrial Digitalization on the Environment

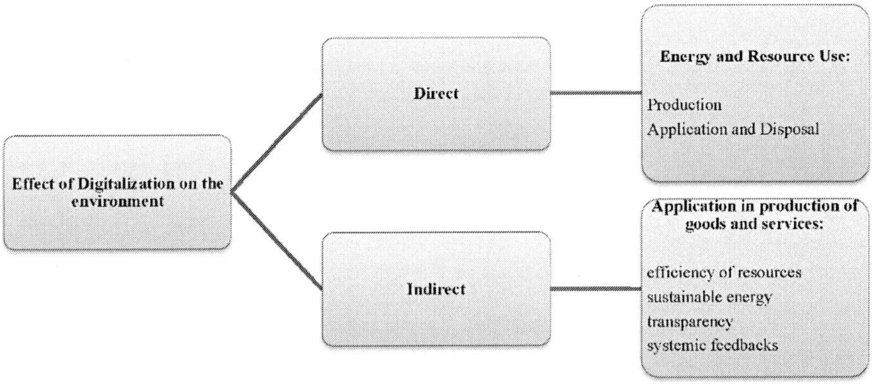

Source: based on Berkhout and Hertin (2001); Erdmann et al. (2004); Beier et al. (2018); Kunkel and Matthess (2020).

4. FDI and Environment

Since the 1990s, a sea change has been seen in foreign investment policies of the government around the world in terms of removal of various restrictions on financial inflows and outflows. A five-fold rise has been witnessed in terms of capital mobility, globalization of production, and extensive privatization. Along with such a growth process, the process of environmental degradation has also accelerated in the form of loss of biodiversity, deforestation, and greenhouse gas emissions. The main force behind the degradation of the environment is the increase in the level of economic activities (Mabey and McNally, 1999; Banga, 2003). Figure 7 shows the effect of FDI on the environment. FDI through capital accumulation impacts economies of scale, the structure of the industry, and pollution density, leading to pollution emission.

Figure 7: Effect of FDI on Environment

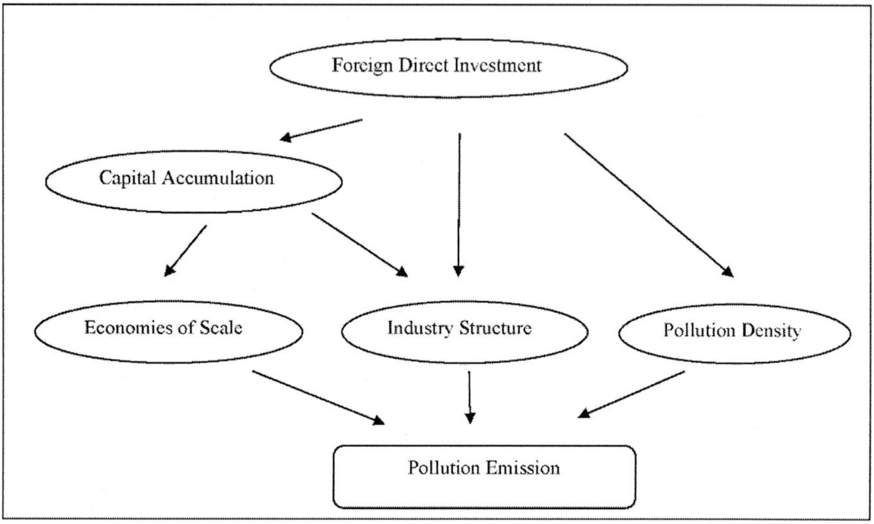

Source: Yang and Chen (2011)

Since the 1990s greenhouse gas emissions around the world have grown 41 percent and rising constantly. The main source of greenhouse gas emissions by humans is the consumption of energy (in sectors such as electricity and heat, transportation, construction and manufacturing, fugitive emission, buildings, and other sources) consisting of around 73 percent (Ge and Friedrich, 2020). In the year 2019, the global carbon dioxide emissions elevated to a record level (Table 1).

Table 1: Countries Share of CO_2 Emission

Rank	Country	Emissions ($MtCO_2$)	% of Global Emissions
1	China	9839	27.2
2	United States	5269	14.6
3	India	2467	6.8
4	Russia	1693	4.7
5	Japan	1205	3.3
6	Germany	799	2.2
7	Iran	672	1.9
8	Saudi Arabia	635	1.8
9	South Korea	616	1.7
10	Canada	573	1.6
11	Mexico	490	1.4
12	Indonesia	487	1.3
13	Brazil	476	1.3
14	South Africa	456	1.3
15	Turkey	448	1.2
	Top 15	26125	72.2
	Rest of World	10,028	27.7

Source: Fleming, S. (2019). Chart of the day: These countries create most of the world's CO_2 emissions. World Economic Forum.

The above table shows that for more than two-thirds of global CO_2 emission only 15 economies are accountable. It shows that developed and developing economies are the main contributors to the emission of CO_2. The changing pattern of consumption and production in both developed and developing economies, as the customers now are more conscious of a healthy environment, is changing the perspective of businesses towards their environmental image (UNCTAD, 2004). Multinational's size is also responsible for the environmental issue other than the type and way to do a particular business. Compared to developed economies, for developing economies, time or the lack of it has a significant role in the generation of issues related to the environment. Most of the policy decisions in developing economies are based on employment and output objectives because of the pressure to have higher investment inflow and growth rates (Polasky et al., 2019).

While in most of the cases it has been found that FDI has an adverse impact on the environment, however, it can also help in the sustainability of the environment through the introduction of cleaner or greener technologies (Zeng and Eastin, 2012; Zhu et al., 2016). The effect of cleaner technology might not be visible in the short run; however, in the long run, the effect of the scale of production might go up leading to a higher income level with a lower level of expenditure on abatement and a higher capital stock (Arango Vieira, 2009). Further, FDI flows will positively impact the environment through scale effect i.e., moving from a small to global scale; technique effect in the form of adoption of cleaner technology; composition effect in a way that shift the preferences to cleaner products and greater environmental protections as income increases (Kathuria, 2018). As Eskeland and Harrison (2003) found that in the case of developing economies, foreign multinationals work taking into consideration the environmental factors compared to the domestic organizations. Therefore, the potential impact of FDI on the environment both positive as well as negative leads to the generation of the term Green FDI. Through green FDI efforts can be made for the growth, protection, and evade the negative effect on the environment. Various institutes are taking steps toward it and the Paris Climate agreement is one of them. Further, technology leapfrogging in which FDI through transferring cleaner technologies can also contribute to development in a sustainable way (Golub, Kauffmann and Yeres, 2011).

5. Conclusion

Environmental Sustainability matter is as significant as other issues like poverty reduction and rising inequality. The well-being of humans is affected by all the issues related with them and the digitalization provides unparallel opportunities to improve it, even during the time of crisis like situations. The enormous potential of digitalization can be utilized to provide services like energy, education, healthcare, the information in association with the environment, and to protect the degradation of the environment. In the area of foreign direct investment where there is an interaction of economies at the international level, digitalization should be approached appropriately. Further, FDI plays a vital role in the present digitalization-based economy in achieving economic growth as well as a sustainable environment. Digitalization in FDI helps in achieving this goal through the ease of doing business, lower costs, effective and efficient communication. However, issues like cyber-security in terms of data threats and information system threats should be taken care of. Moreover, probable structural changes are also expected in the market for labor, use of artificial intelligence in employment, science, and education, the emergence of virtual spaces, and increased level of surveillance potential, which will directly or indirectly affect the social and economic scenario in the future.

Sustainability of the environment can be achieved through FDI by the introduction of less emission-based technologies like end-of-pipe technology and clean technology. The management of environmental concerns should be more than about previous issues related to pollution. Presently, most of the concerns are related to the size of the concerned transnational corporation besides their way of conducting business. In the case of developing countries, the problem of environmental concern originates because of lack of time for it as the policy decisions of these economies are mostly to fulfill objectives like employment generation and instant output. The environmental quality can be maintained only when high standards of governance can be maintained through stringent environmental laws. The government policies along with the growth contribution should scrutinize the expected impact of proposed FDI's costs and benefits to the environment. Further, technological innovation is not a one-time thing, it should be a continuous process through increasing research and development intensity of a nation, so that, new and advanced technologies came into existence to protect the environment in a better way. Therefore, home and host economy policies should be framed with careful considerations to achieve long term sustainability. The present study is solely based on the secondary database and captures mostly the macro aspect of FDI, digitalization, and environmental sustainability; it does not look into the micro perspective of the same. Therefore, further research can be based on primary data from firms' outlook.

References

Arango Vieira, Luis Carlos. (2009). El impacto de las inversiones extranjeras directas en las economías en desarrollo y el ambiente. *Revista Ingenierías Universidad de Medellín*, *8*(14), 111-128. Retrieved from http://www.scielo.org.co/scielo.php?Script=sciarttext&pid=S1692-33242009000100008&lng=en&tlng=es

Ashraf, A., Doytch, N. and Uctum, M. (2020). Foreign direct investment and the environment: disentangling the impact of greenfield investment and merger and acquisition sales. *Sustainability Accounting, Management and Policy Journal*. Retrieved from https://doi.org/10.1108/SAMPJ-04-2019-0184

Baldegger, R.J. (2019). Internationalization and Digitalization of MSMEs or Is it MSME Digitalization of Internalization. ICSB Gazette, Issue 43. Retrieved from https://icsb.org/wp-content/uploads/2019/11/Gazette43.pdf

Banga, R. (2003). Impact of government policies and Investment agreements on FDI inflows. Indian Council for Research on International Economic Relations, Working Paper no. 116. Retrieved from https://www.icrier.org/pdf/WP116.PDF

Beier, G., Niehoff, S. and Xue, B. (2018). More Sustainability in Industry through Industrial Internet of Things?.*Appl. Sci.*, 8 (2), p. 219

Berkhout, F. and Hertin, J. (2001). Impacts of Information and Communication Technologies on Environmental Sustainability: Speculations and Evidence. Report to the OECD, Brighton, p. 21.

Bildirici, M. E. (2020). Terrorism, environmental pollution, foreign direct investment (FDI), energy consumption, and economic growth: Evidences from China, India, Israel, and Turkey. *Energy & Environment.* Retrieved from https://doi.org/10.1177/ 095830 5X20919409

Bruno, C. and Lorenzo, F. (2018). FDI in the digital economy: a shift toasset-light international footprints. UNCTAD. Munich Personal RePEc archive (MPRA). Retrieved from https://mpra.ub.uni-muenchen .de/95201/1/MPRA_paper_95201.pdf

Casella, B. and Formenti, L. (2018). FDI in the digital economy: A shift to asset-light international. Transnational Corporations 25(1):101-130. DOI: 10.18356/cb688e94-en

Clarke, R.A., Stavins, R.N., Greeno, J.L., Bavaria, J.L., Cairncross, F., Esty, D.C., Smart, B., Piet, J. Wells, R.P., Gray, R., Fischer, C. and Schot, J. (1994). The Challenge of Going Green. Harvard Business Review. Retrieved from https://hbr.org/1994/07/the-challenge-of-going-green

Das, P.K. (2018). An Introduction to the Concept of Environmental Management: Indian Context. *International Journal of Innovation and Economic Development, 2(4),* 25-34.

Demena, B. A. and Afesorgbor, S.K. (2020). The effect of FDI on environmental emission: Evidence from a meta-analysis. Energy Policy, Volume 138, 111192. Retrieved from https://doi.org/10.1016/j.enpol.2019.111192

Eden, L. (2016). Multinationals and foreign investment policies in a digital world. E15Initiative, International Centre for Trade and Sustainable Development and World Economic Forum, Geneva. Retrieved from www.e15initiative.org.

Elkjaer, T. and Damgaard, J. (2018). How Digitalization and Globalization have Remapped the Global FDI Network. Prepared for the 16th Conference of the International Association of Official Statisticians (IAOS) OECD Headquarters, Paris, France. Retrieved from http://www.oecd.org/iaos2018/programme/IAOS-OECD2018_Elkjaer-Damgaard.pdf

Erdmann, L., Hilty, L., Goodman, J. and Arnfalk, P. (2004). The Future Impact of ICTs on Environmental Sustainability. European Commission, Joint Research Centre.

Eskeland, G.S. and Harrison, A.E. (2003). Moving to greener pastures? Multinationals and pollution haven hypothesis. Journal of Development Economics, 70 (1), pp.1-23

Everett, T., Ishwaran, M., Ansaloni, G.P. and Rubin, A. (2010). Economic Growth and Environment. Defra Evidence and Analysis Series, Paper 2, Department for Environment Food and Rural Affairs. Retrieved from https://assets.publishing.service.gov.uk/government/uploads/system/uploads/attachment_data/file/69195/pb13390-economic-growth-100305.pdf

Fleming, S. (2019). Chart of the day: These countries create most of the world's CO_2 emissions. World Economic Forum. Retrieved from https://www.weforum.org/agenda/2019/06/chart-of-the-day-these-countries-create-most-of-the-world-s-co2-emissions/

Folnovic, T. (2020). Environmental Pollution. Agrivi. Retrieved from https://blog.agrivi.com/post/environmental-pollution

Ge, M. and Friedrich, J. (2020). 4 Charts Explain Greenhouse Gas Emissions by Countries and Sectors. World Resources Institute. Retrieved from https://www.wri.org/blog/2020/02/greenhouse-gas-emissions-by-country-sector

Global e-Sustainability Initiative. (2020). SMARTer 2030 - ICT Solutions for 21st Century Challenges. Retrieved from https://smarter2030.gesi.org/

Golub, S. S., Kauffmann, C. and Yeres, P. (2011). Definingand Measuring Green FDI: An Exploratory Review of Existing Work and Evidence. OECD Working Papers on International Investment,11/02. Retrieved from http://dx.doi.org/10.1787/5kg58j1cvcvk-en

Hitam, M.B. and Borhan, H.B. (2012). FDI, Growth and the Environment: Impact on Quality of Life Malaysia. Procedia- Social and Behavioral Sciences 50, 333-342. Retrieved from https://doi.org/10.1016/j.sbspro.2012.08.038

IEA. (2017). Digitalization and Energy. *International Energy Agency*, Paris. Retrieved from https://www.iea.org/publications/freepublications/publication/DigitalizationandEnergy3.pdf

Internet World Stats. (2020 Q1). Retrieved from https://www.internetworldstats.com/stats.htm

Iqbal, B. A., & Yadav, A. (2019). Business models: An illustrative study of e-commerce businesses in India. In Handbook of research on business models in modern competitive scenarios. Chapter 22 (pp. 398–408). https://doi.org/10.4018/978-1-5225-7265-7.ch022

Iqbal, B.A. and Yadav, A. (2021). Fourth Industrial Revolution: Its Role and Contribution in Employment Generation and Skills Development. *Journal of Global Economy, Trade and International Business,* Vol. 1, No. 1, 2021, 85-96. DOI:10.47509/JGETIB.1.1.2021.85-96

Jain, R. (2018). Digitalization has led to an increase in investments. Business Today. Retrieved from https://www.businesstoday.in/opinion/columns/digitization-has-led-to-an-increase-in-investments/story/277989.html

Jugurnath, B. & Emrith, A. (2018). Impact Of Foreign Direct Investment On Environment Degradation: Evidence From SIDS Countries. *Journal of Developing Areas*. Tennessee State University, College of Business, vol. 52(2), pages 13-26. Retrieved from https://doi.org/10.1353/jda.2018.0019

Kathuria, V. (2018). Does Environmental Governance Matter for Foreign Direct Investment? Testing the Pollution Haven Hypothesis for Indian States. *Asian Development Review*, vol. 35, no. 1, pp. 81–107. Retrieved from https://doi.org/10.1162/adev_a_00106

Kumar, D and Kumar, D. (2016). Societal Responsibility and Economic Viability. Societal Responsibility and Economic Viability. Management of Coking Coal Resources, 193-259. Retrieved from https://doi.org/10.1016/B978-0-12-803160-5.00006-X

Kundishora, S.M. (2008). The Role of ICT in Enhancing Local Economic Development and Poverty Reduction. World Bank. Retrieved from https://siteresources.worldbank.org/CMUDLP/Resources/Role_ICT_paper.pdf

Kunkel, S. and Matthess, M. (2020). Digital transformation and environmental sustainability in industry: Putting expectations in Asian and African policies into perspective. *Environmental Science & Policy*, volume 112, pages 318-329. Retrieved from https://www.sciencedirect.com/science/article/pii/S146290112030157X

Kvochko, E. (2013). Five Ways Technology can help the Economy. World Economic Forum. Retrieved from https://www.weforum.org/agenda/2013/04/five-ways-technology-can-help-the-economy/

Li, Z. Dong, H., Huang, Z. and Failler, P. (2019). Impact of Foreign Direct Investment on Environmental Performance. Sustainability, MDPI, 11, 3538.

Mabey, N. and McNally, R. (1999). Foreign Direct Investment and the Environment: From Pollution Havens to Sustainable Development. WWF-UK Report. Retrieved from https://www.oecd.org/investment/mne/2089912.pdf

Manyika, J., Lund, S., Bughin, J., Woetzel, J., Stamenov, K., and Dhingra, D. (2016). Digital Globalization: The New Era of Global Flows. McKinsey and Company. Retrieved from https://www.mckinsey.com/~/media/McKinsey/Business%20Functions/McKinsey%20Digital/Our%20Insights/Digital%20globalization%20The%20new%20era%20of%20global%20flows/MGI-Digital-globalization-Full-report.ashx

Mote,R., Pawar,A., and Dani,A. (2016). Review of security and privacy techniques in cloud computing. In Proceedings of First International Conference on Information and Communication Technology for Intelligent Systems, vol. 1, pp. 543–552.

Muralikrishna, I.V. and Manickam, V. (2017). Introduction. Environment Management, Science and Engineering for industry, Science Direct, 1-4. Retrieved from https://doi.org/10.1016/B978-0-12-811989-1.00001-4

OECD (2002). Foreign Direct Investment for Development: Maximizing Benefits Minimizing Costs. Retrieved from https://www.oecd.org/investment/investmentfordevelopment/1959815.pdf

OECD (Organization for Economic Corporation and Development). (2018). Financial Markets, Insurance and Pensions: Digitalisation and Finance. Retrieved from http://www.oecd.org/finance/Financial-markets-insurance-pensions-digitalisation-and-finance.pdf

Polasky, S., Kling, C.L., Levin, S.A., Carpenter, S.R., Daily, G.C., Ehrlich, P.R., Heal, G.M., and Lubchenco, J. (2019). Role of economics in analyzing the environment and sustainable development. Proceedings of the National Academy of Sciences Mar, 116 (12) 5233-5238; DOI: 10.1073/pnas.1901616116

Press, G. (2015). A Very Short History of Digitalization. Forbes. Retrieved from https://www.forbes.com/sites/gilpress/2015/12/27/a-very-short-history-of-digitization/#442589f349ac

Quibria, M. G., and T. Tschang. (2001). Information and Communication Technology and Poverty: An Asian Perspective. ADB Institute Working Paper No. 12, Tokyo.

Quibria, M. G.; Ahmed, Shamsun N.; Tschang, Ted; Reyes-Macasaquit, Mari-Len (2002): Digital Divide: Determinants and Policies with Special Reference to Asia, ERD Working Paper Series, No. 27, Asian Development Bank (ADB), Manila. Retrieved from http://hdl.handle.net/11540/1935

Sasana, H., Sugiharti, R.R. and Setyaningsih, Y. (2018). The impact of Foreign Direct Investment to the Quality of the Environment in Indonesia. E3S Web of Conferences 73, 10025. https://www.e3s-conferences.org/articles/e3sconf/pdf/2018/48/e3sconf_icenis18_10025.pdf

Sinha M., Chaudhury A.R., Sengupta P.P. (2020) An Empirical Analysis on FDI and ICT in India. In: Satapathy S., Bhateja V., Mohanty J., Udgata S. (eds) Smart Intelligent Computing and Applications. Smart Innovation, Systems and Technologies, vol 160. Springer, Singapore.

Sinha, M., Keshari, P.K., Chaudhary, A.R. and Sengupta, P.P. (2019). FDI and Employment in the Era of Digitaliation: Evidence from Developing Economies. Forum for Global Knowledge Sharing. Retrieved from http://fgks.in/index.php/resarch-papers

Sinha, M., & Sengupta, P. P. (2019). FDI Inflow, ICT Expansion and Economic Growth: An Empirical Study on Asia-Pacific Developing Countries. *Global Business Review*. DOI: https://doi.org/10.1177/0972150919873839

Souter, D. and MacLean, D. (2012). Changing our Understanding of Sustainability: The impact of ICTs and the Internet. International Institute of Sustainable Development. Retrieved from https://www.iisd.org/pdf/2012/changing_our_understanding_of_sustainability.pdf

Stephenson, M. and Sen, N. (2020). How digital investment can help the COVID-19 recovery. World Economic Forum. Retrieved from https://www.weforum.org/agenda/2020 /04/covid-19-digital-foreign-direct-investment-economic-recovery/

Strategy &. (2012). Maximizing the Impact of Digitalization. Retrieved from https://www.strategyand.pwc.com/m1/en/reports/maximizing-the-impact-of-digitization.pdf

To, A.H., Ha,D.T.T., Nguyen, H.M. and Vo, D.V.(2019). The impact of Foreign Direct Investment on Environment Degradation: Evidence from Emerging markets in Asia. International Journal of Environmental Research and Public Health.

doi:10.3390/ijerph16091636

Trucano, M. (2010). Perspectives on the use of information and communication technologies (ICTs) to benefit education in developing countries: Excerpts from the World bank's EduTech blog. Retrieved from http://siteresources.worldbank.org/EDUCATION/Resources/EduTech Blog2009_all_the_posts.pdf

UNCC (United Nations Climate Change). (2016). ICT Sector Helping to Tackle Climate Change. Retrieved from https://unfccc.int/news/ict-sector-helping-to-tackle-climate-change

UNCTAD. (2004). Making FDI Work for Sustainable Development. United Nations Conference on Trade and Development and Sustainable Business Institute at the European Business School. Retrieved from https://unctad.org/en/Docs/ditcted9_en.pdf

UNCTAD (United Trade Conference for Trade and Development) (2017a). World Investment Report 2017: Investment and the Digital Economy. New York and Geneva.

UNCTAD (2017b). World Investment Report, 2017, Technical Annex to Chapter IV. http://unctad.org/en/PublicationChapters/wir2017ch4_Annex_en.pdf.

UNCTAD. (2019). World Investment Report 2019: Special Economic Zones. Retrieved from https://unctad.org/en/PublicationsLibrary/wir2019_en.pdf

UNCTAD. (2019). Digital Economy Report 2019: Value Creation and Capture: Implications for Developing Countries. Retrieved from https://unctad.org/en/PublicationsLibrary/der2019_en.pdf

UNEP (United Nations Environment Programme). (2015). Sustainable Consumption and Production: A Handbook for Policymakers. Retrieved from https://sustainabledevelopment.un.org/content/documents/1951Sustain able%20Consumption.pdf

Unruh, G. and Kiron, D. (2017), "Digital transformation on purpose", MIT Sloan Management Review, November 6, available at https://sloanreview.mit.edu/article/digital-transformation-on-purpose/

Wautelet, T. (2017). The impact of digitalization on International companies: A case study of LEGO. Masters' Thesis, European University for Economics and Management. Retrieved from https://www.researchgate.net/publication/319273016

Yang, Boqiong; Chen, Jianguo (2011): An empirical model of the environmental effect of FDI in host countries: Analysis based on Chinese panel data, IAMO Forum 2011, Halle (Saale), June 23 - 24,

2011: Will the 'BRICs Decade' continue? – Prospects for trade and growth, Leibniz Institute of Agricultural Development in Central and Eastern Europe (IAMO), Halle (Saale). Retrieved from https://www.econstor.eu/ bitstream/10419/50803/ 1/ 670767255.pdf

Zekos, G. (2005). Foreign Direct Investment in a digital Economy. European Business Review. Vol. 17 (1), pp. 52-68, Emerald Group Publishing Limited. DOI 10.1108/09555340510576267

Zeng K., Eastin J. (2012). Do developing countries invest up? The environmental effects of foreign direct investment from less-developed countries. World Dev., 40 (11), pp. 2221-2233.

Zhu H., Duan L., Guo Y. and Yu, K. (2016). The effects of FDI, economic growth and energy consumption on carbon emissions in ASEAN-5: evidence from panel quantile regression. Econ. Model, 58, pp. 237-248.

COVID-19: SMEs, Export Promotion Services and Attention-Based View

Hamza El Guili[1], Lasse Torkkeli[2] and Anisur R. Faroque[3]

[1]PhD candidate in Management Science National School of Trade and Management, University of Abdelmalek Essaâdi (Tangier, Morocco)

[2]Adjunct Professor of International Business at Turku School of Economics at University of Turku

[3]Post-doctoral Researcher at LUT School of Business and Management

1. Introduction

Small and medium-sized enterprises (SMEs) generally represent more than 90% of firms in countries. In some contexts, SMEs have their operations limited to their local economy, but in many countries, a growing number of SMEs are internationally active (Kalinic & Clegg, 2017). In recent years, SMEs have begun to be a main source of industrial enhancement, and technological innovation, leading to the emergence of new industries. The degree of their contribution to national economies is noticeable yet difficult to understand (Cernat *et al.,* 2014), however in the 21st century the impact comes increasingly often from SMEs engaging in exporting: Exporting is the main and usually the initial mode of foreign market entry for SMEs, because exporting offers a comparatively greater degree of flexibility, firms' limited risk exposure and minimal resource commitment (Young *et al.,* 1989). Moreover, exporting activities are becoming crucial for governments due to the contribution of such activities to the economic advancement of nations, by improving industries' productivity and job creation (Czinkota, 1994). Thus, the widespread drop in trade barriers and investment, combined with markets' globalization, and the technological advances in communications, has been allowing SMEs to prepare for becoming direct actors in international business after their establishment (Oviatt & McDougall, 2005), and consequently expanding the number of international SMEs.

However, international business remains complex and challenging (Johanson & Vahlne, 2009), and the emergence of the COVID-19 pandemic starting in early 2020 has slowed, and in some sectors even halted international business activities, with SMEs in particular hard-hit, as they tend to exhibit risk-taking in order to reach their exporting target (Fernández-Mesa & Alegre, 2015). Compared to larger organizations, SMEs are not only characterized with the smallness of size, but also display inexperience and sometimes ignorance of the international context, while lacking motivation and knowledge (Wright *et al.*, 2007). Thus, it is crucial for SMEs to overcome these difficulties, and in order to do so they need to use the appropriate combination of resources and capabilities to optimize their international and export activities. Indeed, for SMEs to survive the pandemic, policy measures to support startups are essential (Kuckertz et *al.,* 2020). This suggests that services to support export promotion through the crisis are now more needed than ever.

SMEs have internal stimuli to carry on international operations (Leonidou et *al.,* 2007), but external motives (e.g., export assistance) have a key role in giving support and sustaining international operations involvement (Owusu- Frimpong & Mmieh, 2007). One of the available solutions employed by these firms among the externally accessible resources to boost their export performance is the export promotion instrument and services (EPS). Those measures are mainly designed to support firms' international activity (Durmuşoğlu *et al*., 2012). The last two decades have witnessed a huge growth of export promotion agencies, enhanced by a factor of three (Lederman *et al.,* 2006). However, EPS evolution has not been followed by an important amount of research in this field (Freixanet, 2012).

Awareness toward EPS has been investigated through different perspectives. The first stream studies the awareness and usefulness of EPS by non-exporters (Kumcu *et al.*, 1995). The second stream examines awareness and usefulness of EPS but from the exporters' perspective (Kedia & Chhokar, 1986), while the third group investigates the two previous research streams from a comparative perspective of both exporters and non-exporters (Albaum 1983; Marandu 1995). Used as a construct in the Response Hierarchy Model of Diamantopoulos et al. (1993), awareness has also been included among key drivers of EPS and their effect on the firm's export performance (Gillespie & Riddle, 2004; Marandu, 1995), level of usefulness (Coudounaris, 2012), EPS use (Marandu, 1995), and export market development (Reid, 1984). However, among the weaknesses of these recent models, they consider that managers are aware of the EPS (Coudounaris, 2012). Our study aims to overcome these gaps by drawing a model based on the attention-based view (ABV) perspective that examines the drivers of EPS awareness, such as national culture, formal export institutions, communicational channels and attention structures, during the COVID-19 pandemic.

It is widely known that the original ABV conceptualization (Ocasio, 1997) has influenced a broad range of areas, such as top management teams (Cho & Hambrick, 2006), corporate governance (Tuggle et al., 2010), international business and multinational management (Bouquet & Birkinshaw, 2008), but this perspective has not been linked to EPS awareness prior to this study. To do so now is also particularly timely, as the COVID-19 crisis has severely impacted some export operations and its accompanying logistic, such as limited labor availability, slow container traffic, absence of public transport and minimum customs operation during the crisis (Solomon et *al.,* 2020). Since March 2020, the economy has been suffering its most severe global recession since the Great Depression (Gopinath, 2020). To this end, it is important to study how SMEs direct their attention to EPS during a global crisis context, where it becomes crucial to be aware of export services, with a view to having better access to resources and support during the internationalization process of SMEs. Similarly, better attention to EPS will enable SMEs to have a clear idea of the various market uncertainties and opportunities in foreign markets. Our study aims to address this gap and expand this area of research through assessing the corresponding research question:

What makes SME managers attentive to export promotion services during an unexpected global crisis such as the COVID-19 pandemic?

By focusing on the ABV of the firm, the present study offers a different and complementary angle on the export promotion use during a global crisis. It concentrates on the neglected roles of SMEs' managers and owner-managers' attention toward EPS, by expanding the centrality of communication in making changes to the firm's attention structures. In doing so, this study also shows that the regulation of attention to EPSs is affected by the flexibility and strength of the attentional organizational structures. While ABV perspective and the EPS have been separately assessed, there is a need to show the importance of such collaborations in order to create new theoretical underpinnings in the export promotion literature, particularly in a context where the international business landscape is reshaping due to the pandemic, offering both opportunities and challenges for SMEs. Next, we present the literature review on the EPSs and the ABV perspective.

2. Export Promotion Services

The movement toward markets' globalization has made exports progressively crucial for countries and their national firms (Sousa & Bradley, 2009). The global scene of international trade, defined primarily by several international policies that threaten world's trade, generates "*an urgent need to open new markets and further develop companies' exporting capacities to face unpredictable or unknown changes*" (Geldres-Weiss & Monreal-Pérez, 2017). The economic globalization followed by the massive flow of products and services implies the apparition of new challenges for companies. In this context, many SMEs cannot exploit the potential of foreign markets by reason of lack of motivation, capabilities and financial/human resources and use EPS to overcome these obstacles, offered both by public and private initiatives (Freixanet, 2012). Lederman et al. (2010) recognize that in most countries, domestic firms succeed in foreign markets when an export promotion agency provides assistance.

The first studies regarding EPS were published in the early 1960s (Leonidou et *al.,* 2011). Several studies concerning EPS emphasize on topics related to their specific characteristics (e.g. Winston & Rembler, 2012), evaluation and impact assessment of EPS' effectiveness (e.g. Ayob & Freixanet, 2014; Freixanet & Churakova, 2018; Wang et *al.,* 2017; Cadot et *al.,* 2015; Van Biesebroeck et al. 2015), the awareness and EPS use (e.g. Crick & Lindsay, 2015) and EPS in international trade (e.g. Akai, et *al.* 2014; Van Biesebroeck et *al.* 2016). For open economies, it is essential that many of its national SMEs become successful exporters (Broocks & Van Biesebroeck, 2017), while in developing countries, EPSs show generally poor administration, bureaucratization, inadequate funding, and a lack of client orientation (Lederman et *al.,* 2010).

Encouraging local firms to export is generally initiated by governments around the world (Leonidou et *al.,* 2015) because nations rely on the actions of SMEs under their domain to start the economic activity (Pradhan & Das, 2015) and improve their prosperity. Thus, governments in both developed and emerging countries offer several educational schemes (e.g. training seminars, export counseling) in order to help the national firms solve their exportation problems (Leonidou *et al.,* 2011). In addition, the government programs are designed to create a positive attitude among owner-managers toward opportunities abroad and by minimizing negative perceptions associated with exporting, such as risks, costs, and complexities of international environment (Leonidou et *al.,* 1998). It is widely known that EPS generally concerns public measures which intend to support companies' exporting activity.

However, assistance could be delivered in several manners and from different structures. For instance, trade shows are used by many SMEs, mainly because they allow firms to engage in markets that would not have access without institutional support and assistance (Freixanet, 2012). Furthermore, trade shows generally represent an event organized by industry trade associations on an annual basis and have various objectives such as facilitating direct contact between distribution channel members and manufacturers (Quaye et *al.,* 2017). Trade missions are perceived as coordinated overseas visits made by business group executives in order to meet potential buyers, frequently after an initial market research made by the visitors' embassy (Quaye et *al.,* 2017). Trade missions, promoted by industry associations and organized international sales tours can also be useful in opportunity creation and in increasing managers foreign market experience (Axinn, 1988). However, the access of participants to tradeshows is regularly restrained and the data is confidential (Spence, 2003).

Trade fairs are also important promotional tools for marketing of firms' products and services (Hansen, 2004). The first international fair was initiated at Crystal Palace in England in 1851, with the presence of 72 states (Short, 1967). A trade fair is a business-to-customer event, where firms attend not only to showcase their services/products, but also to sell and market them. Some trade fairs such as Hanover Book Fair, attract participants from all over the world and enable diffuse interactions between the participants (Quaye et *al.,* 2017).

Some scholars emphasized the role of foreign trade offices (FTOs) as programs that aim to encourage SMEs to engage in foreign markets when their experience with the market is limited (Spence, 2003). Because large firms can generally be able to afford the assistance through private consultants (Shatz, 2003), most FTO clients are exporting SMEs (Feldman & Kelley, 2002). For SMEs, the foreign trade offices are reactive in terms of responding to their needs through offering specifically tailored services (Hannaford, 2000).

There are several typologies that allow us to categorize EPS assistance. Faroque and Takahashi (2015) divide it into (1) financial export assistance, that usually includes direct and indirect financial incentives (e.g. lower taxes, duty-free import/export provisions, cash incentives), and (2) technical assistance, that would generally help exporting SMEs in the design and production processes, by offering innovative products/services to international buyers (Faroque & Takahashi, 2011). On the other hand, Gencturk (2010) categorizes EPS into indirect- governmental support that boosts exports through incentives (e.g. incentives to innovation) and direct- including programs' objective aiming to increase exports. In this paper based on the attempts made by scholars to classify EPS assistance, we divide EPS into two categories (1) government and public support and (2) semi-private and private initiatives. In sum, government and public support is provided by government export promotion programs or agencies, while semi-private and private support derives from several sources (Trade shows, Trade and industry associations, Trade fairs, Trade missions and Foreign offices). We next move to discuss how the extent to which SMEs are attentive to these impacts their exporting.

3. Attention based view of the firm

According to the attention-based view (ABV), the context in which cognition and action are situated decides what aspects of the environment managers/decision makers attend to and which opportunities are adopted within the firm (Ocasio, 1997; Ocasio & Joseph, 2005), which can be a useful lens to explore the awareness of export promotion programs within an organization. The attention concept is known to have a rich history in organization science. Initially, Simon (1947) first targeted attention on the structuring, channeling and allocation of attention as a basic concept to the study of administrative behavior, which became organization theory later (March & Simon, 1958). The ABV of the firm (Ocasio, 1997) gave a metatheory of organizational adaptation and action that concentrated on attention by linking back to the Simon's (1947) conception of how organizations form the attention of individual decision makers. Contrary to Simon's concept, which considered attention as an origin of control of individuals, ABV focused on how attention in organizations embodies organizational adaptation (Ocasio, 2011).

The ABV of the firm displays the decision makers' attention and its role within firm behavior (Ocasio, 1997; Simon, 1947). According to Ocasio (1997), the ABV posits that decision makers' eventual actions depend mostly on answers and the issues on which they fix their attention, and this focus usually depends on a certain context. On the other hand, the decision context is shaped by the system of rules, resources, and social relationships that appear within the organizational setting (Ocasio, 1997). It is generally known that the ability of attention of decision makers to focus on issues and answers is limited (Simon, 1947). When decision-makers are in a situation with more information to deal with, their attention becomes selective (Cyert & March, 1963).

Only issues and answers capturing their attention will arouse their actions (Simon, 1947), considering attention gives people with a time to act (Ocasio, 1997). Therefore, selective focusing of attention allows the focus of energy on a limited set of issues and tasks, making the speed of decision-makers' action easier (Ocasio, 1997). Moreover, selective focusing of attention has as a consequence of neglect of useful and important options and information (Barnett, 2008). Ocasio's (1997) model apprehends six elemental components:

(1) The environment of decision;
(2) Issues and answers;
(3) Procedural and communicational channels;
(4) Firm's attention structures;
(5) Decision-makers; and
(6) Organizational moves.

One of the key aspects of the ABV is that an organization's behavior can be examined by searching for how firms regulate and make the distribution their decision makers' attention (Ocasio, 1997). In a similar vein, the ABV claims that "attention structures" such as the rules of the game, the players and resources regulate the firm's attention to certain issues (Ocasio, 1997), arguing that the of attention's structural distribution gives managers with a structured identities and interests (Ren & Guo, 2011). First, the players are a key element that shapes the firm's attention via the specific beliefs, skills and values (March & Olsen, 1976). Studies have examined how demographics of top management teams (Cho & Hambrick, 2006) and board members (Tuggle et *al.,* 2010) as well as cultural dimensions of key decision makers (Souitaris & Maestro, 2010) influence their focus of attention.

Then, the rules of the game influence decision makers in achieving the firm's goals and represents an assortment made of norms, incentives, and values on how to succeed (Stevens et *al.* 2014). Past research has concluded that the company's level of formality in board meetings (Tuggle et *al.,* 2010), and the incentive systems used to reward executives (Cho & Hambrick, 2006), have an influence on the attention allocation of decision makers. Finally, organizational resources that include tangible and intangible assets available to the firm to realize its objectives also determine the direction of the attention (Stevens et *al.* 2014).

4. Framework of EPS and attention during a global crisis

We now present the conceptual framework describing how attention is related to the impact of EPS during a global crisis. During the COVID-19 pandemic, entrepreneurs and international business might fail to deal with the uncertainty about the pandemic's broader impact on their businesses and the economy as a whole, on the short and long terms (Sharma et *al.,* 2020). Therefore, attention structures adjust the legitimization of issues such as EPS awareness and the distribution of procedural and communication channels. Furthermore, managers who are export-oriented are more likely to be attentive to EPS and the environmental changes that take place mainly more relevant to their export activities than to changes that occur in the sectors that are less central to their representations (Lant et *al.,* 1992; Fiol & O'Connor, 2003). When top managers fail to actively be attentive to EPS and environmental changes, they are unlikely to implement strategic responses (Huff & Schwenk, 1990; Terreberry, 1968), as it becomes important for many entrepreneurs to quickly bounce back, while many countries are now moving towards gradual economic and social easing of restrictions.

The attention structures—the firm's rules, players and resources—and communication channels respond to environmental stimuli to generate strategic change and adaptation (Barnett, 2008; Joseph & Ocasio, 2012). Prior research gives a limited understanding of how firms analyze and seek new paths of expansion (Joseph & Wilson, 2019), notably the international expansion. An attention lens gives logic for opportunity processing (Ocasio, 2011), and therefore, suggests a more complete framework to understand how firms notice and focus on new opportunities- such as awareness of relevant EPS providers during a pandemic- that may not conform to a firm's existing belief system (Joseph & Wilson, 2019).

Past ABV studies (e.g. Ocasio & Joseph, 2005; Joseph & Ocasio, 2012; Tuggle et *al.,* 2010; Bouquet & Birkinshaw, 2011; Maula et *al.,* 2013) have examined the attention structure's influence on decision making, as well as the effect of attentional processing in support of firm behavior (e.g., Kaplan & Tripsas, 2008; Nadkarni & Perez, 2007; Rerup, 2006; Shepherd et *al.,* 2017; Zbaracki & Bergen, 2015). However, these two research streams have been separately assessed. To this end, we propose the following model:

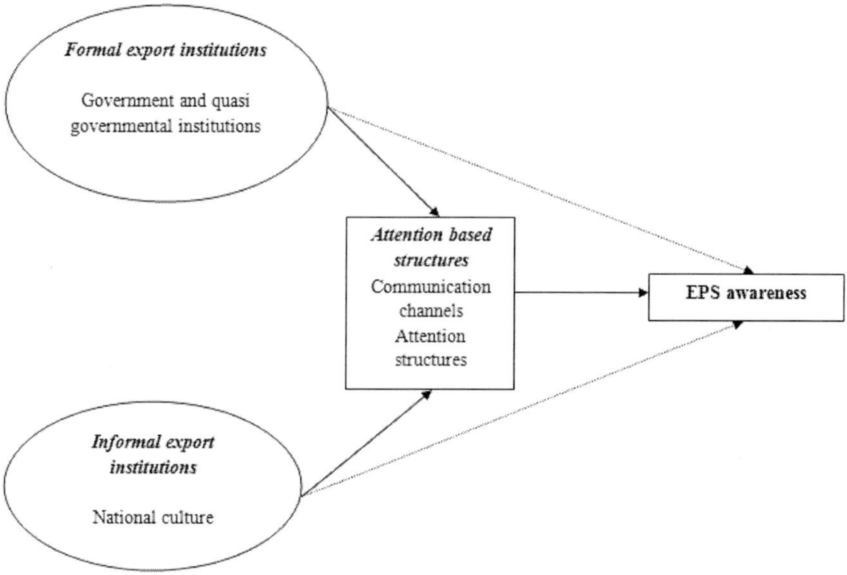

Figure 1. A dynamic model of export promotion services based on the ABV perspective during the COVID-19 pandemic.

4.1 EPS awareness and formal export institutions

It is common knowledge that the awareness creation toward exporting and the promotion incentives creation are among the various roles of EPS (Seringhaus & Rosson, 1990). As Leonidou et al. (2015, p. 22) concluded "*it is critical to increase awareness and appreciation of these programmes among small business firms through appropriate media that target these firms, including articles in trade journals and newspapers, organization of open seminars, workshops, and conferences, and the provision of a hotline service with easy access to government export specialists*".

Rabino (1980) was among the initial scholars who associated the institutional environment with EPS, by analyzing the Domestic International Sales Corporation (DISC) program implemented in the USA during 1971 to attract exports through tax incentives. The firm's internal environment includes the firm's goals, achievements and objectives. As Leonidou et *al.* (2011) claim, organizational factors such as the firm's size and managerial factors such as the export orientation are relevant regarding the EPS awareness. On the other hand, external environmental elements comprise, among others, the governmental attitudes and possible actions from formal export institutions. Most of the empirical studies focusing on measuring the EPS' impact on SMEs' awareness have taken place in export-intensive countries, such as the UK, the USA, and Canada, neglecting less export-intensive countries, where exporting SMEs face several problems compared to traditional exporting nations, and this is due to the issues of relationship between EPS institutions and the mechanism of awareness (Coudounaris, 2018).

Gonzalez and Humberto (2009) assert that concerning the role of the government and export institutions in the internationalization of SMEs, international business theories need to make a greater effort to analyze the potential importance of domestic institutional factors on SMEs' awareness. A large body of the internationalization research emphasized on analyzing a firm's export potential or on describing its export behavior, (e.g.,Wiedersheim-Paul et *al.* 1978; Morgan & Katsikeas, 1997; Bilkey, 1982; Ilmakunnas & Nurmi, 2007). However, scholars paid little attention to what happens in SMEs during the pre-export stages and especially, when export activities start from the decision stage to the export process consolidation (Ruiz, 2007). More specifically, as Ruiz (2007, p.9) claim: "*... literature has not deepened on the study of pre-export stages and the identification of potential exporters in developing countries.*". Analyzing the relationship between EPS formal institutions and SMEs' awareness will provide a vital chance to reinforce the "forgotten mechanism" of awareness during the pre-export and export stages, and strengthening therefore the relationship between partners, specifically EPS formal institutions and exporting SMEs (Coudounaris, 2018).

While the extreme measures imposed by the pandemic contributed to slowing its spread, they have threatened, on the other hand, the survival of exporting SMEs across all sectors and industries (Lu et *al.,* 2020). For instance, Prasad et *al.* (2014) found that small firms were less able to bolster international supply chain disruptions during a global crisis. Tokui et *al.* (2017) found that during the Great East-Japan Earthquake in 2011,

SMEs suffered significant damage from the supply chain disruption effects. Thus, Lee and Warner (2006) concluded that epidemics such as SARS, resulted in a demand shock and particularly affected consumption, which led to high market uncertainties for SMEs.

Therefore, as exporting SMEs and managers around the world are currently struggling with uncertain markets due to COVID-19 pandemic, export managers of firms should be encouraged to be attentive to EPS (Coudounaris, 2018). Simultaneously, governmental officials in Ministries of Trade and formal export institutions should increase the relationship with exporting SMEs, by allowing more communication regarding the export programs (Coudounaris, 2018).

4.2 EPS awareness and national culture

Scholars have tended to focus on the individual entrepreneur profile, by identifying the entrepreneur's characteristics. Other researchers have identified the importance of environmental factors such as national culture (Alegre & Berbegal-Mirabent, 2015). National culture has been explored as one of the antecedents of entrepreneurial activity (Wiengarten *et al.,* 2015). Beliefs, values and the collective programming of mind constitute the national cultural system (Nicholls et *al.,* 1999). Authors (e.g. Tayeb, 1994, p.432) define the national cultural system as "*a set of historically evolved, learned and shared values, attitudes and means. The term nation refers to culture, social, economic and political institutions influence how organizations are managed in different environments*".

The ABV argues that the structural distribution of attention in the firm gives managers a structured set of interests and identities (Ren & Guo, 2011), notably the attention toward EPS, suggesting that cultural dimensions of key decision makers (Souitaris & Maestro, 2010), influence their focus of attention (Stevens et *al.,* 2014). Gonzalez and Humberto (2009, p.127) posited that a better understanding of national culture aimed at internationalization is more likely to "*grant better, more ample learning processes, to implement new practices and develop sustainable competitive advantages on the international scene".* The role of national culture in influencing international business management practices and approaches has largely been documented (Alvesson, 2011). The national culture is connected to the need for a change in mindset: More specifically, a mindset where efforts towards internationalization are not only seen as costs, but instead as strategic and longterm investments. Studies have shown that national cultural systems greatly impact the corporate cultural system (Tayeb, 1994) in many ways.

For example, national culture influences managerial decision-making in uncertain environments (e.g. during the export process during a global crisis), leadership styles and human resource management practices (Li et al. 2002). Similarly, national cultures affect managerial functions such as motivation and communication (Nicholls et *al.,* 1999). Cultural differences have a significant role in influencing the SMEs' awareness, due to the differences between the characteristics that influence a human group's response to its environment (Hofstede, 1997). Cultural differences, if not understood and appreciated well, can also lead to failures in business (Ghemawat & Reiche, 2011), including the "attention failure" toward EPS. With being more widespread and contagious comparing to SARS (Meo et al., 2020), COVID-19 impacted the global economy trajectory, where SMEs are facing decreasing international and national demand (Szymkowski, 2020). Consequently, an important number of countries decided to take protectionist measures by closing their borders, which severely impacted international trade (Salcedo & Cherelus*.,* 2020).

Entrepreneurs' preferences to EPS during this global pandemic are established by the national culture in which they are socialized (Habel et *al*., 2020), knowing that one main component of the national culture is the long-term orientation, defined as "*the fostering of virtues oriented towards future rewards, in particular, perseverance and thrift*" (Hofstede, 2001, p. 359).We believe that in countries that are high in long-term orientation, a positive interaction between the national culture and EPS awareness will be noted during COVID-19 pandemic progression.

4.3 Attention structures and EPS awareness

Our study aims to provide a new theoretical underpinning to the export promotion (EPP) literature, in line with Gonzales and Humberto (2009, p.128) findings: "*The proposed analysis goes well beyond traditional EPP assessment methodologies that are mainly based on separate evaluations or measurement of awareness, usage of EPP services or results in terms of changes in national exports".* The purpose of export promotion today requires a new thinking, based on the understanding of the SMEs' context during the internationalization processes, to analyze EPS awareness. The ABV suggests that the context of the firm, such as the COVID-19 pandemic, impacts attention allocation (Ocasio, 1997). The firm's external context gives stimuli that link the focus of decision makers' attention and also influence the extent to which any given stimulus will be responded to (Stevens et *al.,* 2014). For exporting SMEs, internal and external change agents stimulate firms' export participation and attention (Bilkey, 1982; Seringhaus & Rosson, 1994). Internal change generally emerges from the organization (e.g., as resources and capabilities), while the external changes point out to external forces – such as a global pandemic or an economic crisis (Wilkinson & Brouthers, 2006).

By focusing on relevant stimuli, attention can facilitate environmental scanning and accelerate the detection and creation of new opportunities, such as the existence of relevant EPS for SMEs. In recent years, research has increasingly focused on applying cognitive perspectives to explain organizational decision-making and adaptation behavior (e.g., Hammedi et *al.,* 2011; Tripsas, 2009). A large body of internationalization literature considers that a firm's expansion across national boundaries presents managers with the task of choosing what is best – the where and how of international strategy – from what is possible (Devinney et *al.,* 2003). It is a decision complicated by noisy, ambiguous information and high uncertainty. Through SMEs' internationalization pathway, decision-makers may learn to attend certain environmental factors while ignoring or neglecting others (Ocasio, 1997). Differences between managers in the cognitive capability of attention also affect which managers more accurately anticipate new opportunities and threats (Helfat & Peteraf, 2015).

Nevertheless, little is known about how managers anticipate actions in foreign environments, and whether and how their perceptions and analyses affect internationalization decisions, and internationalization models neglect whether and how decision makers' cognitively-constrained processes shape firms' internationalization (Maitland & Sammartino, 2015). Therefore, managerial cognition's role in assessing foreign environments and determining internationalization decisions remains under-explored and poorly understood (Aharoni et *al.,* 2011; Buckley et *al.,* 2007; Hennart & Slangen, 2015). In the export promotion literature, EPSs could be considered as unsuccessful when firms are not aware of the existence of these services or have poor knowledge about the programs (Naidu & Rao, 1993). Kedia and Chhokar (1986) call for a better understanding of awareness and assert that exporters have a partial knowledge of the EPS. Consequently, the awareness toward these programs was generally low among the exporters and without significant impact. Bruning (1995) examined the relationship between EPS and exporter's awareness, while in their findings, Jindal and Gakhar (2017) revealed that a critical difference is noted in exporters' awareness level, based on experience and selected sector. Unlike other aspects in the international business research, the relevance of awareness mechanisms was ignored in the export stimulation field, even if exporters in the present days have to deal with challenging situations such as the firm survival or exit in a global pandemic due to a lack of accomplishing their export goals (Coudounaris, 2012).

According to the ABV, the structural distribution of attention gives managers with a structured set of interests and identities that allow them to focus on issues facing the firm. As an issue draws the focus of attention, decisions are made to address that specific issue. In this regard, this study examines three main attention structures: (1) organizational "resources", (2) the "rules of the game" that carries out the firm's reality interpretation, and (3) the "players" that regulate the attention focus through their skills, beliefs and values (Ocasio, 1997).

First, in terms of the "players" (i.e. *SMEs' owner-managers' international experience),* the ABV is generally a perspective theory that analyzes how decision-makers allocate their attention to SMEs' issues in an attempt to understand firm behavior (Galbreath, 2018). A vital component of the SME's attention regulation refers to the individuals who are considered as players, referred to as "*individuals ultimately do the attending*" (Ocasio, 1997, p.189). The SMEs' owner-managers' international experience is specifically relevant in making strategic changes (Zhang & Rajagopalan, 2010). Past research has concluded that by endowing owner managers with host countries' knowledge and networks, international experience is valuable for a firm's internationalization and increases its competitive advantage in international markets (e.g., Hsu et *al.,* 2013).

In order to be attentive to EPS during the COVID-19 pandemic, owner-managers should be able to anticipate and maintain a certain degree of flexibility by thinking strategically and working effectively with others (Zhang & Rajagopalan, 2010). Specifically, entrepreneurs should be able to be aware of existing EPS, identify opportunities related to them, develop strategic initiatives to overcome the global uncertainties (Crossland et *al.,* 2014; Hambrick & Mason,1984). As discussed earlier, owner-managers are likely to have valuable knowledge of international markets and complex general competencies (Le & Kroll, 2017). With greater international experience, SMEs' owner-managers are more likely to be more attentive to EPS and to identify relevant opportunities in the global market (Le & Kroll, 2017).

Second, "the rules of the game" (*SMEs' team debate)* are defined as "*the formal and informal principles of action, interaction, and interpretation that guide and constrain decision makers in accomplishing the firm's tasks and in obtaining social status, credits, and rewards in the process*" (Ocasio, 1997, p. 196). It is generally known that debates are an established norm whereby teams in workgroups have the freedom to express different viewpoints, opinions and approaches to decisions and decision-making (Schweiger & Sandberg, 1989). Without debate, the breadth of a team's skills and experiences may remain underutilized (Galbreath, 2018). For instance, when the debate between teams working on export and internationalization strategies within SMEs increases, a divergent knowledge comes to the top, such as the relevance or the importance of a specific EPS and can be exploited and explored. Because open debate is more likely to drag out the rich and diverse group experiences, it is thought to draw attention to critical issues and optimize owner-managers' decision-making (Nielsen & Huse, 2010), related to EPS. Today, SMEs' entrepreneurs seek foreign markets opportunities to overcome the domestic decreasing demand and also to be able to keep jobs, as unemployment rates are rising substantially (Hall, 2020). While SMEs' teams' debate is expected to draw attention to EPS, this "rules of the game" norm is also expected to enable owner-managers to direct their attention to viewpoints, perspectives and alternative ideas about EPS that could be useful for the firms during this pandemic. As such, the nature of teams' debate as mentioned above is more likely to be pertinent as an attention-directing structure related to EPS (Ocasio, 1997).

Third, "SMEs' Resources": Ocasio (1997, p. 198) defines in his model resources as "*the human, physical, technological, and financial capital available to the firm at any moment in time for its objectives*". Resources generally shape the alternatives consideration and have an influence on the answers' repertoire of owner-managers (Ocasio, 1997). Specifically, firm resources and capabilities are important, and are themselves determinants, in part, of organizational attention (Ocasio, 1997). However, export strategies will typically need the acquisition and development of new organizational capabilities and resources and are largely dependent on attentional structures and processes (Ocasio et al., 2018). For instance, an SME that has established an important manufacturing/subsidiary network in different markets will be able to reduce its dependence on a specific market, and also to shift its operations from one location to another during the COVID-19 pandemic, and therefore facing just a slow-down, and not a complete shutdown of its activity (Sharma et *al.,* 2020). However, many

SMEs lack the necessary resources to establish, operate, and maintain such a system (Kaynak & Kothari, 1984), unlike multinational corporations.

Leonidou et *al.* (2011) posit that the adoption of EPS helps the firm enhance the resources required to manage export operations. Based on the above, slack resources are more likely to enhance decision makers' attention by including or excluding different options as the availability of resources provided by EPS, and thereby offering the possibility to achieve a wide variety of tasks (March & Shapira, 1992). As such, slack resources perform extra resources available to the organization that enable owner managers of SMEs to change their focus of attention (Chen & Miller, 2007), notably to the available EPS during the COVID-19 pandemic. For SMEs that lack cash flow and have no savings, government support during a crisis is important to ensure SME survival and recovery (Biggs et al., 2012). SMEs without slack resources will tend to emphasize on short-term goals forcing decision makers to improve allocation efficiency (George, 2005), while SMEs with important slack resources will tend to use it as a buffer that can redirect the decision makers' attention to other goals (Stevens et *al.,* 2014), notably the use of EPS as a means to take profit from international market opportunities during the COVID-19 pandemic, mainly because it requires minimal resources and allows for greater structural and strategic flexibility (Czinkota & Ronkainen, 2007).

4.4 Communication channels and EPS awareness

The focus of attention is affected by so-called communication and procedural channels (Ocasio, 1997). These channels can be described according to their spatial, temporal, and procedural dimensions. They involve both formal and informal activities, communications, and synergy, which focus decision-makers' attention on specific issues and answers (Ocasio, 1997; Ocasio & Joseph, 2005). Communication channels have various forms: gatherings, formal meetings, workshops, conferences. Thus, they can take the form of written, verbal, and technological interaction between participants (Ocasio, 1997; Joseph & Ocasio, 2012). They include formal and informal meetings (Ocasio, 1997), such as reports (e.g., action memoranda, annual reports) and administrative protocols (e.g., personnel evaluations or requests for proposals). Pre-export stages usually include face-to-face meetings, telephone conversations, written communications, email exchanges, and administrative procedures (e.g. budgeting). When an SME wants to increase the amount of attention that its managers or CEOs devote to improve their understanding of the available EPS, it might establish procedures and meetings that clearly draw managerial attention toward such issues. Moreover, communication through social interactions within communication channels allows organizational individuals to collectively adapt themselves with strategic activities (Ocasio *et al.*, 2018), related notably to export activities.

Despite the increase of interest in the integration of the ABV perspective in the understanding of firms' behavior, the understanding of communicative practices in communication channels and specifically the extent to which they reinforce existing patterns of organizational attention is still limited (Ocasio et al., 2018). During the COVID-19 pandemic, several SMEs made efforts on reshaping and readapting their communication channels, to ensure their managers to have the specific and right tools to keep employees well informed and updated about their firms' economic and social situation, especially that many employees switched to remote work, that could be generalized to the business community.

The COVID-19 pandemic is expected to provide SMEs an opportunity to be more attentive to EPS, because the communication channels of pre-export and export stages have undergone great changes, such as the use of modern enterprise video communications for meetings (e.g. Zoom, WebEx etc.), which enable a better access to international opportunities. Therefore, it is important to explain how diverse and modern communicative practices both generate and transform attentional engagement in new and different forms of communication channels and how they help managers to be more attentive to EPS in the COVID-19 pandemic.

5. Conclusion

This study has drawn from the theory of ABV to present a framework for understanding how SMEs trying to manage their exports during a global crisis are expected to behave towards export promotion. The COVID-19 pandemic is significantly impacting SME activities in developing and developed countries, with the scope of the impact being more important than any large-scale environmental hazard (Lu et *al.,* 2020). In this regard, governments need to develop specific policies for exporting SMEs, by notably establishing the adequate support measures to revive the export activities of their SMEs, given that in many countries, whether developed or less developed, exporting is a substantial activity for economic survival.

In general, SMEs face liability of smallness whereas global disasters and pandemics create supplementary risks, such as resource availability and liquidity problems (Eggers, 2020). Therefore, to face export challenges during the COVID-19 pandemic, SMEs should be more flexible in their decision-making and also be more attentive to their business environment, by allocating their attention to various EPS that could be relevant and beneficial for them in this regard. Despite that the literature of export promotion identifies that government programs are essential in shaping awareness of opportunities and organizational capabilities, the relevance of the awareness mechanism was mainly ignored in recent literature in the field of export (Coudounaris, 2018). As many of exporting SMEs shut down and millions of people lose their jobs around the world, governments are being obliged to compensate them with financial aid to help them through this unprecedented crisis.

A large body of research on the ABV remains initially structural (Ocasio *et al.,* 2018), because this perspective has seldom been applied in empirical research, especially in survey studies, due in part to practical measurement challenges (Ocasio, 2011). Therefore, one of the contributions of this study is the operationalization of attentional processing and communicational channels. It is a common knowledge that attention decisions of SMEs' managers depend on the context in which they are present (e.g. COVID-19 pandemic) which includes the attention structure at the organization level and the communication channels through which SMEs' managers obtain information about the environment (Ocasio, 1997; 2011).

In order to seek business continuity and sustainability of their exporting, we call the private/semi-private sector and governments' agencies to develop specific SME-focused assistance policies, taking into account the new parameters related to international businesses, notably the impact of the COVID-19 pandemic on economies. Based on this study, we also call for export providers to predict the risk associated with each stage of the export during the borders' reopening, to manage the uncertainty associated with this process, to avoid a total shutdown of exporting SME activities in the case of a second wave of COVID-19 that can cause worse economic consequences (Sharma et *al.,* 2020).

Our study aims to underline the importance of setting up and updating effective and modern communication channels in order to create a positive and more institutionalized interaction between EPS providers and SMEs, taking into account the major communication changes in international business during a global pandemic, which imposed new communication mechanisms. Hence, our model includes the ABV perspective because we believe it is vital for SMEs to put in place effective attention structures to be more attentive to EPS, including (i) a better understanding of awareness by SMEs' entrepreneurs, (ii) an improved SMEs' teams debate about the relevance of EPS, in order to guide the firm into an unpredictable environment, and (iii) a better management of the SMEs' slack resources during export.

Finally, our model includes the national culture because we believe that regarding the internationality of the COVID-19 pandemic's impact on economies, each country has its own measures to manage its export policy. To this end, we highly recommend the application of cross-country comparison studies and also cross-industry comparisons for a better understanding of EPS awareness during the COVID-19 pandemic.

References

Aharoni, Y., Tihanyi, L., & Connelly, B. L. (2011). Managerial decision-making in international business: A forty-five-year retrospective. *Journal of World Business*, *46*(2), 135–142.

Akai, N., Ogawa, H., & Ogawa, Y. (2014). Endogenous Choice of Subsidy Instruments in Imperfectly Competitive Markets: A Unit Subsidy versus an Ad Valorem Subsidy. *Annals of Economics and Statistics*, *113–114*, 81–98.

Albaum, G. (1983). Effectiveness of government export assistance for US smaller-sized manufacturers: Some further evidence. *International Marketing Review*.

Alegre, I., & Berbegal-Mirabent, J. (2015). Entrepreneurship and the Influence of History: How Much Impact Do Country-Specific Historical Factors Have on Entrepreneurship Initiatives? In *Entrepreneurship, Regional Development and Culture* (pp. 35–52). Springer.

Alvesson, M. (2011). Organizational culture. *Handb. Organ. Cult. Clim.*

Axinn, C. N. (1988). Export performance: Do managerial perceptions make a difference? *International Marketing Review*, *5*(2), 61–71.

Ayob, A. H., & Freixanet, J. (2014). Insights into public export promotion programs in an emerging economy: The case of Malaysian SMEs. *Evaluation and Program Planning*, *46*, 38–46.

Barnett, M. L. (2008). An attention-based view of real options reasoning. *Academy of Management Review*, *33*(3), 606–628.

Biggs, D., Hall, C. M., & Stoeckl, N. (2012). The resilience of formal and informal tourism enterprises to disasters: Reef tourism in Phuket, Thailand. *Journal of Sustainable Tourism*, *20*(5), 645–665.

Bilkey, W. J. (1982). Variables associated with export profitability. *Journal of International Business Studies*, *13*(2), 39–55.

Bouquet, C., & Birkinshaw, J. (2008). Weight versus voice: How foreign subsidiaries gain attention from corporate headquarters. *Academy of Management Journal*, *51*(3), 577–601.

Broocks, A., & Van Biesebroeck, J. (2017). The impact of export promotion on export market entry. *Journal of International Economics*, *107*, 19–33.

Bruning, E. R. (1995). Strategic positioning for export market development: The role of managerial attitudes, export development programmes and firm characteristics. *Journal of Strategic Marketing*, *3*(2), 127–143.

Buckley, P. J., Clegg, L. J., Cross, A. R., Liu, X., Voss, H., & Zheng, P. (2007). The determinants of Chinese outward foreign direct investment. *Journal of International Business Studies*, *38*(4), 499–518.

Cadot, O. Carrère, C., & Strauss-Kahn, V. (2011). Export diversification: What's behind the hump? *Review of Economics and Statistics*, *93*(2), 590–605.

Cernat, L., Norman-Lopez, A., & Ana, D. T. (2014). *SMEs are more important than you think! Challenges and opportunities for EU exporting SMEs*. Directorate General for Trade, European Commission.

Chen, W.-R., & Miller, K. D. (2007). Situational and institutional determinants of firms' R&D search intensity. *Strategic Management Journal*, *28*(4), 369–381.

Cho, T. S., & Hambrick, D. C. (2006). Attention as the mediator between top management team characteristics and strategic change: The case of airline deregulation. *Organization Science*, *17*(4), 453–469.

Coudounaris, D. N. (2012). Effective targeting of national export promotion programmes for SMEs. *International Journal of Globalisation and Small Business*, *4*(3–4), 242–283.

Coudounaris, D. N. (2018). Export promotion programmes for assisting SMEs. *Review of International Business and Strategy, just-accepted*, 00–00.

Crick, D., & Lindsay, V. (2015). Service and service-intensive New Zealand internationalising SMEs: Managers' perceptions of government assistance. *Marketing Intelligence & Planning*, *33*(3), 366–393.

Crossland, C., Zyung, J., Hiller, N. J., & Hambrick, D. C. (2014). CEO career variety: Effects on firm-level strategic and social novelty. *Academy of Management Journal*, *57*(3), 652–674.

Cyert, R. M., & March, J. G. (1963). A behavioral theory of the firm. *Englewood Cliffs, NJ*, *2*, 169–187.

Czinkota, M. R. (1994). Executive insights: A national export assistance policy for new and growing businesses. *Journal of International Marketing*, *2*(1), 91–101.

Czinkota Michael, R., & Ronkainen Ilkka, A. (2007). *International marketing*. Tomson South-Western, a part of The Tomson Corporation. Printed in the ….

Devinney, T. M., Midgley, D., & Venaik, S. (2003). Managerial beliefs, market contestability and dominant strategic orientation in the eclectic paradigm. *International Business and the Eclectic Paradigm. London: Routledge.*

Durmuşoğlu, S. S., Apfelthaler, G., Nayir, D. Z., Alvarez, R., & Mughan, T. (2012). The effect of government-designed export promotion service use on small and medium-sized enterprise goal achievement: A multidimensional view of export performance. *Industrial Marketing Management*, *41*(4), 680–691.

Eggers, F. (2020). Masters of disasters? Challenges and opportunities for SMEs in times of crisis. *Journal of Business Research*, *116*, 199–208. Scopus.

Faroque, A. R., & Takahashi, Y. (2011). *Export assistance: The way back and forward: An empirical investigation into developing country "born globals"*. Springer Science & Business Media.

Faroque, A. R., & Takahashi, Y. (2015). Export marketing assistance and early internationalizing firm performance: Does export commitment matter? *Asia Pacific Journal of Marketing and Logistics*, *27*(3), 421–443.

Feldman, M. P., & Kelley, M. R. (2002). How states augment the capabilities of technology–pioneering firms. *Growth and Change*, *33*(2), 173–195.

Fernández-Mesa, A., & Alegre, J. (2015). Entrepreneurial orientation and export intensity: Examining the interplay of organizational learning and innovation. *International Business Review*, *24*(1), 148-156.

Fiol, C. M., & O'Connor, E. J. (2003). Waking up! Mindfulness in the face of bandwagons. *Academy of Management Review*, *28*(1), 54–70.

Freixanet, J. (2012). Export promotion programs: Their impact on companies' internationalization performance and competitiveness. *International Business Review*, *21*(6), 1065–1086.

Freixanet, J., & Churakova, I. (2018). The impact of export promotion programs on firms' export competencies and performance in a transition economy: The case of Russian manufacturers. *Journal of East-West Business*, *24*(4), 287–318.

Galbreath, J. (2018). Do boards of directors influence corporate sustainable development? An attention-based analysis. *Business Strategy and the Environment*, *27*(6), 742–756.

Geldres-Weiss, V. V., & Monreal-Pérez, J. (2017). The Effect of Export Promotion Programs on Chilean Firms' Export Activity: A Longitudinal Study on Trade Shows and Trade Missions. *Journal of Promotion Management*, 1–15.

Gencturk, E. F. (2010). Export assistance programs. *Wiley International Encyclopedia of Marketing*.

George, G. (2005). Slack resources and the performance of privately held firms. *Academy of Management Journal*, *48*(4), 661–676.

Ghemawat, P., & Reiche, S. (2011). National cultural differences and multinational business. *Globalization Note Series*, *11*, 1–18.

Gillespie, K., & Riddle, L. (2004). Export promotion organization emergence and development: A call to research. *International Marketing Review*, *21*(4/5), 462–473.

González, S., & Humberto, J. (2009). Assessing exporting culture in Colombian SMEs: A look at the Export Promotion Program (EPP). *Cuadernos de Administración*, *22*(39), 99–134.

Gopinath, G. (2020). The great lockdown: Worst economic downturn since the Great Depression. *IMFBlog–Insights & Analysis on Economics & Finance*.

Habel, J., Jarotschkin, V., Schmitz, B., Eggert, A., & Plötner, O. (2020). Industrial buying during the coronavirus pandemic: A cross-cultural study. *Industrial Marketing Management*, *88*, 195–205.

Hambrick, D. C., & Mason, P. A. (1984). Upper echelons: The organization as a reflection of its top managers. *Academy of Management Review*, *9*(2), 193–206.

Hammedi, W., van Riel, A. C., & Sasovova, Z. (2011). Antecedents and consequences of reflexivity in new product idea screening. *Journal of Product Innovation Management*, *28*(5), 662–679.

Hall (2020). Coronavirus shutdown poses threat to 59m jobs in Europe, report warns. (2020). Retrieved from https://www.ft.com/content/36239c82-84ae-4cc9-89bc-

Hannaford, W. (2000). Special report: States and foreign trade offices. *The Nor'Easter: The Council of State Governments/Eastern Regional Conference, Spring*, *9*.

Hansen, K. (2004). Measuring performance at trade shows: Scale development and validation. *Journal of Business Research*, *57*(1), 1–13.

Helfat, C. E., & Peteraf, M. A. (2015). Managerial cognitive capabilities and the microfoundations of dynamic capabilities. *Strategic Management Journal*, *36*(6), 831–850.

Hennart, J.-F., & Slangen, A. H. (2015). Yes, we really do need more entry mode studies! A commentary on Shaver. *Journal of International Business Studies*, *46*(1), 114–122.

Hofstede, G. (1997). *Cultures and Organizations: Software of the Mind*. McGraw-Hill.

Hofstede, G. (2001). *Culture's consequences: Comparing values, behaviors, institutions and organizations across nations*. Sage publications.

Hsu, C.-W., Lien, Y.-C., & Chen, H. (2013). International ambidexterity and firm performance in small emerging economies. *Journal of World Business*, *48*(1), 58–67.

Huff, A. S., & Schwenk, C. (1990). Bias and sensemaking in good times and bad. *Mapping Strategic Thought*, *89*, 108.

Ilmakunnas, P., & Nurmi, S. (2010). Dynamics of export market entry and exit. *Scandinavian Journal of Economics*, *112*(1), 101–126.

Jindal, G., & Gakhar, K. (2017). Awareness of export promotion programs – a perspective. *International Journal of Latest Trends in Engineering and Technology*, *Volume 8*(Issue 2).

Johanson, J., & Vahlne, J.-E. (2009). The Uppsala internationalization process model revisited: From liability of foreignness to liability of outsidership. *Journal of International Business Studies*, *40*(9), 1411–1431.

Joseph, J., & Ocasio, W. (2012). Architecture, attention, and adaptation in the multibusiness firm: General electric from 1951 to 2001. *Strategic Management Journal*, *33*(6), 633–660.

Joseph, J., & Wilson, A. J. (2018). The growth of the firm: An attention-based view. *Strategic Management Journal*, *39*(6), 1779–1800.

Kalinic, I., & Clegg, J. (2017). SME Internationalization, Public Policy and the Growth Agenda. In *Growth Frontiers in International Business* (pp. 33–46). Springer.

Kaplan, S., & Tripsas, M. (2008). Thinking about technology: Applying a cognitive lens to technical change. *Research Policy*, *37*(5), 790–805.

Kaynak, E., & Kothari, V. (1984). Export behaviour of small and medium-sized manufacturers: Some policy guidelines for international marketers. *Management International Review*, 61–69.

Kedia, B. L., & Chhokar, J. (1986). Factors inhibiting export performance of firms: An empirical investigation. *Management International Review*, 33–43.

Kuckertz, A., Brändle, L., Gaudig, A., Hinderer, S., Reyes, C. A. M., Prochotta, A. & Berger, E. S. (2020). Startups in times of crisis–A rapid response to the COVID-19 pandemic. *Journal of Business Venturing Insights*, e00169.

Kumcu, E., Harcar, T., & Kumcu, M. E. (1995). Managerial perceptions of the adequacy of export incentive programs: Implications for export-led economic development policy. *Journal of Business Research*, *32*(2), 163–174.

Lant, T. K., Milliken, F. J., & Batra, B. (1992). The role of managerial learning and interpretation in strategic persistence and reorientation: An empirical exploration. *Strategic Management Journal*, *13*(8), 585–608.

Le, S., & Kroll, M. (2017). CEO international experience: Effects on strategic change and firm performance. *Journal of International Business Studies*, *48*(5), 573–595.

Lederman, D., Olarreaga, M., & Payton, L. (2006). *Export promotion agencies: What works and what doesn't*.

Lederman, D., Olarreaga, M., & Payton, L. (2010). Export promotion agencies: Do they work? *Journal of Development Economics*, *91*(2), 257–265.

Lee, G. O., & Warner, M. (2006). The impact of SARS on China's human resources: Implications for the labour market and level of unemployment in the service sector in Beijing, Guangzhou and Shanghai. *The International Journal of Human Resource Management*, *17*(5), 860–880.

Leonidou, L. C., Katsikeas, C. S., Palihawadana, D., & Spyropoulou, S. (2007). An analytical review of the factors stimulating smaller firms to export: Implications for policy-makers. *International Marketing Review*, *24*(6), 735–770.

Leonidou, L. C., Katsikeas, C. S., & Piercy, N. F. (1998). Identifying managerial influences on exporting: Past research and future directions. *Journal of International Marketing*, 74–102.

Leonidou, L. C., Palihawadana, D., & Theodosiou, M. (2011). National export-promotion programs as drivers of organizational resources and capabilities: Effects on strategy, competitive advantage, and performance. *Journal of International Marketing*, *19*(2), 1–29.

Leonidou, L. C., Samiee, S., & Geldres, V. V. (2015). Using National Export Promotion Programs to Assist Smaller Firm's International Entrepreneurial Initiatives. *Handbook of Research on International Entrepreneurship Strategy: Improving SME Performance Globally*, 239–252.

Li, J., Xin, K., & Pillutla, M. (2002). Multi-cultural leadership teams and organizational identification in international joint ventures. *International Journal of Human Resource Management*, *13*(2), 320–337.

Lu, Y., Wu, J., Peng, J., & Lu, L. (2020). The perceived impact of the Covid-19 epidemic: Evidence from a sample of 4807 SMEs in Sichuan Province, China. *Environmental Hazards*.

Maitland, E., & Sammartino, A. (2015). Managerial cognition and internationalization. *Journal of International Business Studies*, *46*(7), 733–760.

Marandu, E. E. (1996). Impact of export promotion on export performance: A Tanzanian study. *Journal of Global Marketing*, *9*(1–2), 9–40.

March, J. G., & Shapira, Z. (1992). Variable risk preferences and the focus of attention. *Psychological Review*, *99*(1), 172.

March, J. G., & Simon, H. A. (1958). Organizations. New York: John Willey & Sons. *MarchOrganizations1958*.

Maula, M. V., Keil, T., & Zahra, S. A. (2013). Top management's attention to discontinuous technological change: Corporate venture capital as an alert mechanism. *Organization Science*, *24*(3), 926–947.

Meo, S. A., Alhowikan, A. M., Al-Khlaiwi, T., Meo, I. M., Halepoto, D. M., Iqbal, M., Usmani, A. M., Hajjar, W., & Ahmed, N. (2020). Novel coronavirus 2019-nCoV: Prevalence, biological and clinical characteristics comparison with SARS-CoV and MERS-CoV. *Eur Rev Med Pharmacol Sci*, *24*(4), 2012–2019.

Morgan, R. E., & Katsikeas, C. S. (1997). Theories of international trade, foreign direct investment and firm internationalization: A critique. *Management Decision*.

Nadkarni, S., & Perez, P. D. (2007). Prior conditions and early international commitment: The mediating role of domestic mindset. *Journal of International Business Studies*, *38*(1), 160–176.

Naidu, G. M., & Rao, T. R. (1993). Public sector promotion of exports: A needs-based approach. *Journal of Business Research*, *27*(1), 85–101.

Nicholls, C. E., Lane, H. W., & Brechu, M. B. (1999). Taking self-managed teams to Mexico. *Academy of Management Perspectives*, *13*(3), 15–25.

Nielsen, S., & Huse, M. (2010). The contribution of women on boards of directors: Going beyond the surface. *Corporate Governance: An International Review*, *18*(2), 136–148.

Ocasio, W. (1997). Towards an attention-based view of the firm. *Strategic Management Journal*, 187–206.

Ocasio, W. (2011). Attention to attention. *Organization Science*, *22*(5), 1286–1296.

Ocasio, W., & Joseph, J. (2005). An attention-based theory of strategy formulation: Linking micro-and macroperspectives in strategy processes. In *Strategy Process* (pp. 39–61).

Ocasio, W., Laamanen, T., & Vaara, E. (2018). Communication and attention dynamics: An attention-based view of strategic change. *Strategic Management Journal*, *39*(1), 155–167.

Oviatt, B. M., & McDougall, P. P. (2005). Defining international entrepreneurship and modeling the speed of internationalization. *Entrepreneurship Theory and Practice*, *29*(5), 537–554.

Owusu-Frimpong, N., & Mmieh, F. (2007). An evaluation of the perceptions and marketing practices of nontraditional exporters in Ghana. *Thunderbird International Business Review*, *49*(1), 57–76.

Pradhan, J. P., & Das, K. (2015). Regional export advantage of rising power SMEs: Analytics and determinants in the Indian context. *Critical Perspectives on International Business*, *11*(3/4), 236–258.

Prasad, S., Su, H.-C., Altay, N., & Tata, J. (2015). Building disaster-resilient micro enterprises in the developing world. *Disasters*, *39*(3), 447–466.

Quaye, D. M., Sekyere, K. N., & Acheampong, G. (2017). Export promotion programmes and export performance. *Review of International Business and Strategy*.

Rabino, S. (1980). An examination of barriers to exporting encountered by small manufacturing companies. *Management International Review*, 67–73.

Reid, S. (1984). Information acquisition and export entry decisions in small firms. *Journal of Business Research*, *12*(2), 141–157.

Ren, C. R., & Guo, C. (2011). Middle managers' strategic role in the corporate entrepreneurial process: Attention-based effects. *Journal of Management*, *37*(6), 1586–1610.

Rerup, C. (2009). Attentional triangulation: Learning from unexpected rare crises. *Organization Science*, *20*(5), 876–893.

Ruiz, J. (2007). Factors influencing export potential of a developing country SMEs: A study of colombian firms. In *Galeras. Working Papers Series* (No. 011; Galeras. Working Papers Series). Universidad de Los Andes. Facultad de Administración. School of Management.

Salcedo, A., & Cherelus, G. (2020). Coronavirus travel restrictions, across the globe. *The New York Times*, *1*.

Schweiger, D. M., & Sandberg, W. R. (1989). The utilization of individual capabilities in group approaches to strategic decision-making. *Strategic Management Journal*, *10*(1), 31–43.

Seringhaus, F. H. R., & Rosson, P. J. (1994). International trade fairs and foreign market involvement: Review and research directions. *International Business Review*, *3*(3), 311–329.

Seringhaus, F. R., & Rosson, P. J. (1990). *Government export promotion: A global perspective*. Routledge.

Sharma, P., Leung, T. Y., Kingshott, R. P. J., Davcik, N. S., & Cardinali, S. (2020). Managing uncertainty during a global pandemic: An international business perspective. *Journal of Business Research*, *116*, 188–192. https://doi.org/10.1016/j.jbusres.2020.05.026

Shatz, H. J. (2003). Statement on state foreign offices. *Public Policy Institute of California. July*, *2*.

Shepherd, D. A., Mcmullen, J. S., & Ocasio, W. (2017). Is that an opportunity? An attention model of top managers' opportunity beliefs for strategic action. *Strategic Management Journal*, *38*(3), 626–644.

Short, A. (1967). Canada Exhibited, 1851–1867. *Canadian Historical Review*, *48*(4), 353–364.

Simon, H. A. (1947). A Comment on" The Science of Public Administration". *Public Administration Review*, *7*(3), 200–203.

Solomon, S., Rao, G. P., & Swapna, M. (2020). Impact of COVID-19 on Indian Sugar Industry. *Sugar Tech*, *22*(4), 547–551. Scopus. https://doi.org/10.1007/s12355-020-00846-7

Souitaris, V., & Maestro, B. M. (2010). Polychronicity in top management teams: The impact on strategic decision processes and performance of new technology ventures. *Strategic Management Journal*, *31*(6), 652–678.

Sousa, C. M., & Bradley, F. (2009). Effects of export assistance and distributor support on the performance of SMEs: The case of Portuguese export ventures. *International Small Business Journal*, *27*(6), 681–701.

Spence, M. M. (2003). Evaluating export promotion programmes: UK overseas trade missions and export performance. *Small Business Economics*, *20*(1), 83–103.

Stevens, R., Moray, N., Bruneel, J., & Clarysse, B. (2015). Attention allocation to multiple goals: The case of for-profit social enterprises. *Strategic Management Journal*, *36*(7), 1006–1016.

Szymkowski, S. (2020). COVID-19 and plant closures: The automotive industry's response to the pandemic.

Tayeb, M. (1994). Organizations and national culture: Methodology considered. *Organization Studies*, *15*(3), 429–445.

Terreberry, S. (1968). The evolution of organizational environments. *Administrative Science Quarterly*, 590–613.

Tokui, J., Kawasaki, K., & Miyagawa, T. (2017). The economic impact of supply chain disruptions from the Great East-Japan earthquake. *Japan and the World Economy*, *41*, 59–70.

Tripsas, M. (2009). Technology, identity, and inertia through the lens of "The Digital Photography Company". *Organization Science*, *20*(2), 441–460.

Tuggle, C. S., Sirmon, D. G., Reutzel, C. R., & Bierman, L. (2010). Commanding board of director attention: Investigating how organizational performance and CEO duality affect board members' attention to monitoring. *Strategic Management Journal*, *31*(9), 946–968.

Van Biesebroeck, J., Konings, J., & Volpe Martincus, C. (2016). Did export promotion help firms weather the crisis? *Economic Policy*, *31*(88), 653–702.

Wang, X., Chen, A., Wang, H., & Li, S. (2017). Effect of export promotion programs on export performance: Evidence from manufacturing SMEs. *Journal of Business Economics and Management*, *18*(1), 131–145.

Wiedersheim-Paul, F., Olson, H. C., & Welch, L. S. (1978). Pre-export activity: The first step in internationalization. *Journal of International Business Studies*, *9*(1), 47–58.

Wiengarten, F., Gimenez, C., Fynes, B., & Ferdows, K. (2015). Exploring the importance of cultural collectivism on the efficacy of lean practices. *International Journal of Operations & Production Management*.

Wilkinson, T., & Brouthers, L. E. (2006). Trade promotion and SME export performance. *International Business Review*, *15*(3), 233–252.

Wilkinson, T. J. (2006). Entrepreneurial climate and US state foreign trade offices as predictors of export success. *Journal of Small Business Management*, *44*(1), 99–113.

Winston, J., & Rembler, E. A. (Eds.). (2012). *Raising U.s. Exports: Federal Promotion Efforts and Considerations* (UK ed. edition). Nova Science Publishers Inc.

Wright, M., Westhead, P., & Ucbasaran, D. (2007). Internationalization of small and medium-sized enterprises (SMEs) and international entrepreneurship: A critique and policy implications. *Regional Studies*, *41*(7), 1013–1030.

Young, S., Hamill, J., Wheeler, C., & Davies, J. R. (1989). *International market entry and development: Strategies and management*. Harvester Wheatsheaf.

Zbaracki, M. J., & Bergen, M. (2015). Managing market attention. In *Cognition and strategy*. Emerald Group Publishing Limited.

Zhang, Y., & Rajagopalan, N. (2010). Once an outsider, always an outsider? CEO origin, strategic change, and firm performance. *Strategic Management Journal*, *31*(3), 334–346.

The Rise of Cleantech in Finland - Emergence, Development and Internationalization: An Organizational Ecology Perspective

Igor Laine[1] and Lasse Torkkeli[2]

[1]Postdoctoral Researcher at LUT School of Business and Management

[2]Adjunct Professor of International Business at Turku School of Economics at University of Turku

1. Introduction

Climate change is a grand global challenge yet simultaneously it provides entrepreneurs and businesses today new opportunities to engage in sustainable entrepreneurship and in international business activities in new sectors (e.g. renewable energy, see Asemokha et al., 2019). Cleantech entrepreneurship (Goldstein, 2018) is major area of sustainable entrepreneurship that has global potential, yet extant studies in the entrepreneurship or international business domains have not managed to provide any explanations on how enterprises across a new arising sustainability-related industry sector such as the cleantech sector grow, succeed and internationalize. This chapter responds to those omissions in knowledge, by discussing the rise of cleantech entrepreneurship, specifically by illustrating it through the theoretical lens of population ecology theory. In doing so, this chapter embraces the population level of analysis on the emergence, development and entrepreneurial internationalization of enterprises in the context of cleantech entrepreneurship, using the empirical context of Finland as an example.

We illustrate how the new breed of cleantech firms, oftentimes small specializing start-ups operating in a narrow niche, seeks to outcompete traditional technology firms which are usually generalist multinationals with diversified markets and technologies at hand. In this study, cleantech sector firms are highlighted as a distinct population of organizations with the emergence, development and internationalization of this population are examined from the perspective of organizational ecology, thus introducing a new approach to explain how entrepreneurship in new types of sectors such as the cleantech sector arises and functions.

Cleantech enterprises can be broadly defined as a companies that "*develop, produce and disseminate goods and services that improve the environmental performance of the system to which they are applied*" (O'Rourke, 2009). The purpose of this study is to propose the theory of organizational ecology as a useful theoretical lens for research in the international entrepreneurship field (e.g., McDougall & Oviatt, 2000; Jones et al., 2011; Servantie et al., 2016). International entrepreneurship is defined as *"the discovery, enactment, evaluation and exploitation of opportunities – across national borders – to create future goods and services"* (Oviatt & McDougall, 2005). We examine cleantech firms as a distinct population of organizations whereas the emergence, development and internationalization of this population are examined from the perspective of organizational ecology (Carroll, 1984; Hannan & Freeman, 1989; Baum, 1999). In doing so, we outline the fundamental elements on which cross-fertilization between this theoretical perspective and research domain of international entrepreneurship might bring important advancements to one another. The current study is a conceptual one, yet serves a solid basis for the development of guidelines for policymakers on building a favourable environment for proliferation of cleantech firms at home and abroad. The new breed of cleantech firms is seen as an emerging population of organizations that seek to outcompete traditional technology firms. Oftentimes these cleantech firms are small specializing born-global start-ups operating in a narrow niche, while their competitors are generalist multinationals with diversified markets and technologies at the place.

The perspective of organizational ecology allows for assessing several key questions on international competitiveness, renewal of industrial clusters, and the ways in which global macroeconomic phenomena such as climate change impact the rise (and fall) of entire industries of business. These key questions are such as:

- Are new firms with cleaner technologies are replacing old firms operating with traditional technologies?
- Is this trend going to continue or is prone to changing environmental conditions?

- Are older firms capable of replacing their conventional more resource-consuming technologies and successfully compete with emerging population of cleantech SMEs?
- How and why are smaller start-ups able to compete with giant diversified firms that also try to introduce cleaner technologies?
- What are the environmental conditions and industrial relations that are favourable to the emergence and growth (including internationalization-based growth strategies) of the cleantech firms?

We next continue with outlining the potential role of organizational ecology theory in international entrepreneurship, followed by describing the Finnish cleantech industry context. That is followed by liking the theory and the context together, by describing how the central phenomena from organizational ecology can explain the rise and development of an emerging sector of industry in the chosen context – i.e., the cleantech sector in the Finnish context. The chapter concludes by considering the arising avenues for future research and the limitations of this particular study.

2. Organizational ecology of international entrepreneurship

While one of the core tenets of international entrepreneurship is related to establishment of new international firms (see Jones et al., 2011), tracking, analyzing, and comparing the numbers and rates of these establishments is an attractive avenue for international entrepreneurship scholars. Having in mind that organizational ecology is specifically inclined to investigation of the establishment of new organizations and their evolvement over time as populations, we see a great intrinsic potential for cross-fertilization between research domain of entrepreneurship and theoretical approach of population ecology.

Despite of this noted relevance of organizational ecology perspective to entrepreneurship in general and international entrepreneurship in particular, *"little theory and research in the field of entrepreneurship uses it, builds on it, or even acknowledges its existence through citations"* (Carroll & Khessina, 2006, p. 167). Further, by drawing from implications of a recent review study that *"population ecology does have the potential to contribute significantly to our understanding of how sustainable organizational populations have a higher rate of survival"* (Salimath & Jones, 2011, p. 893) we apply this theoretical perspective to investigate the population of international cleantech firms from Finland.

According to population ecology, change at the population level occurs as a result of environmental selection of the fittest firms within the particular environment through births and deaths of different organizations (Hannan & Freeman, 1989). However, at the firm level *"adaptive change is not impossible, or even rare, but it is severely constrained"* (Carroll, 1988, p. 2) by inertial micro and macro processes (Hannan & Freeman, 1977). From this point of view, born global firms (Rennie, 1993; Knight & Cavusgil, 1996; Knight & Cavusgil, 2004) , international new ventures (Oviatt & McDougall, 1994) and other focal actors of international entrepreneurship scholarship (Reuber, Dimitratos, & Kuivalainen, 2017), are simultaneously exposed to liabilities of newness, smallness, and foreignness (Zahra, 2005). However, these firms strive to outcompete incumbent firms that are intrinsically fit to local environments. By shifting the competition from local to global arena these firms are able to redefine characteristics of what is considered environmental fitness for entire populations of firms in various industries and localities of the world. Hence, with their rapid entry to foreign markets, international entrepreneurial firms act as unexpected change agents triggering adaptive processes at the level of entire organizational populations within affected countries and global niches.

An ecological level of analysis operates between micro (individual and organizational) and macro levels and helps to examine *"emergence, growth and decline of a population of organizations as a result of the driving forces of the environment"* (Manigart, 1994, p. 527) such as structural, political, and environmental economic conditions (Bygrave, 1993; Van de Ven, Hudson, & Schroeder, 1984). Entry of international entrepreneurial firms, thus, can be seen as another driving force of the environment that is oftentimes impossible to anticipate and take into account in risk management. Whereas a firm might be able to monitor its local competitors and other multinationals (e.g. by following areas of their patent fillings), activities of these young and unknown companies may surprise the incumbents, while the possible effect of these unwanted entrants on developments of entire populations might be compared to other external shocks such as economic crises.

On the other hand, if we consider outward perspective and respective populations of international entrepreneurial firms from a particular country, the growth of a population over its original locality through internationalization of belonging organizations has not been discussed to any large extent. However, the international aspect of entrepreneurship might be considered aligned with population ecology approaches, whereas internationalization of a population as a survival-seeking strategy, when external forces such as intensified competition compel entrepreneurs to look for opportunities abroad (Westhead, Wright, & Ucbasaran, 2001). When growing numbers of firms from the same industry or sector, or even entire populations in the most critical case, are driven to international markets, such developments create a compelling case for population ecology to provide a substantial insight for international entrepreneurship scholarship.

3. The emergence of the cleantech sector entrepreneurship in Finland

We have purposefully selected the Finnish cleantech sector as a case for our study due to several reasons. First, cleantech sector in Finland is one of the officially and publicly supported directions of industrial development that enjoys considerable informational coverage, transparency and publicity, thus offering the possibility to build up an information-rich case (Patton, 2015). Finland is also on top in most of the main cleantech-related rankings and reports (The Global Cleantech Innovation Index, The Environmental Performance Index, The Global Competitiveness Report, The Good Country Index) for a number of years, thus allowing us to take into account comparable indicators relative to the position of the country in a global cleantech sector. Finally, we have been following the development of several Finnish cleantech companies as well as participating to cleantech-related forums (e.g. Cleantech Forum Europe, Helsinki, May 16-18, 2017), thus being aware of and close to current developments and debates within cleantech sector and its community.

Reflecting the aim of our study, the process of data analysis is naturally abductive implying constant exchange between theory and empirical data (Dubois & Gadde, 2002, 2014). The process of data analysis for this study has started with building the case from secondary archival data. Then, these data were examined through the lens of organizational ecology perspective, providing a preliminary theoretical description of the contextualized phenomena under study. Further, these preliminary theoretical arguments were discussed, triangulated with interview data and refined if needed.

While there is no generally accepted academic definition of *cleantech*, the term is widely used by practitioners and refers to as a sector in which new technology and related business models offer competitive returns for investors and customers as well as providing solutions to face global challenges. In line with this definition, Cleantech Finland, the hub of Finnish cleantech expertise and sustainable innovations, has two main criteria a firm must fulfil to be referred to as a cleantech company. The two criteria relate to a firm's strategic commitment (the company has made or is ready to make a strategic commitment to developing its cleantech operations) and a solution to an environmental challenge (the company has a solution to a significant environmental challenge, either directly or as part of the value chain).

With regards to cleantech investments, according to the recent report by Cambridge Associates (2020), who have tracked results of 1,553 investments in 965 cleantech companies since 2000 through September 2019, internal rate of return on cleantech investments after showing negative results of -1,3% during "cleantech bubble" years from 2005 to 2009 regained and currently reached rather impressive figures (average of 7.9% and 24.7% during 2010-2013 and 2014-2017 respectively). Showing similar positive trend in the volume of investments (Cambridge Associates, 2020), the global cleantech sector was clearly in the up-cycle by the date of the report. Nowadays, however we can only speculate how profitable were these investments in the realms of the global pandemic and associated economic downturn.

The environment of cleantech firms deserves special attention and is distinctive in terms of their customers, suppliers, competitors and regulators. While many governments are now trying to build a favourable environment for the development of cleantech sector in their countries, they have done so with various degrees of success. A specialized index focused on cleantech, the Global Cleantech Innovation Index (GCII), explores and compare countries in their ability to cultivate hotbeds for entrepreneurial companies developing sustainable solutions. According to the GCII, high scores are achieved when countries are *"addressing growing demand for renewable energy and other clean technologies, connecting start-ups with multiple channels to increase their success rates, and increasing international engagement across the cleantech ecosystem"* (Sworder, Salge, & Van Soest, 2017, p. 3). Finland (see Box 1) along with other Scandinavian countries has long been an early adopter of environmental technologies, and according to the latest Global Cleantech Innovation Index (GCII) report maintains a second top position (Sworder et al., 2017).

In terms of early signals of cleantech innovations such as country's records of environmental technology patents and early stage venture capital, Finland has got the top position in Emerging Cleantech Innovation dimension of the index. As it comes to already commercialized cleantech firms, Finland is number eight, with a score that is just slightly above the average. Having these two dimensions together, we may expect further improvement in the number of cleantech companies in Finland as a number of currently emerging cleantech innovations reach commercial phase.

Finland reaffirms its reputation as a cleantech leader, scoring above the mean for all metrics. While Finland ranks well on the Global Innovation Index, placing 5th overall, it does not score as high as its Nordic neighbors for perceived opportunities and early-stage activity. For *cleantech-specific drivers*, Finland takes the 2nd place overall, with strong performances for its cleantech R&D budget and the number of cleantech funds present. It is not, however, attractive for renewable energy investment, where only Indonesia, Russia and Greece score lower. *Emerging cleantech* is Finland's strong point, with strong performances across all indicators. For *evidence of commercialized cleantech*, Finland's performance is nuanced, with a strong showing for renewable energy jobs and M&A activity, but relatively low cleantech imports and exports.	

Source: The Global Cleantech Innovation Index 2017

Vignette 1. Finland on a Global Cleantech landscape

While according to the GCII 2017, Finland scores highly, the evolvement of its cleantech population under current circumstances of increasing uncertainty and budget cuts remains largely unclear. In this respect, exploring the evolvement of the population of Finnish cleantech firms from organizational ecology perspective can bring valuable insights and respond to a number of interesting questions. We next assess the development and internationalization implications for the Finnish cleantech sector through the lens of organizational ecology.

4. Organizational ecology in the rise of Finnish cleantech

We can explain the rise, development and internationalization of cleantech entrepreneurship in a country context through the lens of organizational ecology in several ways. First, organizational ecology theory presumes that an ecosystem has a limited *carrying capacity*, which the population will reach after exponential growth (Figure 1). According to the Global Cleantech Innovation Index (2017), Finland is among the top 10 countries in the world in inputs to cleantech innovation and has relatively high levels of cleantech-specific innovation drivers (Vignette 1). We can therefore conclude that the public support for new cleantech entrepreneurship in the country is substantial, and the local funding and R&D support programs are heavily geared towards helping commercialize new innovations and startups. In terms of population ecology, this development implies an exponential growth curve for the total cleantech population size, as outlined in Figure 1 below.

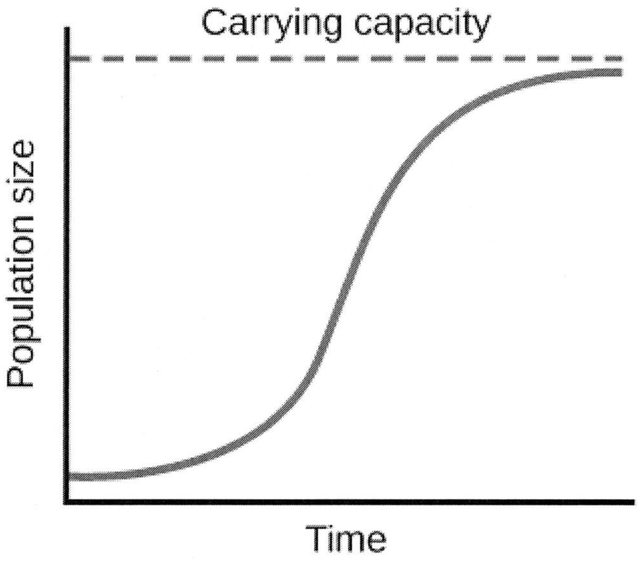

Figure 1. Population curve

In line with the organizational ecology theory, it can be expected that the exponential growth of cleantech enterprises will eventually level out due to the carrying capacity for the cleantech sector in the country context being reached. In the cleantech context, this development will arise due to two main factors: First, failure rates among growth-oriented startups such as born globals are high, as growth-orientation in a high-technology-oriented small open economy such as Finland tends to necessitate international expansion (Kuivalainen et al., 2015). Internationalization is a risky decision, and small businesses are forced to deal with a variety of barriers to exporting (Leonidou, 2004). As the challenges cleantech entrepreneurship tries to help solve – challenges such as the climate change and pollution – are global by default, the majority of enterprises in the cleantech-sector are internationalization-seeking. The public support is extended to those enterprises that survive the risky seeking of growth from international markets.

Second, cleantech innovations (such as those directly related to renewable energy) tend to exhibit substitute effects (Sørensen, 1991). This implies that, as a dominant design (Anderson & Tushman, 1990) emerges, the substitutes in the population tend to "die out" in larger numbers. An example of such a development in the cleantech context is the increasing price- and technological efficiency of solar power technology, achieved through several decades of governmental and other types of institutional support globally. Potential customers aiming to invest in renewable energy production are choosing between different substitutes (e.g., solar, wave or wind power) and eventually, new entrepreneurs seeking to succeed through non-dominant design alternatives with a less competitive cost curve are expected to struggle. The result is the stabilizing of the organizational population to the carrying capacity of the environment.

Another concept from population ecology that helps explain the emerge of cleantech entrepreneurship sector is the *niche-width perspective*. Responding to the question whether Finland can become a superpower in global cleantech the founder and principal shareholder of the Nordic energy company St1 Mika Anttonen claimed that Finland can't be a superpower of the whole sector (Eiramo, 2014):

> *"We need to do the math and choose where we can be the best in the world. We need to seek excellence and not be OK with average."*

This statement goes in line with niche-width perspective within organizational ecology (Hannan & Freeman, 1977; Popielarz & Neal, 2007) that discuss competition between generalists and specialist organizations under various industrial conditions. The concept of the niche was defined by Hannan and Freeman as *"the area in constraint space (space whose dimensions are levels of resources, etc.) in which the population outcompetes all other local populations"* (1977, p. 947). The main premise of the perspective is depicted in Figure 2 below: Specialists tend to have a head start in driving down their cost curve, whereas organizations aiming for a generalist approach will only become cost-competitive with the specialists over time. From the context perspective, the niche-width perspective posits that generalists have the advantage only when the level of environmental variability is high with coarse-grained (seldom and large) variations, whereas specialism is favoured for the more stable environment as well as for the high level of environmental variability with fine-grained (periodic and small) variations (Singh, 1990). In the case of cleantech sector, the niche is mainly constrained by capital investments and demand factors (both currently increasing), whereas investors and customers of cleaner technologies are constituent actors representing the environment. Notably, the niche itself is seen as global whereas constraint resources are spread around the world.

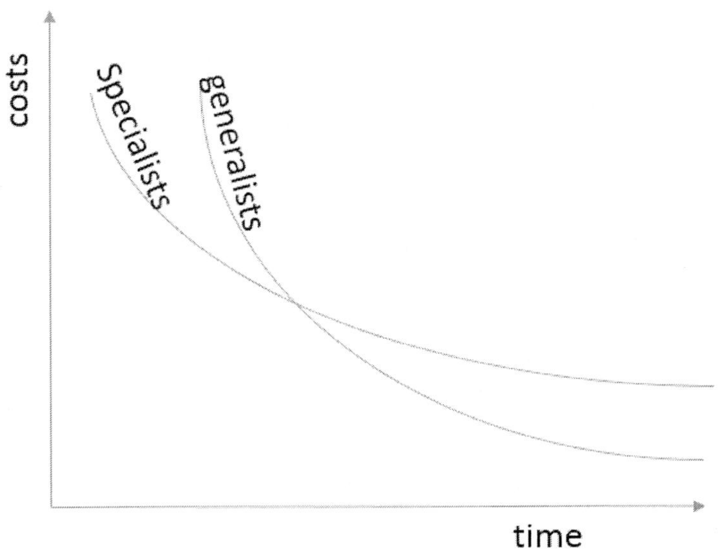

Figure 2. Cost curve

Based on the above-stated arguments we can conclude that specializing approach suggested by Mika Anttonen is only put at risk when the level of environmental variability is high with coarse-grained variations. Another important constraining factor is the regulative environment with national and supranational governments playing the central role. With regards to regulation-related variationsin cleantech sector, CEO of Rettig Group Hans Sohlström stressed that (Eiramo, 2014):

> "[In cleantech sector,] *regulation itself is usually not the problem,* [while it is] *the rapid cycle of change in regulation that makes long-term planning nearly impossible.*"

The pattern of regulative changes described above can be characterized as fine-grained and therefore based on implications of population ecology specialist approach is suggested to be a viable option regardless of levels of environmental variability.

The distinction between fundamental and realized niches can be applied to the internationalization of cleantech firms. While the fundamental niche includes all environmental conditions under which a species may thrive, realized niche covers only those areas where species actually thrive (Popielarz & Neal, 2007, p. 69). Therefore, internationalization of cleantech firms, for example from Finland, implies an expansion of the realized niche in the direction towards covering more of its fundamental niche. Moreover, with increasing number of countries encouraging cleaner technologies the territory of the fundamental niche for cleantech firms tends to expand, thus driving their further internationalization.

The third concept from organizational ecology that helps clarify the emergence and internationalization of cleantech enterprises is the *resource partitioning theory*. This theory suggests that increasing concentration of generalist firms at the centre of a market leaves opportunities for specialists in peripheral markets (Carroll, Dobrev, & Swaminathan, 2002). The fundamental dynamic is illustrated in figure 3. Population can and do move between the periphery and center through e.g. foundation of new spin-offs and other type of startups; through successful growth of existing organizations; and through mergers and acquisitions between existing organizations, for instance when the acquiring organization is located in the center and the acquired one previously in the periphery.

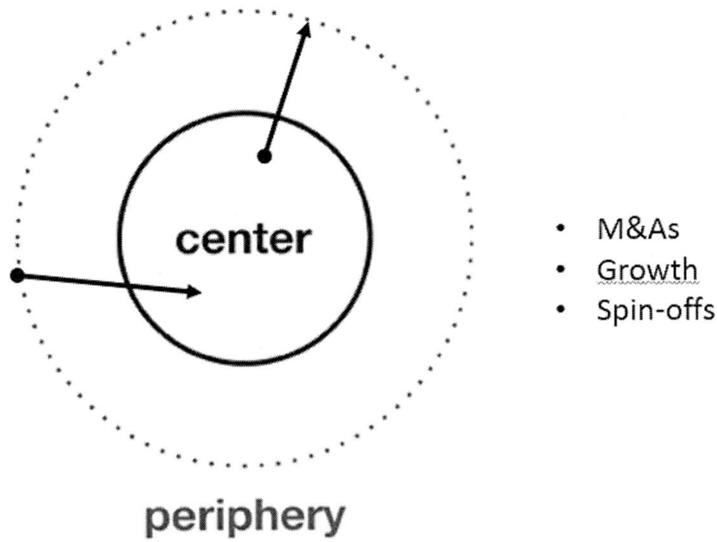

Figure 3. Center and periphery

We can apply this concept to explain the rise and internationalization of the cleantech sector as follows: Throughout many industries where emerging cleantech firms are now trying to establish themselves, large industrial mammoths like General Electric, IBM, BASF, Siemens, Caterpillar and ENI have been fighting for their dominant positions at the centre of the market for many decades. When these large industrial corporations are involved in severe competitive wars with other large players in a red ocean traditional technology markets, next disruptors are developing their products and services in the blue ocean periphery (Figure 4). Although these traditional actors are largely driven by inertial forces, their attention to the periphery through deliberate acquisition strategies might pick and move a certain cleantech venture into the centre of the market.

Notably, according to data collected by the Research Institute of the Finnish Economy (Kotiranta, Tahvanainen, Ritola, & Adriaens, 2015) from a sample of 192 companies, Nokia owns about 9700 from a total of 13000 cleantech patents, thus illustrating uneven structural partition of intellectual property among cleantech firms. Also, according to the same study, the share of turnover attributed to six Finnish cleantech giants, namely Wärtsilä,

Neste Oil, Nokia, UPM-Kymmene, Stora Enso and ABB Oy, comprise 65% of the entire cleantech sector (Kotiranta et al., 2015). Whereas Finnish cleantech sector is generally overrepresented by large industrial manufacturing firms, more service-based customer-driven cleantech SMEs are yet to thrive (Kotiranta et al., 2015). This concentration trend in Finland correspond to a global trajectory where increasing tendency of "positive" acquisitions by larger corporations has been highlighted in the recent Global Cleantech 100 report as a signal of a market upturn (Ault & Sworder, 2017).

The population and cost curves, together with the dynamics explained by the center-periphery logic thus provide a framework through which through macro-level dynamics at the level of an industrial sector can be further explained. Based on our work, we posit that it is precisely the new arising industry sectors which provide solutions to global challenges, such as the cleantech sector, that are the best "fit" to be studied through the lens of organizational ecology and its concepts. We next consider the conclusions and implications arising from this study.

5. Conclusion

The chapter has examined emergence, development and internationalization of cleantech sector in Finland from organizational ecology perspective. It is evident that the perspective of organizational ecology is an appropriate toolbox to describe the rise, development and internationalization of industry sectors in general, and it is particularly suitable as a theoretical lens to explain the rise of new sustainable entrepreneurship industries such as the cleantech sector. As such, it provides a novel lens through which explain entrepreneurial activities, as well as entrepreneurial internationalization and international business; Entrepreneurship studies have mainly assessed entrepreneurial phenomena from the individual or enterprise-specific aspects, namely through seeking to explain the discovery or creation (and subsequent seizing) of entrepreneurial opportunities (Alvarez & Barney, 2007; Bruyat & Julien, 2001; Shane & Venkateraman, 2000).

Similarly, international business research has tended to focus on the multinational firm as the unit of analysis, seeking to explain internalization (Buckey & Casson, 2008), international expansion through firm-specific advantages (e.g., Birkinshaw et al., 1998) or firm-specific learning (Johanson & Vahlne, 1977; 2009). More recent treatises have considered the role of external enablers (Davidsson et al., 2020) or the institutional environment (e.g., Tihanyi et al., 2012) in contemporary international business and entrepreneurship. Very few if any studies have considered the population dynamics at the level of entire industrial sectors. The present study contributes to the research on 21st century entrepreneurship and international business by providing a foundation through which the population ecology theory can be linked to emergence, development and internationalization of emerging fields of industry, by having used the Finnish cleantech sector as an empirical example to illustrate the possibility.

On a broader level, we note that, although human progress has long been powered by technological advancements, the shift towards cleaner technology since the early 1980s have started to change the established technological and competitive landscapes in a variety of industries. Whereas the emergence of the global cleantech sector was then initiated by purely economic reasons such as using less resource or/and producing less waste, the environmental societal discourse has been seen as a secondary factor reinforcing the trend (Millennium Ecosystem Assessment, 2005). The emergence of the cleantech sector in the early 2000s, when the term was first coined in the investment and venture capital circles, is one of the key turning points in global industrial development (Caprotti, 2012; O'Rourke, 2009). This makes the cleantech sector a valid starting point for the incorporation of population ecology theory and concepts to entrepreneurship.

A limitation of this study is naturally the fact that, upon choosing an empirical context, one also has to not choose other potentially illustrative contexts. However, we argue that, although the case of the present study is bound to a particular country, we took a broader perspective viewing it as an embedded unit with a global cleantech sector. Even though our study is about a single case, the population of Finnish cleantech firms, data collection relation to the case have been conducted at multiple levels, including individual, firm, industry, country and a global industrial sector (Fletcher & Plakoyiannaki, 2011).

Although this study has deliberately relied upon a particular theoretical perspective to analyze a contemporary empirical phenomenon, we admit the existence of other relevant (compatible or contradicting) theoretical perspectives. Despite our belief that for a stated research goal our choice of theoretical perspective seems to provide valuable insight, careful consideration of alternative perspectives should be undertaken at the further stage of our study. Furthermore, whereas the main aim of this study has been drawing from theory to practice, investigation of organizational populations under unprecedented conditions such as Coronavirus outbreak might bring solid theoretical contributions to a population ecology. In particular, under the current situation of external shock caused by Coronavirus outbreak, investigations into survival rates of international entrepreneurial firms in general and cleantech firms in particular across countries seem especially important.

We suggest that the next step in integrating population ecology and contemporary 21st century entrepreneurship and international business is to proceed from this conceptual and macro-level analysis to studies employing primary data from meso and micro levels of analysis. Both the international business (Marschan-Piekkari et al., 2004) as well as the international entrepreneurship (Ji et al., 2019) research domains have established traditions for qualitative case-based analysis (see Eisenhardt, 1989; Yin, 2017). Future studies could shed light on the dynamics of population ecology concepts at the organizational level, for instance by illustrating how the entrepreneurs themselves experience center-periphery or cost curve transitions. Finally, policy makers across countries would certainly welcome recommendations for policy and funding decisions based on optimal investment across different generalist-specialist division, the expected shape and current phase of a population curve in the given industry sector, and on optimal support systems for facilitate functioning center-periphery transitions across industry sectors. To facilitate continued deepening of the necessary knowledge in order to achieve those recommendation, empirical studies employing both qualitative and quantitative methods, and concentrating both on the entrepreneurial and policy makers' perceptual level are called for. The emergence and internationalization of cleantech entrepreneurship is at the heart of contemporary international business and entrepreneurship globally, and the present study has taken on the task of seeking to explain the phenomenon through a novel theoretical lens. Yet this is but the first step; more research is needed to clarify the big picture on cleantech entrepreneurship and the optimal ways in which population ecology should be applied empirically in business and management studies in general.

References

Anderson, P., & Tushman, M. L. (1990). Technological discontinuities and dominant designs: A cyclical model of technological change. *Administrative science quarterly*, 604-633.

Asemokha, A., Ahi, A., Torkkeli, L., & Saarenketo, S. (2019). Renewable energy market SMEs: antecedents of internationalization. *critical perspectives on international business*.

Alvarez, S. A., & Barney, J. B. (2007). Discovery and creation: Alternative theories of entrepreneurial action. *Strategic entrepreneurship journal*,

1(1-2), 11-26.

Ault, T., & Sworder, C. (2017). *Global Cleantech 100: A Barometer of the Changing Face of Global Cleantech Innovation*. San Francisco, CA.

Baum, J. A. (1999). Organizational ecology. *Studying Organization: Theory and Method*, 71-108.

Birkinshaw, J., Hood, N., & Jonsson, S. (1998). Building firm-specific advantages in multinational corporations: the role of subsidiary initiative. *Strategic Management Journal*, *19*(3), 221-242.

Bruyat, C., & Julien, P. A. (2001). Defining the field of research in entrepreneurship. *Journal of business venturing*, *16*(2), 165-180.

Buckley, P. J., & Casson, M. C. (2009). The internalisation theory of the multinational enterprise: A review of the progress of a research agenda after 30 years. *Journal of international business studies*, *40*(9), 1563-1580.

Bygrave, W. D. (1993). Theory building in the entrepreneurship paradigm. *Journal of Business Venturing*, *8*(3), 255–280. https://doi.org/10.1016/0883-9026(93)90031-Y

Cambridge Associates. (2020). Clean Tech Company Performance Statistics, *As of Sept*. Retrieved from https://www.cambridgeassociates.com/wp-content/uploads/2019/07/Cambridge-Associates-Clean-Tech-Company-Performance-Statistics-4Q18.pdf

Caprotti, F. (2012). The cultural economy of cleantech: Environmental discourse and the emergence of a new technology sector. *Transactions of the Institute of British Geographers*, *37*(3), 370–385. https://doi.org/10.1111/j.1475-5661.2011.00485.x

Carroll, G. R., Dobrev, S. D., & Swaminathan, A. (2002). Organizational processes of resource partitioning. *Research in Organizational Behavior*, *24*, 1–40. https://doi.org/10.1016/S0191-3085(02)24002-2

Carroll, G. R., & Khessina, O. M. (2006). The Ecology of Entrepreneurship. In *Handbook of Entrepreneurship Research* (pp. 167–200). New York: Springer-Verlag. https://doi.org/10.1007/0-387-23622-8_9

Davidsson, P., Recker, J., & von Briel, F. (2020). External enablement of new venture creation: A framework. *Academy of Management Perspectives*, *34*(3), 311-332.

Dubois, A., & Gadde, L.-E. (2002). Systematic combining: an abductive approach to case research. *Journal of Business Research*, *55*(7), 553–560. https://doi.org/10.1016/S0148-2963(00)00195-8

Dubois, A., & Gadde, L.-E. (2014). "Systematic combining"—A decade later. *Journal of Business Research*, *67*(6), 1277–1284. https://doi.org/10.1016/j.jbusres.2013.03.036

Eiramo, J. (2014). Finland on the way to becoming a cleantech superpower. *Sitra*. Retrieved from https://www.sitra.fi/en/news/finland-way-becoming-cleantech-superpower/

Eisenhardt, K. M. (1989). Building theories from case study research. *Academy of management review*, *14*(4), 532-550.

Fletcher, M., & Plakoyiannaki, E. (2011). Case selection in international business: key issues and common misconceptions. In R. Piekkari & C. L. Welch (Eds.), *Rethinking the case study in international business and management research* (pp. 171–191). Cheltenham, UK: Edward Elgar Publishing.

Goldstein, J. (2018). *Planetary improvement: cleantech entrepreneurship and the contradictions of green capitalism*. MIT Press.

Hannan, M. T., & Freeman, J. (1977). The Population Ecology of Organizations. *American Journal of Sociology*, *82*(5), 929–964. https://doi.org/10.1086/226424

Ji, J., Plakoyiannaki, E., Dimitratos, P., & Chen, S. (2019). The qualitative case research in international entrepreneurship: a state of the art and analysis. *International Marketing Review*.

Johanson, J., & Vahlne, J. E. (1977). The internationalization process of the firm—a model of knowledge development and increasing foreign market commitments. *Journal of international business studies*, *8*(1), 23-32.

Johanson, J., & Vahlne, J. E. (2009). The Uppsala internationalization process model revisited: From liability of foreignness to liability of outsidership. *Journal of international business studies*, *40*(9), 1411-1431.

Jones, M. V., Coviello, N., & Tang, Y. K. (2011). International entrepreneurship research (1989–2009): a domain ontology and thematic analysis. *Journal of Business Venturing*, *26*(6), 632-659.

Knight, G. A., & Cavusgil, S. T. (1996). The born global firm: A challenge to traditional internationalization theory. In S. T. Cavusgil & T. K. Madsen (Eds.), *Advances in international marketing* (Vol. 8, pp. 11–26). JAI Press Inc. Retrieved from http://books.emeraldinsight.com/display.asp?K=9780762301645

Knight, G. A., & Cavusgil, S. T. (2004). Innovation, organizational capabilities, and the born-global firm. *Journal of international business studies*, *35*(2), 124-141.

Kotiranta, A., Tahvanainen, A., Ritola, M., & Adriaens, P. (2015). Leveraging Physical Assets for Value Creation Through Cleanweb Firms - The Finnish Cleantech Space in Transition. *SSRN Electronic Journal*. https://doi.org/10.2139/ssrn.2611231

Kuivalainen, O., Saarenketo, S., Torkkeli, L., & Puumalainen, K. (2015). International entrepreneurship among finnish SMEs. In *Handbook of Research on International Entrepreneurship Strategy*. Edward Elgar Publishing.

Leonidou, L. C. (2004). An analysis of the barriers hindering small business export development. *Journal of small business management*, *42*(3), 279-302.

Manigart, S. (1994). The founding rate of venture capital firms in three European countries (1970–1990). *Journal of Business Venturing*, *9*(6), 525–541. https://doi.org/10.1016/0883-9026(94)90020-5

Marschan-Piekkari, R., & Welch, C. (Eds.). (2004). *Handbook of qualitative research methods for international business* (pp. 5-24). Cheltenham: Edward Elgar.

McDougall, P. P., & Oviatt, B. M. (2000). International entrepreneurship: the intersection of two research paths. *Academy of management Journal*, *43*(5), 902-906.

Millennium Ecosystem Assessment. (2005). *Ecosystems and Human Well-being: Synthesis.* Island Press, Washington, DC.

O'Rourke, A. R. (2009). *The Emergence of Cleantech*. Yale University.

Oviatt, B. M., & McDougall, P. P. (1994). Toward a Theory of International New ventures. *Journal of International Business Studies*, *25*(1), 45–64. https://doi.org/10.1057/palgrave.jibs.8490193

Oviatt, B. M., & McDougall, P. P. (2005). Defining international entrepreneurship and modeling the speed of internationalization. *Entrepreneurship Theory and Practice*, *29*(5), 537-553.

Patton, M. Q. (2015). *Qualitative Research and Evaluation Methods* (4th ed.). Thousand Oaks, CA: SAGE Publications, Inc.

Popielarz, P. A., & Neal, Z. P. (2007). The Niche as a Theoretical Tool. *Annual Review of Sociology*, *33*(1), 65–84. https://doi.org/10.1146/annurev.soc.32.061604.123118

Rennie, M. W. (1993). Born global. *The McKinsey Quarterly*, (4), 45-53.

Reuber, A. R., Dimitratos, P., & Kuivalainen, O. (2017). Beyond categorization: New directions for theory development about entrepreneurial internationalization. *Journal of International Business Studies*, *48*(4), 411–422. https://doi.org/10.1057/s41267-017-0070-3

Salimath, M. S., & Jones, R. (2011). Population ecology theory: implications for sustainability. *Management Decision*, *49*(6), 874–910. https://doi.org/10.1108/00251741111143595

Servantie, V., Cabrol, M., Guieu, G., & Boissin, J. P. (2016). Is international entrepreneurship a field? A bibliometric analysis of the literature (1989–2015). *Journal of International Entrepreneurship*, *14*(2), 168-212.

Shane, S., & Venkataraman, S. (2000). The promise of entrepreneurship as a field of research. *Academy of management review*, *25*(1), 217-226.

Singh, J. (1990). Theory And Research In Organizational Ecology. *Annual Review of Sociology*, *16*(1), 161–195. https://doi.org/10.1146/annurev.soc.16.1.161

Sørensen, B. (1991). Renewable energy: a technical overview. *Energy Policy*, *19*(4), 386-391.

Sworder, C., Salge, L., & Van Soest, H. (2017). *The Global Cleantech Innovation Index 2017: Which countries look set to produce the next generation of start-ups?* Järfälla, Sweden.

Tihanyi, L., Devinney, T., & Pedersen, T. (Eds.). (2012). *Institutional Theory in International Business*. Emerald Group Publishing.

Van de Ven, A. H., Hudson, R., & Schroeder, D. M. (1984). Designing New Business Startups: Entrepreneurial, Organizational, and Ecological Considerations. *Journal of Management*, *10*(1), 87–108. https://doi.org/10.1177/014920638401000108

Westhead, P., Wright, M., & Ucbasaran, D. (2001). The internationalization of new and small firms: a resource-based view. *Journal of Business Venturing*, *16*(4), 333–358. https://doi.org/10.1016/S0883-9026(99)00063-4

Yin, R. K. (2017). *Case study research and applications: Design and methods*. Sage publications.

Zahra, S. A. (2005). A Theory of International New Ventures: A Decade of Research. *Journal of International Business Studies*, *36*(1), 20–28. https://doi.org/10.1057/palgrave.jibs.8400118

PART 3:

THE ROLE OF THE INDIVIDUAL IN INTERNATIONAL BUSINESS AND ENTREPRENEURSHIP

BUSINESS MODELS IN CONTEXT: ENTREPRENEURS (RE)MODELLING THEIR BUSINESS TOWARDS AN INTERNATIONAL VENTURE

AGNES ASEMOKHA[1] AND SATU VESIN[2]

[1]Junior Researcher at LUT School of Business and Management

[2]Project Researcher at LUT School of Business and Management

1. Introduction

Throughout history, firms have struggled to catch up and survive with the ever-changing market and technological trends, customer requirements, and interests. Today, across various industrial disciplines, the fast-paced contemporary world of business, globalisation, and disruptive technological advances create uncertainty in the markets and increasingly render business models (BM) obsolete. Our generation is witnessing the rise of the so-called platform and online business models that disrupt the competitive landscape of many traditional industries like never before.

On top of this, the recent global pandemic (COVID-19) and new political phenomena (e.g., Brexit) contest existing regulations, trade liberalisation, and global transparency, thereby blurring the industrial and international boundaries that have existed in the past decades (McDougall and Oviatt 2000; Osterwalder et al. 2005). — and profoundly changing the competitive game of international businesses in unexpected ways. As a result, to catch up with the times, managers must be increasingly proactive and willing to change their business models (Nielsen et al. 2018). These issues necessitate an impending shift from 'conventional' managerial approaches and typical business model architectures towards more innovative and robust business model designs (McGrath 2010) that are flexible enough to accommodate rapid change.

The research on business models has so far enriched our understanding of the working mechanism of a business (Teece 2010; Zott and Amit 2011). However, in academics and practice research, business models have been progressively adopted as a sole or complementary unit of analysis for researching and understanding a firm and its activities (Zott and Amit 2011; Pohle and Chapman 2011). Previous studies have also mostly focused on business models as an isolated construct (Stampfl and Prügl 2011) without considering the context and role of the decision-maker or how their decisions affect the (re)configuration of business models as a firm goes through the stages towards internationalising.

In the early phase of venture creation, entrepreneurs face the daunting task of designing or reconfiguring their business model. In this phase, entrepreneurs carefully identify the important central components (value creation, delivery and capture mechanisms) and change initiatives that support the reconfiguration of the business model to satisfy the environment (Cavalcante 2014; Cavalcante et al. 2011). Here, an entrepreneur's rationale of how a venture creates delivers and captures value (Osterwalder and Pigneur 2010) and the continual renewal and adaptation of business models are relevant for obtaining a sustained competitive advantage (Achtenhagen et al. 2013). However, despite the importance of entrepreneurs' roles in designing and creating the core processes that shape their ventures, these individuals have not been extensively researched especially in the business model discourse.

Studies highlight that the complexity of an organisation's construction is what makes every firm's business model unique (e.g., Denyer et al. 2008; Westerman et al. 2006). As a result, business models are not necessarily static but have a propensity to change (Cavalcante 2014). Furthermore, to understand the value creation, delivery and capture of businesses, we must acknowledge that ventures do not exist in isolation from their *context*. For example, specific contexts (i.e., industry, level of home country development) may influence business models (Child et al. 2017; Foss and Saebi 2017), further suggesting that contextual knowledge is an essential underlying dimension of business model creation and change. Interestingly enough, entrepreneurship and new venture creation are often 'de-contextualised' in both scholarly and practitioner accounts, both of which feature the need for more studies that potentially constitute and/or transcends context (Hjorth et al. 2008; Brännback and Carsrud 2016). Nevertheless, entrepreneurs and the context in which they operate are heterogeneous in nature; consequently, the firms these individuals create are always context-bound. Without analysing entrepreneurs' *qualitative heterogeneity* and the context in which they initiate and lead their firms, we are left with an incomplete picture of the very backdrop of entrepreneurship (Ucbasaran et al. 2001) and business model creation and/or change.

Like the launch and development of a viable business, successful internationalisation requires a firm to effectively change or reconfigure its business model to fit international market requirements and contexts (Onetti et al. 2012; Child et al. 2017). By extension, entrepreneurs are consistently at the crossroads (Kets de Vries 1977) in their decision making and when it comes to devising the appropriate pathways and operations to ensure that the firm succeeds in its internationalisation pursuit. In alignment with the above notions, scholars have highlighted that entrepreneurs' mental frameworks influence how they interpret their context of doing business, make decisions and approach new opportunities in risky and uncertain environments (Shane and Venkataraman 2000; Maine et al. 2015). International entrepreneurship (IE) scholars suggest that the thinking process, structure, and behaviour of the entrepreneur are shaped by their prior experiences, which have implications for the pre-start-up and start-up mindset (Milanov and Maissenhälter 2015; Korhonen and Leppäaho 2019). Thus, there is a need to explore the international(ising) entrepreneur's all-encompassing role, their prior contextual experiences, and their cognitive schemas (Milanov and Maissenhälter 2015; Korhonen and Leppäaho 2019; Rissanen et al. 2019; Massa et al. 2017) while looking at the configuration and reconfiguration of their business models.

The current study explores how entrepreneurs make sense of their business model and change it as they internationalise or seek to do so. Thus, the study approaches the entrepreneurs as focal actors who make sense of their firms' international opportunities. The contribution of our qualitative inquiry lies at the intersection of the business model and IE literature, focusing on the entrepreneur(s) as they navigate both the individual- and firm-level context to gain a deeper understanding of the dynamics and changes that occur in their business models. Our study addresses the calls for more contextual exploration of SME internationalisation activities (Michailova 2011; Child et al. 2017, Foss and Saebi 2017) and entrepreneurship (Baker and Welter 2018; Zahra et al. 2014)—by qualitatively investigating how entrepreneurs make sense of the relationships, events, and situations they are part of (Rasmussen et al., 2001)—and how their context plays a role in the creation and exploitation of international opportunities (Mainela et al. 2014; Mainela and Puhakka 2009). In addition, we add insight into the meaning of contextualising the actions and interactions of the entrepreneurs as they (re)model their business towards an international venture. By offering four typologies of how individuals' experiences and contextual business model creation and iteration ground their approaches as they internationalise their ventures, we give both researchers and practitioners ways to understand the entrepreneur-level reasoning. Hence, the study transcends individual occurrences and also provides a gestalt-interpretation of the activities of different international entrepreneurs and how their actions concurrently influence the business model as well as determines their internationalisation processes (e.g., Acedo and Jones 2007; Autio et al. 2000; Di Gregorio et al. 2008)

2. Literature Review

2.1. Business models and business model change in the internationalisation of SMEs

Derived from the diverse theoretical and contextual lenses within management studies and practice, the untethered conceptualisation of a business model has led to increasing research on the concept (George and Bock 2011; Massa et al. 2017, Foss and Saebi 2017). Scholars in management and practice highlight that the concept of business models is valuable for exploring and providing evidence, that articulates how entrepreneurs create value (for customers) as well as for exploring the systems through which firms deliver and capture value (Teece 2010; Pohle and Chapman 2010; Zott et al. 2011, Clauss 2017).

Business models typically begin with an 'idea,' which develops and transforms over time into an envisioned architecture. The business model embodies the firm's core processes embedded in the value dimensions: value proposition, value capture, and value delivery mechanisms (Clauss 2017). The value creation reflects organizational decisions that define resource allocation, identify and capitalize on new business opportunities, and introduce new products and services in the market. Value proposition deals with how the firm provides value to its customers; Value capture focuses on how the business makes profits [Amit and Zott 2001; Teece 2010; Clauss 2017].

Thus, business models serve the interlinked purpose of providing stability for standardising a firm's core processes while also being flexible enough to accommodate change (Cavalcante 2014). Because of the unique nature of a firm's business model, multiple companies may operate in the same business field yet possess business models that are very different from each other. In essence, every business model has a unique identity that aims to satisfy organisational functions and achieve the business' vision and goals (Denyer et al. 2008; Westerman et al. 2006; Massa et al. 2017). Therefore, the ideas and principles that drive the development of a firm's standard processes (the activities related to achieving a specific result) are embedded in the mindset and action of the entrepreneurs (Andersson 2015), who must organise the activities of the firm (George and Bock 2011; Cavalcante et al. 2011), emphasising the role of the cognition schemas of the individual pushing the firm to action (Andersson 2015; Cavalcante et al. 2011; Massa et al. 2017). Most studies show that changes to the business model can mostly be attributed to business model innovation or the innovation of products and services, while a change can also be because of market position, regulatory policies, changes in the firm's processes, and internationalisation activities (Björkdahl and Holmén 2013; Child et al. 2017).

IE scholars agree on the significance of business models as a fundamental contributor to competitive advantage, strategic agility, and performance both home and abroad and across various industrial spheres (Onetti et al. 2012; Child et al. 2017; Asemokha et al. 2019; Rissanen et al. 2019). International entrepreneurial firms are known to make pivotal changes in their business models, proactively seeking new opportunities while taking significant risks for a more competitive future (Asemokha et al. 2019). As such, business models serve the interlinked objectives of providing stability for the development of firm routines and activities while also providing flexibility to allow change (Cavalcante et al. 2011, Asemokha et al. 2019) as they venture into new international markets. However, a manager's ideas and/or cognition may influence their mental framings of organisational processes. Hence, how managers think is critical in creating and developing a business model (Massa et al., 2017). This means that the sense-making of the entrepreneur and resulting implication, (that is, decision making,) within the bounded context of the business model provides more nuanced and holistic insights into the activities that shape the internationalisation of ventures (Arend 2013; Baden-Fuller and Morgan 2010; Doganaova and Eyquem-Renault 2009). For example, entrepreneurs as managers must weigh the pros and cons in relation to the perceived foreign market context and determine the implications this has for business model development or change.

As entrepreneurs enter or seek to enter foreign markets, the situation revolving around the competitive market situations, shifting customer needs and environmental uncertainties (Teece 2010, Foss and Saebi 2017) affect how entrepreneurs do business. As a result, decision-makers, or entrepreneurs can leverage or adapt their business models to initiate change (Asemokha et al. 2019) and satisfy the international market context by curating their value capture and delivery options (i.e., the channels to use, competitors' activities and institutional conditions) to suit foreign market contexts (Child et al. 2017). Business models also serve as an abetment tool for enacting international opportunities, as well as for articulating the value chain, the costs/margins structure and vantage positions that can best support a firm's competitive strategy (Onetti et al. 2012; Teece 2010; Björkdahl and Holmén 2013, Mainela et al. 2014). Therefore, to be profitable, the focal firm must continually strive to modify its operational processes in response to customers' needs and market opportunities while coping with market uncertainty and managing the competitive environment (Cavalcante et al. 2011; Torkkeli et al. 2012; Sarasvathy 2001). Moreover, because business models reflect the practice of how a venture transitions in its (international) entrepreneurship journey (George and Bock 2011) —the business model should be able to support an organisation's strategic functions, especially when it comes to surviving in new and uncertain international environments (Arend 2013).

2.2. International entrepreneurs and business models in context

Scholars have categorised entrepreneurs in numerous ways. Ucbasaran et al. (2001) classify entrepreneurs as either novice or habitual entrepreneurs or even based on human capital factors (such as prior entrepreneurial experience, business ownership and capabilities) which influences venture performance, (Ucbasaran et al. 2001, 2008). Habitual entrepreneurs (i.e., serial entrepreneurs), as their name implies, possess previous portfolio business ownership experience and tend to have more expansive knowledge and skill bases, hence fostering a diverse human capital profile (Ucbasaran et al. 2008). Novice entrepreneurs are characterised as first-time entrepreneurs with no or limited business experience or ownership. Although a novice may leverage the accumulated experiences from their current venture, they may not have enough experience—especially relating to the issues and processes associated with identifying and exploiting entrepreneurial opportunities (Ucbasaran et al. 2001, 2008). Despite this categorisation of entrepreneurs, studies add that such human capital factors (e.g., prior experiences) enhance entrepreneurial rationality thereby influencing sensitivity to relevant contingencies and/or reinforcing mental framing that determines entrepreneurial characteristics (Schweizer 2012; Child and Hsieh 2014) and identification and pursuit of international opportunity (Ucbasaran et al. 2008).

Moreover, the embryonic phases of new venture creation or product or service commercialisation and internationalisation are considered daunting tasks due to uncertainty and diverse resource and capability (e.g. financial, technical, managerial) constraints (Trimi and Berbegal-Mirabent, 2012). These constraints undoubtedly affect entrepreneurial activities, and in many cases, to address uncertainty and market imperfections, entrepreneurs rely on their limited experiences as they seek international opportunities. This leads to potential changes in the business model of their firm (Drucker 1988). Trimi and Berbegal-Mirabent (2012), also argue that in dynamic settings, critical features (for product, operations, and structure), such as innovation speed, product development, customers' behaviours, competition, regulations, stakeholder activities, and other environmental factors, considerably impact an organisation (cf. Goktan and Miles 2011; Mulders and van den Broek 2012), all of which are embedded in the business model.

Nevertheless, studies show that an objectively similar environment and/or temporal circumstances can mean very different things to different individuals (Johns 2017). For example, the differences in how founders enact the same objective environments—such as the contemporary historical time context, economic trends, or peculiarities—lead to differences in the meaning that the context holds for them and, in turn, how this changes their behaviour. In this vein, intrinsic differences in the entrepreneurs' definitions of a situation drive their firms' strategic response, that is, business model change, to the challenges they face. According to Child et al. (2017), home market context, industry context, and entrepreneurial experience contribute as valuable predictors in explaining an SME's international business model. However, so far, the context and inception of the business idea (i.e., ideation stage) have been largely neglected in business model research. Scholars highlight that the contextualisation of business model changes in relation to a firm's internationalisation cannot be dismissed because of its underlying importance, especially in small venture development (Child et al. 2017).

In the current study, contextualisation is defined as placing the entrepreneurs and their new ventures into their *'natural settings to understand their origins, forms, functioning, and diverse outcomes'* (Zahra et al. 2014, 481); hence, this is where a context encompasses the *'dynamic array of factors, features, processes or events which influence the phenomenon that is examined'* (Michailova 2011, 130). In relation to business model literature, there is no universalised normative model for creating new organisations

(Brännback and Carsrud 2016) or a sound business plan that will endure the decontextualisation of it (Baker and Welter 2018, 380):

> *Even Steve Blank, the inventor of the 'lean start-up model', acknowledges the context-specificity of his model, which stems from his experiences as a serial technology entrepreneur and investor in Silicon Valley.*

Earlier studies have rationalised that the entrepreneur's executive choices regarding the components and links in a business model generate 'fit' or an 'optimal design' for value creation or capture within a given context (Martins et al. 2015; Child et al. 2017). Hence, the entrepreneur and their role as a critical decision-maker determine what 'contextual factors' are pertinent to the chosen business model (Nielsen and Nielsen 2011).

2.3. Entrepreneurs (re)modelling their business towards an international venture

A common assumption in internationalisation studies is that the national and cultural differences of new markets pose various contexts of uncertainty and surprises on the individual and firms—that is, the various embedded situations for problem-solving, as their operations begin to cross borders and internationalise (Johanson and Vahlne 1977). Following the views of entrepreneurship, such as effectuation (Sarasvathy 2001; Read et al. 2016), International entrepreneurship (IE) scholars have become more interested in the individual entrepreneurs who convert uncertainties into opportunities based on the means available and who do so without trying to predict the future (Mainela et al. 2014).

Much like in the general entrepreneurship literature (Gartner 1989), IE research also points out that entrepreneurs are the key driver of new venture creation (Coviello 2015) and that their perceptions of the circumstances for their venturing efforts (Ozgen and Baron 2007; Zahra et al. 2005) manifest in their firms' process of engaging with international opportunities (e.g., Fletcher 2004; Hohenthal et al. 2003; Mainela and Puhakka 2009). Moreover, a variety of theoretical approaches have been adopted to understand how international entrepreneurs and their behavioural orientations, mindsets and the ways they identify and exploit business opportunities both at home and abroad affect the journey of their business (Mainela et al. 2014; Zucchella et al. 2018).

In practice, IE phenomenon originates from the entrepreneurs' everyday context, actions and interactions (i.e., routines and more improvised forms of action) towards the internationalisation of their firms (Mainela et al. 2014). Thus to complement the firm-level focus in IE research, that is, the venture type and antecedents to internationalisation (Jones et al. 2011; Oviatt and McDougall 2005), one hypothesis has been that exploring the of internationalisation of new ventures should also reflect on the role of individual-level sense-making, actions, and practices in concretising international opportunities (Rasmussen et al. 2001; Acedo and Jones 2007). Thus, due to the above-mentioned complementarity, we surmise that the way entrepreneurs interpret their own contemporary, and contextual events or circumstances can influence the organisational routines and related internationalisation intentions or activities— all of which are functions of their business models (George and Bock 2010; Linder and Cantrell 2011; Cavalcante et al. 2011).

3. Methodology

In the current qualitative study, we explore how entrepreneurs make sense of their business model and change it as they internationalise or seek to do so. Thus, we examine the entrepreneur and the context of the business model's early and iteration phases regarding the company's internationalisation journey. Furthermore, we focus on the context of these phases as a valuable point of reflection for how different contextual dimensions (social, temporal, spatial, industry, and organisational) of their entrepreneurial journeys (Zahra et al. 2014) drives the sensemaking behind the business model of the internationalising firm. Accordingly, we set out to investigate four companies at the verge or in the early phases of their internationalisation journeys; to do so, we use a critical realist case study approach (Ragin 2009), which aims to contextualise explanations by using a more subjective search of the causes in the focal phenomenon (Piekkari et al. 2009; Welch et al. 2011). Drawing from a sensemaking perspective in IE (e.g., Rasmussen et al., 2001), we investigate the entrepreneurs' narratives and descriptions of their experiences and the current situations with the company, along with the entrepreneurs' projections of the company's visions and future directions in relation to reaching international markets. In conjunction with this, we are interested in the contextual conditions from which the initial business model (ideas) had emerged and were configured (Ragin 2009), along with the business model changes that had taken place or would possibly take place in the future based on the entrepreneurs' views of the current situation.

3.1. Data and case descriptions

The cases were selected based on preset criteria, which included being recently established small companies in their early internationalisation stage. Data were generated through semi-structured thematic interviews from the company founders and co-founders Welch and Piekkari 2006). The firms were in the early phases of establishment and internationalization, the interviews lasted for about an hour each and the recorded interviews were transcribed verbatim for the initial content analysis. The interview transcripts totalled up to 210 minutes and 67 pages of text. For triangulation and more robust analysis, we also used data from other sources, such as webpages and data collected from an IE master's degree course (i.e., founders' narrative script), in which the interviewees were attending as case companies. Table 1 summarises the case descriptions, providing an overview of each company.

3.2. Analysis

In this study, the entrepreneurs' accounts function as "sensemaking instruments" (Brown et al., 2015) of their international entrepreneurial experiences and behaviour, which again provided us means for analysing how these entrepreneurs chose to encode information about their past experiences, the surrounding world and themselves in it (e.g., Korhonen and Leppäaho 2019). Based on semi-structured interviews with the CEOs and/or founder-entrepreneurs of the companies, our qualitative exploration could focus on the contextualisation of the early phases of creating their business models and the changes they made—that is, phases of rethinking their value creation, value delivery and value capture—in relation to their internationalisation journey. Our analysis process was manifold and resembled an abductive process of moving between the data and literature.

For the initial level of analysis, we organised the data based on the interview guide (structuring the data based on the overall idea of the business, that is, service and product and value propositions). This part included the founders' background and the time prior to founding in relation to the processes the ventures had been going through, here with a keen focus on the early years of business inception and internationalisation activities. An inquiry of any change the entrepreneurs had detected in their firm's journey was embedded in the interview guide.

Table 1. Overview of case companies

Case Descriptions	
Kalamar Kalamar was founded by four entrepreneurs in 2015, who combined their past work experience (in corporate management operation) to find a solution for a company's management system using business information to facilitate strategic processes effectively. Each of the founders had vast experience in different management disciplines, such as corporate management and software business. Kalamar provides a cloud-based living strategy platform or product (a connection between strategic work, management system, and management teamwork) used mostly on B2B business. The 'Living Strategy' concept is the main value proposition and service offering of the business. The platform allows their client to collect useful data for customers' needs from different sources and gather them into one place. The platform also helps users (customers) organizes and analyses collected data to improve executive reasoning and choices. Thus, supports managers in strategic planning and decision making for the best possible outcomes.	**Sunsu** Sunsu two-man company founded in 2015, providing streamlined e-commerce solutions and services for the B2B client by providing them with custom solutions (clients in the home market) on how to sell their products in international markets, primarily to Russia, Japan, and China —thereby bridging international boundaries by creating the possibility for Finnish products to be exported conveniently into international markets. In a way, the company acts as an intermediary to its clients by effectively providing services and relevant information needed to customers to cross their products and services. Their business solutions include e-commerce, sales management, logistics, and consulting. The company provides an all-in-one package that allows their clients to explore international markets successfully by leveraging their solutions, thereby minimizing significant internationalisation investment costs, which is crucial in facilitating international activities between their clients across borders.
Modula Solutions Modula solutions is a start-up that manufactures furniture. Founded in 2016 by a Finnish couple, whose initial vision was to expand the unique and innovative business abroad. The core products are cushion blocks (Furniture made of BiT elements modular sofas for customization) connected by magnets - a type of frameless furniture. The product is easily maintained, safe, and caters to families or residential owners of small apartments/ spaces. The product is designed to be used both indoors and outdoors, such as small apartments, offices, public spaces, and building multipurpose play areas in parks for children. The company has tried to carry out its production in Poland, but so far, the company has sold products only in its home country. However, moderate the overall sales have been, the ambition to expand further internationally, especially in Asian countries, is high. Having a small product selection and given the competitive market space in the furniture business, the company has limited customer options, which may pose a challenge.	**Kurros** Kurros was founded by an entrepreneur in 2014. It is a digital platform offering virtual specialized social services for the elderly. The company collaborates with professional service providers using teleconference technology to provide real-time stimulating services via its web store, where customers purchase services and participate in interactive activities with professionals. Kurros main business activities have been focused within the home country, particularly focus on Finnish customers and service providers. The company also uniquely and strategically internationalizes by mainly targeting Finnish customers in international markets. However, Kurros has intentions to expand its business soon to other countries. So far, the company does not have direct competitors due to its unique and innovative new type of digital services they provide for the elderly.

Building on the more content-oriented initial analysis, we began to map out and connect the different contextual elements in the early 'idea generation' phase (of the venture) and how the early visions of internationalising the company conditioned the remodelling of the companies' value proposition, value delivery and value capture. This second level of analysis involved a preliminary restructuring of the data, including identifying the coding and thematic categorisation of experiences (in NVivo) and business model changes. Such a categorisation allowed us to dig deeper into the initial findings and make sense of business model changes in context. Although we identified numerous business model changes in many business model elements, we sensitised our analysis mainly by tracing the events in which the entrepreneurs were facing opportunities and/or challenges for their internationalising business hence, initiating change to their business accordingly.

Based on the iteration of the data, the latter part of our analysis helped to unravel the primary business model changes happening in relation to the different dimensions of the entrepreneurs' context, sensitising us to see more of the multidimensionality and entwining of contexts in which the business ideas and models had come about; this helped give shape to the entrepreneurs' 'creativity and approaches' to internationalisation. Through our analytical process of contextualising the individual entrepreneur, the different phases of changes in the business models and their internationalisation journeys directed us to make more nuanced understandings of the different temporal, social, spatial, organisational, and market/industry dimensions of the context (Zahra et al. 2014) in the entrepreneur-level reasoning of the past, present and imagined future of internationalising business models. The interview accounts reflect the individuals' relations with their partner and customer base and the value such social contexts bring to (re)thinking the business model in the form of renewed products and/or services suitable for the markets abroad. For example, the" *timing of economic crisis triggering internationalization"* another example "*the entrepreneur was working alongside a financial institution to help create a solution to facilitate international transactions"*. These findings informed our contextual interpretation that of the founders, the iterative work that founders/entrepreneurs engage in within these entrepreneurial contexts has implicit or explicit implications on the business model and consequent internationalization efforts.

Finally, coming back to the individual, our analysis continued by contextualising the sensemaking accounts of the founders to depict their alternative interpretations of their international entrepreneurial behaviour

(Korhonen and Leppäaho 2019) in conjunction with rethinking their business models. By offering four typologies of the entrepreneurs, our iteration of the data and analysis further supports our findings of the business model changes regarding how the individual firms have approached international opportunities in their unique contextual setting.

4. Findings

This section begins with our findings of how the contextualisation of the founder(s) and business model change—that is, the phases of rethinking value creation, value delivery, and value capture in relation to early internationalisation—comes through in the entrepreneurs' subjective sense-making of their contextual experiences of the past, the current situation and projections of the company's future directions. Accordingly, we first set out to tap into each case individually. Then, we continue into our findings as a cross-case type of analysis, where the aim is to show how contextualisation matters in how and why business models are thought of and how they could—and maybe should—change during the internationalisation journey of their firms.

4.1. Individuals creating value in context

Our findings indicate how the entrepreneur's past background, experience, and social context drive the company's initial point of departure in value creation and propositions. As an individual-level and entrepreneur-based process, the contextual mechanisms of the initial business idea are found in the person's close relations, expertise, and competence.

Sunsu and the Tactical Entrepreneur

Sunsu company was co-founded by co-workers. The interviewed founder had owned a series of companies in the past, and his expertise was fundamental to the creation of the company. All the founders were experts in different professional fields, such as international marketing and logistics. The founders' combined expertise provided the bedrock within which the business model and the firm's core services were embedded. Both founders seemingly approached business decisions with *skill and tact*: in a sense, they seemed to have a more diverse idea of what it meant to fail or succeed in business. We detected that these seasoned founders were brave enough to ignore the status quo. Although they would encounter specific institutional barriers and challenges in the home and international market, they would try to interact with external institutional actors (i.e., the financial instruments providers) and seek standard solutions. They proactively in collaborated with external stakeholders and partners to create reforms and align these reforms with their internal strategies to change their core processes, further influencing their value delivery and capture. The founders had extensive network connections that they leveraged when aiming to scale their business model internationally. Combined, the founders pioneered their vision to bring their business venture towards international success:

> *[...] we (founders) have several kinds of backgrounds and specialties. When we get an idea, we start to discuss them. ...and reflect on how it could be done? Then we decide if to take it forward or if they were just ideas! However, some of them (ideas) we start to develop and find solutions_(thus)a new possibility for business and so on. [...] After that, we decide if it an opportunity to pursue or if they were just ideas and may not be feasible going forward.*

Modula Solutions and the Inventor Entrepreneur

The founder of Modula solutions was the least formally educated. Prior to starting the business, he had no educational background except for a couple of courses in programming in a polytechnic. His prior work experience included social and health care work for eight years, from which he went onto establishing his company. The founder considered himself an inventor with an extensive product portfolio and process ideas from diverse industrial sectors. The entrepreneur claimed some of his ideas were executed, and others were unexecuted and still in his mind.

The company's business idea was conceived by realising the need for furniture for social settings and his personal need in his home's aesthetics. By combining his inventions and the ideas of his spouse, they developed the initial product. As a co-founder, his spouse brought in her competence as a seamstress and later managed the company's administrative activities. The research and testing of the product took five years before it was launched to the market. The entrepreneur described himself as a person with multiple ideas who creates new devices and tools to solve practical problems. In this sense, the entrepreneur displayed the typical 'inventor mentality', where the product is created prior to thinking of ways to commercialise, sell, and market it.

The founder was keen on selling his 'innovation' abroad, yet the strategies to achieve this appeared to be lacking. The company was also heavily reliant on funding firms and networks to help catapult product development and internationalisation initiatives. He also manifested the *Novice Entrepreneur's* attributes because the ways to scale and create the business model had not been considered at the time of the interview. Thus, they faced the challenges of finding the appropriate customers, resources, and organisational and management capability to shift from being just a product to an operational and running business:

> *[...] I have done these inventions since 2006. [...] I like to observe things a little bit from the side to see without any heavy burden and create solutions easily. I would like to work very closely with research and development in the future. Not as a CEO at all, so I'd be doing product development.*

Kurros and the Control Entrepreneur

The founder of Kurros had a university education and professional background in international marketing. Her previous work experience stemmed from an international company exporting medical equipment. Having worked in the social health care sector, during which the founder had participated in projects testing virtual services, she combined two kinds of contextual knowledge and interests into her business opportunity. Therefore, we can say this entrepreneur was building her business idea and model based on the previous expertise: by transforming a conventional solution into a unique service solution, she could serve a niche segment. Although the core service (i.e., physiotherapy) we see is not new, the delivery method of the value proposition (i.e. virtual physiotherapy service) is. By providing tremendous comfort and convenience to customers via digitalising her service, she was able to disrupt conventional delivery approaches in physiotherapy. The delivery and channels become innovative when put into the temporal context of the market at the time. However, the founder reveals a sense of rigidity or control in the decision making of how the entrepreneur approaches the internationalisation of the firm:

> *I have done that for 20 years, so I know what it is. If I want to do [...] a profitable export business, I would need to have resources. I need to have a person who will be totally devoted. In a way, I have been very quiet about it because I don't want to do a lousy job. I want to start the export when we are ready for it!*

Kalamar and the Experimental Entrepreneur

The founder of Kalamar had a university education and prior experience in a software firm, consulting business, and sporting industry. He was involved in establishing a currently successful start-up (software business) in Finland from scratch. His previously owned company provided financial consultancy services during the *internet boom and/or early dot-com bubble*.

During this time, he helped companies understand how to utilise the opportunities provided by the internet. This entrepreneur stated that he learned how to run small- and medium-sized companies and gained international trade and manufacturing experience while working in a family-owned business in the sports industry. The co-founders' previous work experience (in finance) and observations at work ignited his idea and developed a next-level strategic management solution for firms, bringing about an opportunity to capitalise on it that led to the company's establishment. Based on their industry knowledge, the founders' initial idea evolved into a new management method to analyse business operations. This entrepreneur(s) portrayed an experimental mindset in their business routines and attitude towards international opportunities:

> *We need to start with some part of the whole idea, and then first try to go to market with one part before we decide to make the process as a whole, which is our competitive edge!*

4.2. Contextualising business model change in international entrepreneurship as an iterative process

The contextual changes because of or within internationalisation trigger how the entrepreneurs and their firms change their business model and/or 'remodel' how they do business: the present situation and future scenarios of the business context (i.e., economic situation market trends, networks) trigger iteration of how value is created, delivered and captured. Accordingly, tracing the context in the entrepreneurs' accounts as a way to explore their business models and frame the changes in them as 'iteration' processes, we can see how and why different contextual dimensions in their internationalisation journeys matter. Tables 2 to 5 show the typologies of these entrepreneurs and the meaning of the context from which the initial idea and business model of the companies unfolded.

Sunsu's process

The founders leveraged their collective interdisciplinary knowledge and capabilities to provide a comprehensive solution to customers. The founder identified the need for the next phase of business model development: transitioning from the product development phase to actively implementing changes in their processes by developing standard routines. Thus, they were developing the necessary standard routines that could help evolve the business model into maturity and make it function like a real company:

[...] we focused very much on this product development, and we are running out of resources. We have done enough product development, (now) we have to change. We have to focus more on sales and marketing, b2b-marketing. This may be the most dramatic change in what will happen if we really have to start working like a real company. We're not this kind of hobby, product development thing. We have to get rid of this start-up level and start to do business. And it means changes in these processes of our company very much.

The company encountered institutional and bureaucratic barriers that delayed some of their stakeholders' payments (transactions) in the initial phases of their internationalisation. Thus, because of the small size of the firm, they had limited resources. Because of the clients' international location, the firms needed to find alternative ways to facilitate international payments. The founders responded to this problem of international payments (i.e., how domestic banks view money transfers from abroad) by seeing an opportunity to rectify challenges they were facing with money inflow from abroad. Thus, they proactively collaborated with the financial institution to find a solution by creating a robust business model that allowed for payment flexibility.

[...] I was the one who was teaching Finnish banks how to handle international payments, money funding, and transfers, but they did not know about this. I found out a legal and reasonable way to make these money transfers flow from Russian payment methods to Finnish companies. [...] It was a very ridiculous situation. [...] But the point is that this is just one case that these challenges what we have, you just have to learn and make the innovation and push it through because you will find the solution.

The founder highlighted the importance of understanding the contextual nuances that exist with customers and how cross-cultural contexts support business processes, allowing them to understand customers' needs properly. Thus, they actively reflected on their cultural tendencies to minimise bias about prospective markets by showing market commitment and learning about the potential target market by collaborating with a person who is knowledgeable about the market culture and context:

[...] How you can create trust with the person. [...] We might have a deal and arrangement that we're doing cooperation, but how well it works. It depends very much about this between the chemistry of those people. This is very much a cross-cultural issue that do you speak in a contextual way or not-contextual way.

Table 2. The entrepreneur of *Sunsu* making sense of relevant context and activities that influence the business model

Sunsu: The Tactical Entrepreneur

Temporal dimensions	Social dimensions	Spatial dimensions	Industry and market dimensions	Organizational, ownership and governance dimensions
Timing of economic crisis in foreign target market. e.g., the crisis and collapse of Russian market economy triggering the birth of ecommerce as a solution.	Revisiting the initial offering and channels by developing new approach to tackle customer and partner concerns.	Leveraging regional advantages and networks from previous business ownerships in domestic and international market (Russia and Japan).	Minimize barrier to entry by working in collaboration with stakeholders and other online marketplace to ensure customer satisfaction and optimization of their business operations.	Due to limited inflow of funding and resources. The company focuses on boosting sales and amplifying their marketing activities in order to thrive.
We were doing this Russian marketing and we faced with challenges of understanding our client requirements on how the internet marketing and sales should be done. However, we knew that e-commerce is growing very fast, and we found out that companies are very willing to buy their own web shop. Then we changed that we started to sell this own shop, because it was clear there was a demand.	Decision making takes in consideration localization strategic marketing, partnership selection and reflects on cross cultural patterns and customer identities in communication and offerings.	For example, collaboration to solve transactions in *Russia, e-commerce;* ***bureaucracy and regulations regarding financial systems, payments.*** ***"if the fashion products are to be sold in Japan, the pictures should be taken by using Japanese models. So, we have a network in Japan where product illustration can be taken. We European people look a little bit different, and the consumers think about how this jacket looks like, when I wear it on. we can provide and consult on these kinds of services, as well.*** Pre-empting latent needs of customers or stakeholder concern and modifying based on the competitive market situation, i.e., how or what kind of quantity of demand is there, the sales strategy search for the partners, and so on.		Effectuation by leveraging on company's the existing resources and capabilities of founders. ***"We have a wide range of expertise in the background of our company, these experts together and so we have covered all these themes what is needed there."***

→

Entrepreneur making sense of relevant internationalization activities and contexts that influence business model change

To remain scalable, the company capitalised on the internationalisation initiatives of funding and governmental agencies for their resources because they could gain recognition (domestically) and legitimacy by being in an alliance with them. The founder also emphasised that 'more challenging in this financial level is this financial flow inside the company'. The founder stated that value is created by prioritising sales and reflecting on how it influences the cost, identifying what kind of things should be done, and the resources and capabilities needed—suggesting that sales are needed to get the necessary funds for investments to pick up. Although the firm's immediate focus was on home market clients, the company expressed an interest in expanding its client base into the Nordic countries, part of Europe, and North America. Sunsu also had a vast network and consistently working towards developing more international and local partnerships, for example, with local logistics providers at both ends of their customer scale. Their multisided platform for customers allowed them to develop relationships with partners and clients that tended to transcend simply creating deals. The respondent maintained that collaborating with their partners and customers fostered solutions that lead to customer lock-in.

Modula Solution's process

The value proposition of Modula Solutions is the design and multifunctionality of the product, and extensive iterations and modifications have been made to the product since the launch of the company. The company was in a critical phase where it needed to transition from product development and develop its business model to scale. The founder identified that they might benefit by expanding their single product line to other sectors where their product would be needed. However, the founder(s) grappled with inadequate finance, resource, and capability to scale the business, acknowledging the need for people with the right capabilities to push that initiative forward.

The company adopted a strategy that emphasised using direct selling in the home market, aiming to use online sales and crowdfunding campaigns to reach international customers. International market selection and operational processes were still unestablished and how to internationalise to these countries had yet to be determined. The value delivery and capture activities, such as source material, manufacture, and reaching the primary target market, were based on intuition and speculation. The founder's technical knowledge was focused on generating new ideas to improve the functionality of the product rather than developing the business model and standardising the company's operational routines, which we identify as the 'inventor's mentality'.

Although Modula Solutions was still seeking long-term collaborations with different suppliers and partners for sourcing materials and manufacturing. To accelerate product development and better understand customer needs, the company took in new ideas and feedback (such as product design ideas and internationalisation decisions) that led to changes in their business model, from both customers and stakeholders.:

> *[...] It's on-going negotiation and idea storm between all the shareholders inside the company all the time. we need a lot more ideas. [...] We are also in the testing period, and we need lots of feedback from the customers. So, we are choosing to go, and the customers are part of forming a new product process. [...] They have ideas of, e.g., new shapes or systems that can be, maybe incorporated into our system. We would like to present a model where we can quite generously pay these idealistic customers who have new ideas.*

The founder acknowledged that cultural context and matters regarding customer requirements differ in different countries. Stating that as a small company, they need more employees and more knowledge on streamlining and localising their offerings to target customers. The founder reflects that they have not been able to secure financial support from business angles or other institutional investors. However, the entrepreneur confirms that they would benefit from getting support from the Government trade promotion organisation, which would be valuable to catalyse their internationalisation plan by connecting them with the right people.

> *'[...] localisation is very important in all international markets. [...] for example, in Asian markets, or even if you are going close to the Mediterranean, the sofas' colors (for customer taste) are totally different. [...] Moreover, the distance is too great, and we need localisation if we have to try to match customer expectations.*

Table 3. The entrepreneur of Modula Solutions making sense of relevant activities that influence the business model

Modula Solution : The Inventor Entrepreneur

Temporal dimensions	Social dimensions	Spatial dimensions	Industry and market dimensions	Organizational, ownership and governance dimensions
Research and testing took five years before sales: Incremental innovation on value offering before product launch to market . ***"We have modified the idea a lot. We have this is the fifth iteration of the connector. So, we have redrawn it several times, and now it's perfect"***	Engaging in research to understand and identify what customer wants. After which they identify what customers are appropriate to target, and then they test such market opportunities by sending the product to customers (families and kids) there to see how they interact with it	Actively seeking long term market actors (as partners and collaborators) to provide supports services, materials and other services. E.g contractors for sewing. textile supplies from Denmark, magnets from US .	Preempting and making regulation driven decisions making in partner selections and product innovation to help them compete with big players especially in an industry that is heavily reliant on materials that leads to so much waste such as wood. ***"environmental protection legislations are getting very tight. Which is good. We are close partners with an organization and a university researching (environmentally friendly foam). when they are ready, we aim to implement it immediately into our products. [...]It is not expensive so the customers, who have bought before these, can change them if they want so the switch can be very quick after that".***	Precautionary measures were pertinent to the founder. Patents to secure the value offering, and against competitors and counterfeiting. ***--" The (future) will come as threats. We are dealing with them as happening now situations. So, that's why we are making precautions. The patent schemes, they are the greatest threat".***
Unclear internationalization plans: ***United States is very important for us, because of the scalability of the product, after that comes U.K. and Germany AND Japan Europe, which is hard. We'll see how the delivery company delivers our products in the States. We want a global crowdfunding campaign, but it's not decided yet, how to do it".***	Providing the value promise to customers for maintenance or replacement if the product is destroyed. Product is presumed to be cheaper and easier to transport, deliver, assemble the product unlike other bulky furniture	New channel to reach customers and lower barriers that may affect purchase decisions due to lack of pop-up stores for customers to test and see the product. ***there will be videos on the web of different weight class people sitting on our product and showing how they are function, how do they feel, which is not done in other products. So we hope that lowers the barrier to order it from the internet***	Information from competitor's activities and triggered their actions (fast follower) ***The campaign in Kickstarter was successful to this entrepreneur in Australia, but he couldn't deliver, as nobody couldn't do that product. We saw that they started at the same time as we did, and we just recently discovered this kind of a systems. So, that's why we are using embedded connectors inside polyurethane.***	

Entrepreneur making sense of relevant internationalization activities and contexts that influence business model change

Kurro's process

Kurro's initial business idea started from a European Union (EU)-funded project. The project unravelled a market opportunity and a need for complementary products and services to meet the country's physical and health needs regarding its changing (ageing) demographics. After the initial idea had been refined, the company was born. The business model was developed around their core product offering, which was the 'innovative virtual platform that integrates professionals and customers providing digital health care and social services' for the elderly in real-time. The fundamental value proposition of the firm was the user-friendliness of the product, cost-effectiveness and convenience. The platform was the channel through which the company interacts, transacts and sell with customers and stakeholders. Thus, the platform anchored the business process, and the company focused on optimising the platform to ensure customer satisfaction. Business model innovation was achieved by co-creating with stakeholders to ensure customer satisfaction and optimisation of the platform towards standardisation:

> *[...] we are listening to the feedback. We're talking with the customers all the time. That's not internal, that's more external, but you get feedback from your customers, and then you innovate from there. [...] but, our people are following the development of different activities (all the time) that bring internal innovation.*

Although the company focused on customers in the home market, the company uniquely approached internationalisation by providing their services and *Natives (i.e. Finnish customers)* living abroad. In other words, they were strategically engaging in internationalisation (drawing from a cultural context) and targeting individuals from similar and/or familiar cultural context abroad. Also, by prioritising the home country customers, and studying their behaviour, they incrementally modified their platform (product offering) before expanding their services beyond the home market context:

> *[...] when we start internationalisation, we are doing it step by step. I think the first internationalisation that we will be doing is expats works. So Finnish people residing out of Finland because there we can supply the services from Finland. Because they want to have services in their own language, then after that it would be Scandinavia. Let's say it would be the countries that have a similar system for elderly care.*

The founder highlighted that the novelty of the platform and other applications might intimidate their customers (i.e., senior citizens) and other users, such as the service provider and service centres. Therefore, because of their clients' demographics, the company tried to minimise stereotypes and social and psychological barriers concerning the use of advanced technology. Thus, they 'educated' their customers on their value offering (e.g., convenience and flexibility) and the accompanying benefits accrued from using this technology and using feedback to improve the offering.

> *[...] launching is something new is always a challenge, and we're creating awareness. We have just launched apps for android phones and tablets. [...] the elderly people were participating in co-creating the apps_ And of course, we are gathering feedback from our customers and trying to improve our services and the selection of our service.*

Due to limited resources, deriving new network relationships, contacts and knowledge about the international markets and exports were the drivers for international market entry. Moreover, the founder exerted substantial control over the business (internationalisation) process, which presented a resemblance of the company being 'rigid' and cautious towards internationalisation, regardless of prior experiences or background:

> *[...] I have discussed with some people that I know my international network. So, I have contacted and tried to see what the situation in their countries is. Let's put it that I know what it is to do export business and I know that it is very demanding and until now I have been kind of waiting.*

Table 4. The entrepreneur of *Kurros* making sense of relevant activities that influence the business model

Kurros: The Control Entrepreneur

Temporal dimensions	Social dimensions	Spatial dimensions	Industry and market dimensions	Organizational, ownership and governance dimensions
Timing of value offering to the market gives the company a head starts and flexibility in the international market ***a forerunner in that way, so the rules are not yet applicable for services that are delivered to using technology so, it is a totally new market***	Strategic partnerships and networks relationships to foster the recognition and visibility of the firm -to make service more mainstream.	Incremental internationalization plans and leverage regional advantage: internationalization begins by doing expats works. So Finnish people residing out of Finland, because there we can supply them the services from Finland. Because they want to have services in their own language then the Scandinavian countries. Also, we will need to have local service providers because we can scale up the business	Some level of uncertainty and the firm still struggles with the acceptance of the service because old industrial processes are still prevalent. Also, no clear regulation and standard for products	Internationalization decisions is controlled and are dependent on entrepreneurs past experiences and social networks to meet new customers gather information on internationalization decision.
			The need for secondary (external) resources to facilitate value delivery. "***Launching is always a challenge and we are creating the awareness. I mean, and when we deliver the services to the tablet device you need to have a good coverage.***"	Recurrent control overseeing of firm and stakeholders' activities influences internationalization and business model initiatives
Due to customer misconception or lack of clarity with the service: The company devotes time towards educating target stakeholders (Clients, service providers) on about the benefits they could have using the technology to minimize psychological barrier due to the novelty of service offering				The founders trying to minimize risks by being ahead with privacy issues. ***"… EU ruling is going to be changed next year so then the rules would be tighter…when think about privacy issues, we have already known, we are taking (privacy issues) into consideration ."***
		The need for localization to facilitate internationalization : ***"We need to have local service providers then of course we need to do localization to our web shop in the local language of […]the target market. . I think that some countries would be subsidiaries and some countries would be licensing."***		
		The company capitalizes on it unique position in the market, product advantage and Market opportunity which is the rapid growing rate of the aging population and need for the resources to take care of them.		

→ *Entrepreneur making sense of relevant internationalization activities and contexts that influence business model change*

Kalamar's process

At the early stage of their product development and being management consultants, Kalamar's entrepreneurs were iterating their value mechanisms (business model) and experimenting based on customer feedback. When they first set out to realise the untapped *business opportunity of consultancy services*, their launch was piloted in Finland and Sweden. The founders changed their business model by leveraging feedback and co-creation with customers. Customer involvement was evident in the innovation of value offering because the founders would use customer feedback as a resource for refining value offering (also, this is a case of the firm having clarity on their business models and channels). The founders tried to get as much information from the market and then prioritise what mattered, testing it before incorporating it into their standard processes (business models):

> *[...] Before introducing the software, it was piloted with seven companies that operate in various industries (e.g., software, consultancy, physiotherapy, assembling equipment for electric scooters for elderly, etc.). The software was tested in order to receive a response and critical feedback on usability and, in general, how potential end customers feel about the product.*

The founders used an established well-thought-out go-to-market plan by identifying and rectifying challenges with their 'product fit' and 'customer needs'. However, though they changed their business model, they did so without compromising the core idea or their main value proposition. Instead, they remained sensitised with the customer context and its needs:

> *When you go deep into the core of the idea, there is not that much change, but of course, how to do it, that has been developing on the way. I guess more, now to be more focused than it used to be when you start it's not quite open for different opportunities and then when you go to market, you have to be more focused, how you really want to solve the problem.*

Due to their limited experience in some prospective markets, their distribution channel or strategy was not extensively reshaped by their business model. Instead, most of the changes and shaping of their business model were because of the product portfolio of their features (i.e., product offering). Moreover, due to the small size of their company, they preferred to experiment with their business model to optimise their core operations within the confines of their resources and capabilities before internationalising:

> *[...] when thinking about how to produce the software and go to market, we reflect, what kind of features would be needed for the customers. Are we too early with those types of features? What is the order on how to produce (the software)? As a small company, we cannot create a perfect product before we got to the market. [...] Although we understand that it is a collection of supportive and continued products.*

The backgrounds and previous experience of the founder(s) contributed to their business knowledge and business strategy. The founders were alert and vigilant to international market changes, reflecting on how various market factors influenced their business model. They continuously innovated their business model because they predicted that the shifts and advances in technology (e.g., artificial intelligence services) might take away their opportunities and threaten their operations. Furthermore, the founders perceived that it was easier to internationalise to similar markets. They recognised that mental resilience fosters initial market entry and/or internationalisation. Thus, the company also adopted bootstrapping as a strategy for the market validation of their offering.

> *We have just a handful of customers right now, and we are selling and working directly with them. [...]So, mostly the changes and shaping of (the business model) has mainly been with the product portfolio of the features.[...] We are in the phase that we have to introduce the first models of the service. We have about 50 % of our service package on production right now. [...] however, though we have few paying customers using the software, we are in the bootstrap phase; that is., we are looking for market validation for the product.*

Table 5. The entrepreneur of *Kalamar* making sense of relevant activities that influence the business model

Kalamar: The Experimental Entrepreneur

Temporal dimensions	**Social dimensions**	**Spatial dimensions**	**Industry and market dimensions**	**Organizational, ownership dimensions**
Pilot stage → Challenge with product fit with customer needs. Experimentation and feedback loop towards standardizing products and operational process.	Mutual benefit using a revenue share model with the distribution network. "*so, we have a partner program. Our consultant's benefits, if they bring customers into the system. But that is our model, how to make money.*"	Weighing options and pursuing internationalization incrementally and location advantage ***Internationalising to the Nordics due to similar regulations and network ties then other countries […] depending on how fast we mature enough to go international. We, are creating a model that we could copy in different countries the same time. we know, that we need to have a presence in each country, if we really want to be successful,***	Leveraging core competence in technical and software business. "agility and efficiency too build up and develop the product. To handle more demanding tasks compared to some of our competitors in our field.	Competitive edge and business model development lies in understanding the combination of core processes
Link between small size of the firm's product development and market entry (intended go to market).	Using feedback to create mock-up service to test the market: we kind of want to get the feedback and then formulate a bit cheap product also allows them to go beyond of customers feedback to understand that what they really want.	Pursuing scalability: ***we of course want to be in scalable business and referring our strength mentioned we reflect how to build scalable software services. So, it means, that now we have a really high cost per customer, because we only have four customers. If we think about the whole structure and we are mostly focusing what them developing, so it really should turn vice versa***	***we try to identify some threats in the marketplace. we see that big players would introduce more intelligent system to do the same thing, which will replace the need of this kind of system we want to keep our eyes open, which means that we would have to radically change our business model.***	***how can we combine different data and tools in one service. challenging old ways of doing business and we know out positioning with competitors[…] we are always developing the core needs and processes for the strategic management process. and that is endless work. But aim to we put our resources focused on the core market.***
Iincremental approach to product and service (portfolio features) change and development to develop products that satisfy customer requirement: Customer involvement is valuable towards product development and standardization over time.			Experienced professionals with keen focus on continuous development in the industry and training of customers for better acquaintance with products also on their standard processes to ensure optimal business model. When we go to market, we focus on the development in supporting services, for customers training train them with software tools and so on.	
In identifying opportunities, *We have different sessions we where we use our own custom tool to identify all the things that are related in our market perspective. Then we rate and discuss and get that dialogue […]to know when and how to proceed with e.g product development, technological opportunities, and marketing opportunities.*	Leveraging network ties to internationalize and establish local market presence. ***We know it is a heavy investment, I to set up the operations in different countries, we have some plans to that with our network. we discuss with our network and friends on the market, if there are any ideas, that's how we do it mostly today. We would like to have understanding that what would be the core local presence that we need to have for supporting the consulting network in the local markets***		Founder sees future in internationalisation process as mental challenge for the company due to system and cultural requirements of host country. Thus, reflecting capabilities to implement effective business model as in home market.	

→ *Entrepreneur making sense of relevant internationalization activities and contexts that influence business model change*

Together with the four main typologies of the international entrepreneurs, we developed a two-by-two table (see Figure 1 below) that categorises the different approaches of entrepreneurs (in this case) in relation to their international experiences(e.g., general work experiences education) and their urge towards changing the business models as they engage or attempt to enter the international market. With our categorisation, we surmise the following:

- The *Tactical Entrepreneur* has prior business ownership and international experience. Although prioritising both product and process development, their expansive experience makes them capable of tactically iterating with their business model holistically. Thus, they tend to be more critical in iterating between the business model dimensions relevant in their internationalisation activities.
- The *Inventor Entrepreneur,* or the *Novice Entrepreneur,* has little or no international experience and is fixated on improving product performance and development. There is no well-defined approach and understanding of their business model development process, both domestically or internationally. The entrepreneur may be somewhat open to business model change but remains fixed in the business' initial idea, making it hard to move to a scalable business model.
- The *Control Entrepreneur* has relevant educational background and some previous international experience. However, this does not fully influence the entrepreneur's impetus to change or internationalise the business model. The entrepreneur demonstrates a sense of rigidity and caution in decision making and in approaching the internationalisation of the firm. Such as targeting predictable or familiar (e.g. 'psychically or culturally safe niches') market segments.
- The *Experimental Entrepreneur* has prior business ownership and relevant educational background, with some or limited international experience. The entrepreneur has a more flexible approach towards changing their business model with an attitude that accommodates uncertainty in their decision-making. Thus, the entrepreneur is experimenting with different value mechanisms and/or business models to find the optimal operational BM before going international.

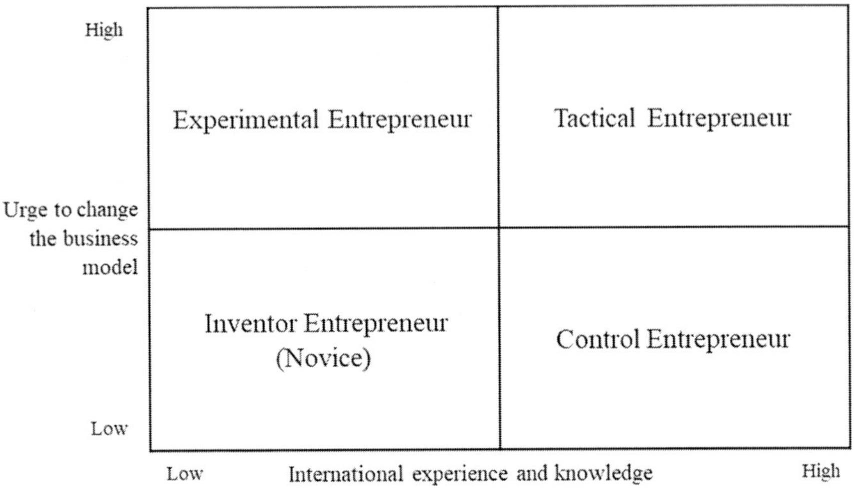

Figure 1. A typology for the case entrepreneur(s) in relation to their international experience(s) and knowledge and urge to change the business model.

According to our analysis, the context in which founders have understood both their current and their future internationalization activities plays a critical role in how the type of business model as a potential 'boundary object' for internationalisation can be interpreted. For example, some of the entrepreneurs with more prior international experience than others were able to reconfigure their approaches, which seemed like a function of their background, previous business ownership, education, and professional knowledge. We also identified that experience (in this context) may not entirely determine internationalisation success. In this case, we find that experience of founders may or may not fully influence business model change or determine 'tact' adopted in approaching international markets. For example, we can observe that both 'novice' and more experienced founders who are still on the brink of developing their service or product offerings (internationally) and did not have standardised value capture and delivery mechanisms in place to scale the business model for an international market.

Although we identified that value capture and delivery processes changed incrementally as the ventures developed their value offerings and organisational routines. In many instances, due to the founder's sincere intent to satisfy customer needs, the founders were keen to hear what the customer wanted —thus paid more attention towards collaborating (with stakeholders) to refine the value proposition. These acts (business model changes) seemed to be reinforced because of the holistic iteration between the value dimensions (e.g., *Experimenter Entrepreneur*). We also identified that more ideas or feedback from stakeholders and customers did not always yield valuable transformation to the business model without precise verification and identification of the value proposition delivery and capture activities to be implemented.

We recognise that although internationalization is an important trajectory in the early stages of venture creation, —If the initiatives for business model change, and interrelated routines, resources and capabilities are not clarified or adequate to satisfy the market-specific requirement, attempts to shift to a more international setting may not be feasible and the venture may fail. Thus, it seemed important to set boundaries that permit iteration between the different value dimensions and clarify the required routines crucial for successful internationalisation and scalability of the business model.

5. Discussion and Conclusions

The current study was designed to explore how entrepreneurs make sense of their business model and change it as they internationalise or seek to do so. Because this is a very much unexplored area, we used a qualitative investigation. Furthermore, our analytical approach of contextualising the individual, and the different related phases business model changes in their internationalisation journeys directed us to make a more nuanced sense of the findings in relation to different social, temporal, spatial, organisational and market/industry) dimensions of context (Zahra et al., 2014).

With our findings, we seek to add to the understanding of the iterative process between the individual and context in which business models and their internationalisation unfold. Our study delves into the nuances of how entrepreneurs interpret the contextual events and circumstances that have influenced the routines and processes unfolding as they internationalise. Our findings provide insights into how entrepreneurs navigate different contexts and how these various contextual dimensions shape their understanding regarding the creation and exploitation of international opportunities (Mainela et al. 2014) and (re)modelling of their business.

The entrepreneur's contextual experiences and capabilities to create and iterate business models for internationalisation

Previously, scholars have denoted the influence of the background and current context in which the entrepreneurs make sense of things, make decisions, and act based on their experiences and perceptions of the world around them (e.g., Crick et al. 2001; Zander 2004). The present study identified that the founders' past and contextual experiences and related capabilities informed how the entrepreneurs navigated through different international contexts and reconfigured their business model. As has been pointed out in the literature, the experience and knowledge of entrepreneurs-cum-founders differ based on various factors, that is, previous business ownership, commitment, and level of involvement (Wasserman 2008), especially previously established, purchased, or inherited firms by the entrepreneur (Ucbasaran et al. 2001). With our findings, we bring new insights into the body of research that suggests that the decision-makers orientation and prior experiences reasonably inform the (re)configuration (Child et al. 2017; Zahra et al. 2014; Jones and Casulli 2014) and subsequent modification of the business model (Asemokha et al. 2019). Although entrepreneurs with more international experience may be systematic and make sound decisions (Collinson and Houlden 2005), entrepreneurs' contextual experience can contribute to or differentiate between the kinds of business models they adopt (Child et al. 2017).

Furthermore, we have pointed out how the entrepreneurs with prior business ownership and international experiences (e.g., the *Tactical Entrepreneur, Control Entrepreneur,* and *Experimental Entrepreneur)* showed a propensity to go with more planned—or causal—actions and business strategies. Nonetheless, we acknowledge that this would not necessarily mean one is more risk-averse because their approaches (of the case firms) were different in terms of their propensity to iterate with the value dimensions of their business models. For example, the *Tactical Entrepreneur's* background allows them to reflect on how they perceive the present in their development of new product or service offerings and what business model is appropriate. Indeed, founders have the expertise and experience to identify an idea that could thrive. Thus, their expertise and commitment allow them to reflect on the requirements, capabilities, and resources needed to push ideas or processes beyond a particular stage or not. In their business operations, the *Experimental Entrepreneur* encourages learning through trial and error (Yli-Huumo et al. 2015; Sonsa et al. 2010; McGrath 2010). In this case, though the *experimental entrepreneurs* were iterating their value dimensions by experimentation, customer feedback and, consequently, modified their business models to validate their value offering for a suitable international market. Thus, the entrepreneurs demonstrated that by learning the ropes and delving deeper to understand the functionality of their business model mechanisms, entrepreneurs are able to identify barriers and develop tactics to deal with uncertainty, hence smoothing out operational activities (Kuemmerle 2002; Wasserman 2008). Thus, in line with studies that predict that the long-term success of a firm depends not only on the effectiveness and execution of the business model but also on the ability to identify and capitalise on new market opportunities (Saebi et al. 2016; Clauss 2017) while adapting their business models (Linder and Cantrell 2000; McGrath 2010, 2011; Chesbrough 2010; Hennart 2014).

With the Control Entrepreneur this study, we surprisingly identified that the entrepreneur's previous international education and work experience, significantly informed, her choice to internationalise 'safely'. Studies attest that some experienced entrepreneurs may fall into so-called *mental ruts and fail to change their business models or leverage their experience or knowledge into superior performance* (see Ucbasaran et al. 2008. p155). Accordingly, the case shows a restrained approach to international opportunity (i.e., potential customers) e.g., by targeting a 'home market culture' abroad. The Control entrepreneur's approach also demonstrates that the entrepreneur leveraged the home market as the initial point of departure for the product offering—unlike incremental internationalisation, where the company internationalises with lower perceived distance. This case can be said to deviate from the typical incremental internationalisation assumption (Johansson and Vahlne 1977). Peculiarly, it resembles a business model that becomes international but targets a 'home market' in a host environment. This shows that the early stage of a venture, creation in the home market, and host context matter in terms of a company's business model (Child et al. 2017) and inevitably ground the underlying (cultural) attitudes and further initiatives that drive the firm forward.

The *Inventor Entrepreneur,* due to his keen technical background, was more fixated on product development ideas, thereby making it challenging to develop routines for a scalable international business model. Although the inventor created a unique product and wanted to scale the business model abroad, his limited prior international experience or capabilities hindered scalability of the business internationally. Furthermore, the inventor entrepreneur's resource and capability constraints seemed to force him to lean towards 'online channels' without determining the 'fit' of the intended value activity to the prospective channels. Instead, the entrepreneur's lack of experience led him to welcome and encourage 'many new ideas from stakeholders', to augment for his lack of know-how rather than understanding how to holistically develop the business model —which may support product development but eventually lead to a lack of focus within other essential aspects of the business model, such as value capture and delivery mechanisms.

Although with the above insights, we uncover that entrepreneurs' propensity or capabilities to iterate their business model for internationalisation may be debatable. Studies purport that previous experiences, shape the entrepreneur's actions and decision making, or entrepreneurial context (Child et al. 2017) influencing how firms control their business operations (Magretta 2002). Our findings perhaps show that managerial capabilities are valuable and dependent on the individuals' sense-making because the previous experience may also lead to substantial control of firm activities, which may slow down the internationalisation process. Essentially, both inexperienced and experienced entrepreneurs may demonstrate unique approaches or capabilities in initiating the business model change. Notably, compared to the other entrepreneurs; for example, the experienced *Tactical Entrepreneurs* and less experienced *Experimental Entrepreneurs* showed dynamic managerial capabilities in approaching international opportunities than others by devising unique pathways to transform recognised opportunities and curating (strategic adjustment) their business model for scalability. Thus, they demonstrated more strategic alertness and tact by adopting experimentation and iteratively testing their value dimension (proposition, creation, delivery, and capture) activities in the market while still possessing a different contextual and experiential background.

Business models as boundary objects for entrepreneurs in internationalisation

Some scholars advocate that the business' architecture has to become more structured, and the founder is then required to create formal and core processes, develop specialised roles and/or routines to satisfy the company's needs (Cavalcante et al. 2011; Wasserman 2008). However, the de-contextualisation of business models at the early phases of a venture or those on the verge of internationalisation may bring a false sense of stability and/or a 'roadmap' to success. Considering the broad scope of firms' entrepreneurial history and future trajectories, especially as they internationalise, business models may act as a 'boundary object' (Doganaova and Eyquem-Renault 2009). As boundary objects, business models serve as the go-to means to explain the action and coordination of the various actors interested in value creation and capture (Cavalcante et al. 2011; Doganaova and Eyquem-Renault 2009).

With our findings, we seek to remind researchers and practitioners that business models as boundary objects may not necessarily constitute the same context for every entrepreneur but serve as a framework to understand and interpret the 'change context' as they engage in business activities. Therefore, in light of our findings, we argue that business models should act in a broader sense as curative and/or confining tools through which entrepreneurs can incrementally or radically visualise the extent of firms' internal and external operations *in context* to optimise business success, even in times of radical change. As a result, the integration of contextual understanding with business model change is a valuable framework that entrepreneurs can leverage while examining their existing core processes for further development in their internationalisation journey. Aligning with research on business models and the internationalisation context, we denote that the process of changing the business model should be considered as context-specific and that it cannot be universally generalised (Rissanen 2019). Furthermore, because of the process' dynamics and sometimes cyclical nature of organizational activities, business model changes may not necessarily be replicable for exactly this reason (Rissanen et al. 2019).

In relation to this, our study has uncovered the important role of customer involvement in the co-creation of business models and their role in expanding the business model as boundary objects. We see that founders can co-innovate their value proposition with customer *feedback* and/or reiterate their initial proposition with value capture and delivery activities, leading to a more viable business model. Scholars agree that customer relationships provide the entrepreneur with valuable information about latent market needs and environmental changes (Chesbrough 2006; Clauss 2017), which entrepreneurs can leverage to create lock-in effects (Amit and Zott 2001). Additionally, in the current study, we see that the entrepreneurs' perceptions of their specific network ties informed their accounts of how they interacted with their business models in international markets. Hence, our findings further contextualise the previous notions in the literature, on the importance of network ties and partner relationships home and abroad augment the founder's knowledge and capabilities, providing them with support and market information to support their business activities as they go abroad (Ucbasaran et al. 2001; Zahra et al. 2014; Asemokha et al. 2020). In relation to this, we also want to point out how, based on their experiences, entrepreneurs contextual knowledge and networks with partners in context, potentially deconstructing institutional barriers by co-creating with reconfiguring stakeholders and customers, leading to the iteration of the business model in the internationalisation context (as seen with the *Tactical Entrepreneur*).

More so, we add that despite customers' indispensability to the business process, their role has not been extensively explored in the business model discourse. More exploring should be done on the customer's role, especially on how their interaction with the entrepreneur leads to the (re)configuration of business models, particularly in international market contexts. Based on our findings, we suggest that entrepreneurs have *a bounded* capability to identify relevant feedback, especially in the initial phase of venture creation, and identification of what is feasible within the parameters of their proficiencies and without spreading resources and capabilities too thin. This may be especially the case in SMEs that have limited resources to reach international markets.

Iterating the business model dimensions when leaving the familiar home market context

According to Wasserman (2008), the successful transition from the idea, product development stage, or even initial sales is said to mark the end of an era; simultaneously, the dramatic broadening of the skills required (especially in the early stages of venture creation) in, for example, internationalisation, may stretch the founders' abilities beyond their limits (Wasserman 2008). Doz and Kosonen (2010) add that even successful ventures run the risk of failing if they continue in their old ways and do not adapt their business model to the changes in competitive situations.

Designing a business model from scratch takes time, and establishing the links (Cavalcante et al. 2011) to ensure the best outcome requires that the decision-makers understand the economic logic that best satisfies the environments and that envelops the business model (Child et al. 2017; Stampfl and Prügl 2011). In the process of the current study, we identified how the founders might have leaned towards similar and familiar ideas based on their expertise and previous contextual experiences. In other words, the choices made by the founders tended to closely hinge on previous experiences, which determines the kind of domestic and international opportunities prioritised. In addition, knowing when to enter the market or industry affects new venture survival and performance, here as measured by growth and productivity (Zahra et al. 2014). In relation, it has been argued that home market maturity influences the timing of companies' internationalisation efforts (Rissanen et al. 2019). More so, the home market's spatial and institutional context affects the companies' approaches to changing their business model when internationalising, but research on this is scarce (Rissanen et al. 2019).

In conclusion, recognizant of how the different entrepreneurs approached business model change and internationalisation, we have enumerated that tensions may exist in how they appropriate value, modify their business model and carry out decision making, especially because of the different contextual factors in temporal, spatial and market contexts. In light of our findings, for entrepreneurs and their firms who are not yet profitable, market uncertainty and different cultural and social contexts may restrict how they make sense of approaching international markets.

5.1. Theoretical contributions

Our contributions lie at the intersection of the business model and IE literature. With the present study, we address the call for a more contextual exploration of SME internationalisation activities (Michailova 2011; Onetti et al. 2012, Child et al. 2017; Foss and Saebi 2017) and entrepreneurship (Baker and Welter 2018; Zahra et al. 2014) by focusing on entrepreneurs who were navigating both the individual and firm-level context to gain a deeper understanding of the dynamics of the business models of their firms. Moreover, in the current study, the heterogeneity of international entrepreneurs (in context) provides a compelling backdrop for exploring the changes occurring in SMEs' internationalising business models. Our work is in line with suggestions of contextualisation but provides more in-depth explanations of unobserved variables (Ragin 2009) by providing the opportunity to integrate existing frameworks and provide a deeper level of reasoning on theoretical and empirical findings (Zahra et al. 2014; Johns 2017).

To lessen some of the 'de-contextualisation' and ambiguity in understanding the configuration and reconfiguration of business models as firms internationalise, we contribute insights into the individual's sense-making in context (i.e., experience and background, current capabilities and networks) and business model changes. By introducing the four cases in light of Zahra et al.'s (2014) categorisation of contextual dimensions in entrepreneurship—the temporal, spatial, industry and market and social contexts—we contribute to the IE literature by qualitatively discussing how the iteration of the dimensions of business models is based on or affects the entrepreneurs' experience and involvement in their immediate context. Although various market forces, antecedents, and contexts (Zahra et al.,

2014; Kuivalainen et al., 2012) heavily affect internationalisation, our findings add to the understanding of how founders may choose the internationalisation approaches that suit their experience-bound capabilities (Milanov and Maissenhälter 2015) and creation and iteration processes.

Second, we shed light on an individual-level inquiry and contextualisation into the literature on business model change; we question the dominant quantitative methodological choices in business model research by conducting a qualitative inquiry of individuals in contexts which are bound to change. By introducing a more nuanced discussion of the contextual dimensions of business model creation and change, our study adds empirical evidence of how the emergence of a business idea is an important and contextually heterogeneous phase of value creation and capture (Eppler et al. 2011; Cavalcante et al. 2011). This view connects the entrepreneur's experiences, current motivations, and future trajectory of the business model as dynamic. More so, because business models are dynamic (Amit and Zott 2001; Chesbrough and Rosenbloom 2002), engaging more heavily with context provides alternative explanations on complex phenomena and providing bounded propositions (Zahra et al. 2014) and findings. Accordingly, rather than serving as distant reporters, we draw from Zahra et al. (2014) to minimise the familiar and broad assertions about the causal mechanisms that underlie a phenomenon, developing a more profound and meaningful understanding of the individual in context.

Third, in light of our findings, we deepen the understanding of how the business model literature in the 'change context' of internationalisation can further address the different kinds of 'static' (the novice *Inventor Entrepreneur* and the expert *Rigid/Control Entrepreneurs*) versus 'flexible' (the novel *Experimenter Entrepreneur* and the expert *Tactical Entrepreneur*) approaches that individual entrepreneurs embody when going about the business model creation and iteration processes. Our study shows that business model (changes) may serve as a 'boundary object' (Doganaova and Eyquem-Renault 2009) that can lead both researchers and practitioners to tap into the founders' personal needs to control their value creation, capture, and delivery as a 'static' model and/or see how to work towards a more flexible business model in internationalisation and its iteration. Thus adding to pivotal studies that have examined and established how international(ising) entrepreneurs' identities ground their entrepreneurially and internationally oriented behaviour (Korhonen and Leppäaho 2019; Massa et al. 2017). With the present study, we further discuss how individuals' experiences and contextual business model creation and iteration ground their (entrepreneurs) approaches with the internationalising firm.

A more practical contribution of the present study is that by making oneself aware of the delimiting 'context' (i.e., experiences, current capabilities and networks), individuals are more able to 'break free' from how their own context inhibits them from changing their business models for international markets. Looking at this in today's present times of uncertainty, particularly this contemporary era of global change, crisis, and political shifts, (for example, Brexit and the US elections) when entrepreneurs are becoming more aware of how varying issues affect their ecosystems. Unexpected contextual matters that affect the whole world, such as global pandemics closing country borders, may force entrepreneurs to rethink and adapt their current and future business models and organizational routines to match changing trends and minimize competition as they internationalize. Besides, when an entrepreneur begins to see how their business model is contextually and socially constructed, the entrepreneur can also see beyond it and step out of its boundaries and rationalise what is perhaps better for the company. Thus, the entrepreneur can better reflect on the capabilities and constraints stemming from a 'context-bound sense-making by using the business model as a boundary object and finding complementary resources to (re)configure the business model beyond their own context, for example, in the international market.

5.2. Practical implications

With the present study, we invite entrepreneurs to a constant and critical re-evaluation of their approach towards international opportunities to see if their methods are feasible and within their business models' boundaries; doing this can train them to welcome times of change without the crippling fear of uncertainty. In relation, entrepreneurs should question their own motives (what motivates one to continue and dig deeper into the possibility) and commitment (what does this require from me; do I have the interest to put my resources into this?). This can guide them in identifying the activities and routines and whether an idea should grow past a particular stage or not. The founders need to self-evaluate their actions and know when to stop collecting ideas if they have too many untethered parts in their operation that do not work well together towards developing the standard processes necessary for the independent functionality and maturity of the business model.

Our study also stresses network ties as a conduit for early internationalisation activities and the execution of ideas. Hence, entrepreneurs—especially those with previous business ownership—should leverage partner knowledge and support-to-support internationalisation. As in the case of the *Tactical*

Entrepreneur, we see an example of how entrepreneurs can deconstruct institutional barriers by co-creating with reconfiguring stakeholders and customers, thereby lowering bureaucracy and regulations (e.g., financial systems, payments or channels). Furthermore, in times of uncertainty, person-level interactions may become more crucial for developing alternative channels and agile tactics to help navigate bureaucracies and minimise institutional barriers. Beyond just having relationships with customers and partners, establishing trust and rationalising contextual communications with potential customers creates lock-in, which may precede securing deals or having a keen focus on the value proposition.

Together with other studies (McGrath 2010; Sosna 2010; Rissanen et al. 2019), we see how some firms may opt to *experiment* with their business models through trial and error before developing an optimal model. Hence, managing business models requires effective leadership and commitment and the capability to experiment with a business model by leveraging feedback loops that provide diverse possibilities for value creation and capture. Beyond solving a problem with a service and product, founders should strive for business model fit by engaging with their customers to better understand industry and market complexities. This means having the capability to iterate back and forth between the value mechanisms (i.e., value proposition, deliver and capture) to ensure that the customers' needs are efficiently met and solved; in addition, ensuring that the business model is viable and delivers and captures profits is of the utmost importance to the success and performance of internationalising ventures.

5.3. Limitations and future research avenues

Business models do not occur in a vacuum, especially for internationalising SMEs. The current study points out that the contextualisation of business models and business model change calls for more in-depth case studies or even single case studies that reveal more of the nuances in creating a new venture. Although a quantitative survey-based inquiry shows that various factors predict and control the business model dimensions, the present study set out to qualitatively investigate some nuances that exist in and between these dimensions. We show that business model research would benefit if the scholars considered in-depth on how these nuances play out in the contextual environment and what implications they have for the business model.

Because international contexts do not occur homogeneously, and entrepreneurs do not interpret them routinely, firms navigate and make sense of multiple international contexts that may not be observed at the surface. Drawing from our findings, there is a need for more in-depth qualitative research on how entrepreneurs make sense of the context in which they make decisions and how they can act to make the arguments and assumptions of the contextual dimensions affecting the business model change. In addition, longitudinal studies would provide an even more processual exploration of the patterns and contextually causal effects of business model changes as founders engage in internationalisation over time. Because our present study was mainly focused on the founders' actions as the context within which they internationalise, we encourage future studies to explore external events such as the activities of customers, partners, investors, legislation, and other external stakeholders shaping the actions of entrepreneurs and how they encounter different market contexts.

Finally, we also note that the firms we investigated had an online or service offering, unlike brick-and-mortar firms, which may have the propensity to provide a more curated value proposition for different clients without altering the primary value offering. We suggest that empirical studies should delve deeper to demarcate how firms with tangible products or firms operating in other industry contexts change their business models.

References

Acedo, F. J., & Jones, M. V. 2007. Speed of internationalization and entrepreneurial cognition: Insights and a comparison between international new ventures, exporters and domestic firms. *Journal of World Business*, 42(3): 236-252.

Achtenhagen, L., Melin, M., & Naldi, L. 2013. Dynamics of Business Models – Strategizing, Critical Capabilities and Activities for Sustained Value Creation. *Long Range Planning*, 46: 427-442.

Amit, R., & Zott, C. 2001. Value creation in e-business. *Strategic Management Journal*, 22(6-7): 493-520.

Andersson, S. 2015. The international entrepreneur–From experience to action. S. A. Fernhaber, & S. Prashantham (Eds.). *The Routledge companion to international entrepreneurship*: 70-83. Abingdon: Routledge.

Arend, R. J. 2013. The business model: Present and future-beyond a skeumorph. *Strategic Organization*, 11(4): 390-402.

Asemokha, A., Musona, J., Torkkeli, L., & Saarenketo, S. 2019. Business model innovation and entrepreneurial orientation relationships in SMEs:

Implications for international performance. Journal of International Entrepreneurship, 17(3): 425-453.

Asemokha, A., Torkkeli, L., Faroque, A. R., & Saarenketo, S. 2020. Business model innovation in international performance: the mediating effect of network capability. *International Journal of Export Marketing*, 3(4): 290-313.

Autio, E., Sapienza, H. J., & Almeida, J. G. 2000. Effects of age at entry, knowledge intensity, and imitability on international growth. *Academy of Management Journal*, 43(5): 909-924.

Baden-Fuller, C., & Morgan, M. S. 2010. Business models as models. *Long range planning*, 43(2-3): 156-171.

Baker, T., & Welter, F. 2018. Contextual entrepreneurship: An interdisciplinary perspective. *Now*.

Björkdahl, J., & Holmén, M. 2013. Business model innovation–the challenges ahead. *International Journal of Product Development*, 18(3/4): 213-225.

Brännback, M., & Carsrud, A. L. 2016. *Understanding entrepreneurial cognitions through the lenses of context.* In A Research Agenda for Entrepreneurship and Context. Edward Elgar Publishing.

Brown, A. D., Colville, I., & Pye, A. (2015). *Making Sense of Sensemaking in Organization Studies.* Organization Studies, 36(2), 265–277.

Cavalcante S., Ketsing P., & Ulhoi J. 2011. Business model dynamics and innovation: (re)establishing the missing linkages. *Management Decision*, 49(8): 1327-1342.

Cavalcante, S. A. 2014. Designing business model change. *International Journal of Innovation Management*, 18(02): 1450018.

Child, J., & Hsieh, L. H. Y. 2014. Decision mode, information and network attachment in the internationalization of SMEs: A configurational and contingency analysis. *Journal of World Business*, 49: 598-610.

Child, J., Hsieh, L., Elbanna, S., Karmowska, J., Marinova, S., Puthusserry, P., Tsai, T., Narooz, R. & Zhang, Y. 2017. SME International Business Models: The Role of Context and Experience. *Journal of World Business*. 52(5): 664-679.

Chesbrough, H. 2010. Business model innovation: opportunities and barriers. *Long range planning*, 43(2-3): 354-363.

Chesbrough, H. 2006. *Open business models: How to thrive in the new innovation landscape*. Harvard Business Press.

Clauss, T. 2017. Measuring business model innovation: Conceptualization, scale development, and proof of performance. *R & D Management*, 47: 385-403.

Collinson, S., & Houlden, J. 2005. Decision-making and market orientation in the internationalization process of small and medium-sized enterprises. *Management International Review*, 45: 413-436.

Coviello, N. 2015. Rethinking research on born globals. *Journal of International Business Studies*, 46(1): 17–26.

Crick, D., Chaudhry, S., & Batstone, S. 2001. An investigation into the overseas expansion of small Asian-owned UK firms. *Small Business Economics*, 16(2): 75-94.

Doganova, L., & Eyquem-Renault, M. 2009. What do business models do?: Innovation devices in technology entrepreneurship, *Research Policy*, 38(10): 1559-1570.

Denyer, D., Tranfield, D., & van Aken, J. E. 2008. Developing design propositions through research synthesis, *Organization Studies*, 29 (3): 393-413.

Di Gregorio, D., Musteen, M., & Thomas, D. E. 2008. International new ventures: The cross-border nexus of individuals and opportunities. *Journal of World Business*, 43(2): 186-196.

Drucker, P. F. 1988. *The coming of the new organization*.

Doz, Y. L., & Kosonen, M. 2010. Embedding strategic agility: A leadership agenda for accelerating business model renewal. *Long range planning*, 43(2-3): 370-382.

Eppler, M. J., Hoffmann, F., & Bresciani, S. 2011. New business models through collaborative idea generation. *International Journal of Innovation Management*, 15(06): 1323-1341.

Fletcher, D. 2004. International entrepreneurship and the small firms. Entrepreneurship and Regional Develop- ment, 16: 289-305.

Foss, N. J., & Saebi, T. (2017). Fifteen years of research on business model innovation: How far have we come, and where should we go?. *Journal of Management*, 43(1), 200-227.

Gartner, W. B. 1989. Some suggestions for research on entrepreneurial traits and characteristics. *Entrepreneurship Theory and Practice*, 14(1): 27-38.

George, G., & Bock, A. J. 2011. The business model in practice and its implications for entrepreneurship research. *Entrepreneurship Theory and Practice*, 35(1): 83-111.

Goktan, B. A., & Miles, G. 2011. Innovation speed and radicalness: are they inversely related?, *Management Decision*, 49(4): 533-547.

Hennart, J. F. 2014. The accidental internationalists: a theory of born globals. *Entrepreneurship Theory and Practice*, 38(1): 117-135.

Hjorth, D., Jones, C., & Gartner, W. B. 2008. Introduction for 'Recreating/recontextualising entrepreneurship'. *Scandinavian Journal of Management*, 24(2): 81-84.

Hohenthal, J., Johanson, J. and Johanson, M. 2003. Market discovery and the international expansion of the firm. *International Business Review*, 12: 659-672.

Johansson, J., & Vahlne, J. E. 1977. The internationalization process of the firm. A model of knowledge development and increasing foreign market commitment. *Journal of International Business Studies*, 8(1): 23-32.

Johns, G. 2017. Reflections on the 2016-decade award: Incorporating context in organizational research. *Academy of Management Review*, 42(4): 577-595.

Jones, M. V., & Casulli, L. 2014. International entrepreneurship: Exploring the logic and utility of individual experience through comparative reasoning approaches. *Entrepreneurship Theory and Practice*, 38(1): 45-69.

Jones, M. V., Coviello, N., & Tang, Y. K. 2011. International Entrepreneurship research (1989–2009): A domain ontology and thematic analysis. *Journal of Business Venturing*, 26(6): 632–659.

Kets de Vries, M. 1977. The entrepreneurial personality: A person at the crossroads. *Journal of Management Studies*, 14(1): 34–57.

Korhonen, S., & Leppäaho, T. 2019. Well-trodden highways and roads less traveled: Entrepreneurial-oriented behavior and identity construction in international entrepreneurship narratives. *Journal of International Entrepreneurship*, 17(3): 355-388.

Kuemmerle, W. 2002. A test for the fainthearted. *Harvard Business Review*, 80(5): 122-127.

Kuivalainen, O., Saarenketo, S., & Puumalainen, K. 2012. Start-up patterns of internationalization: A framework and its application in the context of knowledge-intensive SMEs. *European Management Journal*, 30(4): 372-385.

Linder, J., & Cantrell, S. 2002. What makes a good business model anyway? Can yours stand the test of change? *Outlook, www. accenture. com.*

Maine, E., Soh, P. H., & Dos Santos, N. 2015. The role of entrepreneurial decision-making in opportunity creation and recognition. *Technovation*, 39: 53-72.

Mainela T., Puhakka, V., Servais P. 2014. The concept of International Opportunity in International Entrepreneurship: A Review and a Research Agenda. *International Journal of Management Reviews*, 16: 105-129.

Mainela, T., & Puhakka, V. 2009. Organising new business in a turbulent context: Opportunity discovery and effectuation for IJV development in transition markets. *Journal of International Entrepreneurship*, 7(2): 111.

Martins, L. L., Rindova, V. P., & Greenbaum, B. E. 2015. Unlocking the hidden value of concepts: A cognitive approach to business model innovation. *Strategic Entrepreneurship Journal*, 9: 99–117.

Massa, L., Tucci, C. L., & Afuah, A. 2017. A critical assessment of business model research. Academy of Management Annals, 11(1): 73-104.

McGrath, R. 2011. Finding opportunities in business model innovation. *The European Financial Review*, 14-17.

McGrath, R. G. 2010. Business models: A discovery driven approach. *Long range planning*, 43(2-3): 247-261.

Michailova, S. (2011). Contextualizing in international business research: why do we need more of it and how can we be better at it? *Scandinavian Journal of Management*, 27(1): 129-139.

Milanov, H., & Maissenhälter, B. 2015. Cognition in international entrepreneurship. In S. A. Fernhaber, & S. Prashantham (Eds.), *The Routledge companion to international entrepreneurship*: 47-69. Abingdon: Routledge.

Mulders, M. A., & van den Broek, C. 2012. Entrepreneurial decision-making and the effect on business models. EFMD, *European Foundation for Management Development*. Accessed at http://www.avansondernemerscentrum.nl/UserFiles/BMG_paper.pdf on 23.11.2020.

Nielsen, B. B., & Nielsen, S. 2011. The role of top management team international orientation in international strategic decision-making: The choice of foreign entry mode. *Journal of World Business*, 46: 185–193.

Nielsen, C., Lund, M., Montemari, M., Paolone, F., Massaro, M., & Dumay, J. 2018. *Business models: A research overview*. Routledge.

Onetti, A., Zucchella, A., Jones, M. V., & McDougall-Covin, P. P. 2010. Internationalization, innovation and entrepreneurship: business models for new technology-based firms. *Journal of Management and Governance*, 14(3): 1-32.

Osterwalder, A., & Pigneur, Y. 2010. *Business model generation: a handbook for visionaries, game changers, and challengers*. John Wiley & Sons.

Oviatt, B. M., & McDougall, P. P. 2005. The internationalization of entrepreneurship. *Journal of International Business Studies*, 36(1): 2–8.

Ozgen, E., & Baron, R. A. 2007. Social sources of information in opportunity recognition: Effects of mentors, industry networks, and professional forums. *Journal of Business Venturing*, 22(2): 174-192.

Piekkari, R., Welch, C., & Paavilainen, E. 2009. The Case Study as Disciplinary Convention: Evidence from International Business Journals. *Organizational Research Methods*, 12(3), 567-589.

Pohle, G., & Chapman, M. 2006. IBM's global CEO report 2006: business model innovation matters. *Strategy & Leadership*.

Ragin, C. C. 2009. Reflection of casing and case-oriented research. In D. Byrne & C.C. Ragin (Eds), *The Sage handbook of case-based methods*: 522-534. London: Sage.

Rasmussan, E. S., Madsen, T. K., & Evangelista, F. 2001. The founding of the born global company in Denmark and Australia: Sensemaking and networking. *Asia Pacific Journal of Marketing and Logistics*.

Read, S., Sarasvathy, S., Dew, N., & Wiltbank, R. 2016. *Effectual entrepreneurship*. Taylor & Francis.

Rissanen, T., Ermolaeva, L., Torkkeli, L., Ahi, A., & Saarenketo, S. 2019. The role of home market context in business model change in internationalizing SMEs. *European Business Review*.

Saebi T., Lien L., & Foss N. J. 2016. What Drives Business Model Adaptation? The Impact of Opportunities, Threats and Strategic Orientation. *Long Range Planning*, 50(5): 567-581.

Sarasvathy, S. D. 2001. *What makes entrepreneurs entrepreneurial*?

Schweizer, R. 2012. The internationalization process of SMEs: A muddling-through process. *Journal of Business Research*, 65: 745-751.

Sosna, M., Trevinyo-Rodríguez, R. N., & Velamuri, S. R. 2010. Business model innovation through trial-and-error learning: The Naturhouse case. *Long range planning*, 43(2-3): 383-407.

Stampfl, G., & Prügl, R. 2011. *Business models in context: conceptualizing the environment of business models*. In Academy of Management Annual Meeting: 13-17.

Teece, D. J. 2010. Business Models, Business Strategy and Innovation, *Long Range Planning*, 43: 172-194.

Torkkeli, L., Puumalainen, K., Saarenketo, S., & Kuivalainen, O. 2012. The effect of network competence and environmental hostility on the internationalization of SMEs. *Journal of International Entrepreneurship*, 10(1): 25-49.

Trimi, S., & Berbegal-Mirabent, J. 2012. Business model innovation in entrepreneurship. *International Entrepreneurship and Management Journal*, 8(4): 449-465.

Ucbasaran, D., Alsos, G. A., & Westhead, P. 2008. *Habitual entrepreneurs*: 17. Now Publishers Inc.

Ucbasaran, D., Westhead, P. & Wright, M. 2001. The Focus of Entrepreneurial Research: Contextual and Process Issues. *Entrepreneurship theory and practice*, 25(4): 57-80.

Westerman, G., McFarlan, F. W. & Iansiti, M. 2006. Organization design and effectiveness over the innovation life cycle. *Organization Science*, 17(2). 230-238.

Welch, C., Piekkari, R., Plakoyiannaki, E., & Paavilainen, E. 2011. Theorising from case studies: Towards a pluralist future for international business research. *Journal of International Business Studies*, 42(5): 740-762.

Welch, C., & Piekkari, R. 2006. Crossing language boundaries: Qualitative interviewing in international business. *Management International Review*, 46(4): 417-437.

Wasserman, N. 2008. The founder's dilemma. *Harvard Business Review*, 86(2): 102-109.

Yli-Huumo, J., Rissanen, T., Maglyas, A., Smolander, K., & Sainio, L. M. 2015. *The relationship between business model experimentation and technical debt*. In International Conference of Software Business: 17-29. Springer, Cham.

Zahra, S. A., Korri, J. S., & Yu, J. 2005. Cognition and international entrepreneurship: implications for research on international opportunity recognition and exploitation. *International Business Review*, 14(2): 129-146.

Zahra, S. A., Wright, M., & Abdelgawad, S. G. 2014. Contextualization and the advancement of entrepreneurship research. *International Small Business Journal*, 32(5): 479-500.

Zander, I. 2004. The microfoundations of cluster stickiness – Walking in the shoes of the entrepreneur. *Journal of International Management*, *10*(2): 151-175.

Zott, C., Amit, R., & Massa, L. 2011. The business model: recent developments and future research. *Journal of management*, 37(4): 1019-1042.

Zucchella, A., Hagen, B. & Serapio, M. 2018. International entrepreneurship: 37-67. Cheltenham: Edward Elgar Publishing Limited.

Individual Productivity in the Foreign Subsidiaries of Emerging Market MNEs: Evidence from a Chinese State-owned Enterprise

JIE CHEN

Post-doctoral Researcher at LUT School of Business and Management

1. Introduction

Outward foreign direct investments (OFDIs) from emerging markets started to attract research interest in the late 1990s (Bryan et al., 1998). OFDIs from emerging markets continuously grow, as emerging market multinational enterprises (MNEs) look outwards and internationalise operations (Gaur et al., 2018). According to the UNCTAD (2017), China has become one of the most promising sources of OFDI. Meanwhile, state-owned MNEs accounted for 1.5 % of all MNEs, but their announced greenfield investments accounted for 11% of the global total in 2016. China is the largest home economy. Chinese state-owned enterprises (SOEs) have started to internationalise operations, established foreign subsidiaries, and contributed significantly to the global growth of OFDIs.

The rise of populism and nationalism in many markets—both advanced and emerging markets—has sparked many to react with xenophobia towards Chinese multinational enterprises, such as Huawei and ZTE (Brubaker, 2020). At the same time, the total amount of OFDI from Chinese SOEs shrank in 2018 and again in 2019 (UNCTAD, 2019). Coronavirus disease 2019 (COVID-19) was first identified in the Hubei Province of China in December 2019. The COVID-19 pandemic has been spreading rapidly across the globe, affects all major economies by the spring of the year 2020. The COVID-19 pandemic is a global healthcare crisis and challenges healthcare systems worldwide. The pandemic also exerts huge pressure on the national economy in all major economics (Kuckertz et al., 2020). Billions of people face lockdowns worldwide. Unemployment rates hit a historical high in many countries. Customer demand is dropping as people face the horror of the coronavirus infection and avoid non-essential spending due to the financial uncertainty and weak job security.

Many Western leaders have consistently accused China of withholding information regarding the pandemic (Miller, 2020). I expect that the xenophobia towards Chinese SOEs would intensify in a post-COVID-19-pandemic global economy. At the time when I wrote the chapter, people still knew little about the future of the pandemic. The COVID-19 was spreading rapidly worldwide. The pre-COVID-19 global socioeconomic environment might never return. Due to the global coronavirus recession and the xenophobia towards Chinese multinationals, I predict that the amount of OFDI from China will continue shrinking from 2020. Despite the difficulty to predict the future of the Chinese SOEs and their greenfield investment, we can learn from what happened in the past—for example in 2017 when the amount of OFDI from China reached the historic high.

On the one hand, the management culture in China indeed has long-standing communication problems. An efficient information-sharing mechanism—between the international departments or with external actors—is yet missing in the government or the Chinese SOEs (Leutert, 2016). Thus, many Chinese SOEs cannot communicate efficiently with external actors—including stakeholders, auditors, and the media—in the same way as public MNEs in the advanced markets.

Similarly, due to the gap between the management culture in China and the Western world, many managers in the Chinese SOEs might also have problems to communicate efficiently with non-Chinese external stakeholders or with non-Chinese employees within the foreign subsidiaries. On the other hand, Chinese manufacturing enterprises predominately carry out manufacturing activities in domestic sites (Zhao & Zou, 2002). But, the recent rise of populism and nationalism in the many extant markets for Chinese SOEs has raised trade tariffs and triggered protectionist trade policies (Lester & Manak, 2018). It has created an impetus for many Chinese state-owned manufacturing enterprises to establish foreign subsidiaries of operations that carry out parts of the manufacture or the final assembly and mitigate the risks associated with uncertain and volatile trade policies (Du & Zhang, 2018). Yet, most Chinese SOEs might not know how to manage and motivate non-Chinese operational workers. On the other hand, international business scholars know little about the internal management of Chinese SOEs, despite its theoretical and practical importance. The extant studies of Chinese SOEs have focused on how they interact with the institutional context or social actors in the home and host countries (Buckley et al., 2007; Cui & Jiang, 2012). The chapter instead analysed internally collected data in three foreign subsidiaries of a Chinese SOE. The results reveal the first-hand information regarding the internal management in the foreign subsidiaries. I found that some Chinese managers might communicate with and motivate the local staff more efficiently. The results also guide the Chinese SOEs—regarding how to fill the gap between the management cultures and to improve the overall information-sharing efficiency—by selecting and promoting the right staff in their foreign subsidiaries.

2. Literature review and hypothesis development

2.1 Management in the Chinese SOEs

The extant literature has notably analysed the management culture in China within the Western framework (Barney & Zhang, 2009). The modern management culture in the Chinese enterprises—combining elements from traditional Chinese culture and elements from the era of a centrally planned economy—is dynamic and has evolved rapidly in the passing four decades (Ralston et al., 2018). On one hand, extant cross-cultural studies (Hofstede, 1993) suggest that the management culture in China generally encourages conformity to the organization and harmony in the manager—worker relationship but focuses less on individual responsibility and conflict resolution. Some traits from the dated management system in the era of a centrally planned economy still exist in many Chinese SOEs. For example, managers do not play an important role in recruitment, selection, and performance management (rewards and punishment) (Ngo et al., 2008). A performance-based reward system has never fully enforced. Instead of improving individual productivity, it is more important for an employee to maintain harmony with the frontline manager and co-workers (Ding & Warner, 2001). Many managers often do not have enough impetus to motivate their employees to increase productivity.

2.2 Recent changes for Chinese SOEs and how they respond

The competitive landscape in the Chinese market has changed significantly, with the proliferation of start-ups (Zhou et al., 2017). The new emphasis on manufacturing efficiency in the concurrent competitive environment cannot always match up with the traditional emphasis on the interpersonal harmony at the workplace. Chinese SOEs also need to face pressure from the increasingly competitive market environment in China. Many Chinese SOEs have responded to the market change and thus reformed their internal management, but the details regarding their internal changes are not yet clear to the research community.

Guided by the Belt and Road Initiative (BRI)—a development strategy adopted by the Chinese central government from 2013, China has enormously increased the indirect foreign aid in the cooperation countries of the BRI—in the form of long-term contracts—to help these countries to forge infrastructure and facilitate further investment. Plenty long-term contracts have been given to the Chinese SOEs (Guo & Clougherty, 2015). Consequently, many Chinese SOEs have undergone a rapid process of globalization. Meanwhile, Chinese SOEs need a reward system that can evaluate employee performance in both domestic and foreign operations. Yet, these Chinese SOEs often have not accumulated enough internal data to design own country-specific reward system, which can calibrate the effect of the cross-country difference. Chinese SOEs can alternatively design a reward system based on the secondary data from the extant studies of the total factor productivity (TFP). The reliability of the system is questionable, as China often does not fit into the existing TFP-based theories of productivity (Ozyurt, 2009).

Managers in the foreign subsidiaries of Chinese SOEs face cultural and language barriers when motivating the non-Chinese employees (Harzing & Feely, 2008). Managers might differ in terms of the capability to cross the barriers and motivate the employees, as they have different educational backgrounds and previous working experiences. In the case company, I found two distinct types of frontline managers. The first type has an engineering background. For example, the manager has an advanced degree in the field of mechanical or automation engineering. He started his career as an engineer or a technician. Communications between the frontline manager and local employees can only carried out through the medium of English. Communications do not always run smoothly due to the language barriers. The second type started their career as a language specialist or a translator. For example, the manager studied foreign languages (e.g. Spanish or Farsi) in one of the four foreign language universities in Beijing or Shanghai. Communications between the manager and local employees can be carried out though the medium of both the local language and English.

2.3 Theoretical framework and hypotheses

In this chapter, I intend to find out the predictors for individual manufacturing productivity in the foreign subsidiaries of a Chinese SOE. A multi-level theoretical framework of this chapter is illustrated in Figure 1.

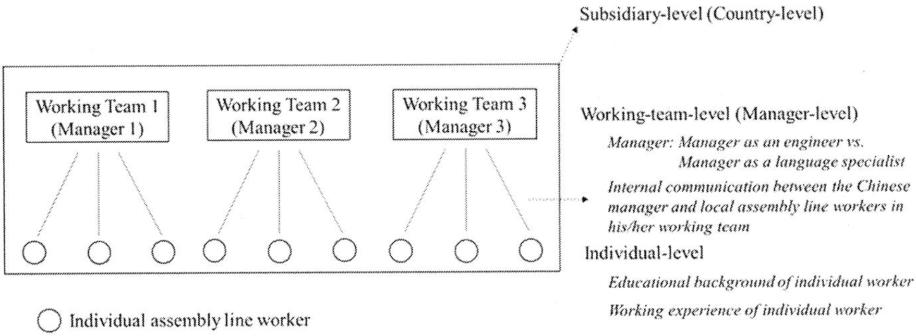

Figure 1. Theoretical framework

There are multiple working teams and assembly lines in each foreign subsidiary. There are three shifts in a working day. An assembly line worker only works in a working team led by the same manager, no matter in which shift or in which assembly line he or she works. The human resource system with an exclusive manager-worker relationship can easily track the responsibility or performance of each frontline manager or assembly line worker. Internal communications between the manager and employees are critical to achieve organizational success and improve the organizational performance (Ruck & Welch, 2012). In the case company, frontline managers, who oversee a working team, are exclusively Chinese expatriates. The case company has not operated in any of the three host countries long enough to select and train the local staff as local frontline managers. On the contrary, the assembly line workers are almost exclusively hired locally according to cost considerations and the immigration laws and regulations in the host country. The language and cultural barriers between the Chinese manager and the local workers need to be bridged that internal communications can run smoothly. Hence, I predict that if a manager has a higher level of internal communication skills, the manager can motivate the assembly line workers in his or her working team in a better and more efficient way. The assembly line workers in his or her working team would thus generate higher individual manufacturing productivity.

H1. The higher the level of internal communication skills that the manager has, the higher the manufacturing productivity his or her team members generate.

I identified two common distinct types of managers in the foreign subsidiaries of the Chinese SOEs—managers as an engineer (thereafter labelled as managers ENG) and managers as a language specialist (thereafter labelled as managers LANG). I intend to test which type of managers can motivate the assembly line workers in his or her working team better than the other. On one hand, managers LANG have better language and cultural knowledge regarding the host country. It is easier for them to cross the language and cultural barriers, build trust with the local assembly line workers, and motivate them to increase their productivity (Katzenbach, 1996). On the other hand, managers ENG have technical knowledge regarding the operations in the assembly lines. A manager ENG can provide better technical training to the workers in his or her team and improve their technical skills. The economic model of technology-skill mismatch is one of the most frequently used models to explain the cross-country differences in manufacturing productivity (Acemoglu & Zilibotti, 2001). Following the economic model of technology-skill mismatch, I predict that workers in a working team led by a manager ENG thus generate higher manufacturing productivity than those led by a manager LANG, as workers in the former group are expected to have better technical skills than those in the latter one. In case of malfunctions and other mechanical faults in the assembly lines, a manager ENG can also provide technical support of better quality to the local assembly line workers in a more efficient way. Short response time to the malfunctions and mechanical faults helps to increase the manufacturing productivity in the assembly line. The dichotomy of managers in the foreign subsidiaries of Chinese SOEs has not been reported in the literature. There is not enough empirical evidence in the literature for us to make a convincing prediction regarding how managers ENG differ from managers LANG specialist in terms of improving the individual manufacturing productivity.

Similarly, individual assembly line workers also differ in terms of technical skills as well as educational background and working experience. Following the economic model of technology-skill mismatch, I believe that the technical skills of an individual worker can predict individual manufacturing productivity. However, in the datasets, there are no variables accurately measuring the technical skills of assembly line workers on the individual level. I then selected two variables from the datasets as the estimation of the individual worker's technical skills. The first variable differentiates the educational background of individual assembly line workers. I predict that workers with post-secondary education in the field of mechanical engineering or automation engineering can be more skilful to deal with malfunctions in the assembly line and thus generate higher individual manufacturing productivity. The second variable measures the number of years that the worker has worked in the automotive assembly line. I believe that workers with more working experience in the automotive assembly line can be more technically skilful and thus generate higher individual manufacturing productivity. For example, a worker who has worked in the assembly line for a year is more productive than the other newly hired worker with no previous experience is. A newly hired worker with previous working experience in the assembly line is also more productive than the other newly hired worker with no previous experience is. Consequently, I generated hypotheses as follows.

H2. Workers who have post-secondary education in the field of mechanical engineering or automation engineering generate higher manufacturing productivity than the workers who do not have.

H3. Workers who have long working experience in the automotive assembly line generate higher manufacturing productivity.

3. Methods

3.1 Data

The case company X is a Chinese state-owned multinational enterprise in the automotive sector. All the data used in the sequential analyses were secondary data collected internally for other purposes. The company X started aggressive international expansion in the passing decade and now has three foreign subsidiaries in Iran, Mexico, and South Africa, respectively. There are multiple automotive assembly lines in each foreign subsidiary. In 2017, there were 281, 188, and 276 employees working in the assembly lines in the Iranian, Mexican, and South African subsidiaries, forming six, four, and six working teams, respectively. Only employees who had worked for six months or more within 2017 in the assembly line were included in the study. Each working team is responsible for each shift in an assembly line. I divided the frontline managers by the educational background and working experience into two categories: managers as an engineer (thereafter labelled as managers ENG) and managers as a language specialist (thereafter labelled as managers LANG). All the frontline managers are Chinese expatriates who grew up and finished college education in China.

The host countries Iran, Mexico, and South Africa are thereafter labelled as IR, MX, and ZA, respectively. The working teams in the three subsidiaries are labelled as IR1-IR6, MX1-MX4, and ZA1-ZA6, respectively. Individual-level data were further differentiated by both the host country and the working team in the sequential analyses except in the regression model. Individual-level data were only differentiated by the host country in the regression model, as the working-team-level sample size (N=46–49) is too small. A binary independent variable "MGR" was created, with the value of one when the frontline manager was a manager LANG and with the value of zero when the frontline manager was a manager ENG.

3.2 The individual manufacturing productivity

The company X uses Design Standard Time Ratio (DSTR) as an index to measure the labour cost in the assembly lines, commonly used in the automotive manufacturing industry (Taylor et al., 2013). DSTR is calculated by the actual working time multiplied by the labour used and then divided by the product of the design standard time and the production volume. The higher the DSTR is, the lower the productivity is. The company X further uses the average DSTR of assembly line workers in six domestic operations centres during the year 2014—2016 as an internally used "standard" DSTR. The individual productivity of an assembly line worker is further defined as the ratio between the "standard" DSTR and the DSTR of that worker. In this chapter, I used the individual productivity of assembly line workers in the year 2017 (descriptive statistics in Table 1).

Table 1. The average individual productivity and the average individual evaluation of the manager's internal communication skills across three overseas subsidiaries and across working teams

	overall	working teams					
	IR	IR1	IR2	IR3	IR4	IR5	IR6
N	281	48	47	46	47	47	47
Manager Type		ENG	LANG	LANG	LANG	ENG	ENG
Productivity (average)	0.948 (0.033)	0.973 (0.023)	0.954 (0.031)	0.951 (0.029)	0.937 (0.036)	0.926 (0.033)	0.945 (0.019)
COMM (average)	0.104 (0.139)	-0.056 (0.111)	0.163 (0.129)	0.213 (0.052)	0.112 (0.093)	0.094 (0.093)	0.105 (0.161)
	MX	MX1	MX2	MX3	MX4		
N	188	47	46	49	46		
Manager Type		LANG	LANG	ENG	LANG		
Productivity (average)	0.918 (0.032)	0.933 (0.029)	0.907 (0.022)	0.913 (0.027)	0.920 (0.041)		
COMM (average)	0.672 (0.304)	0.885 (0.115)	0.617 (0.184)	0.339 (0.334)	0.864 (0.083)		
	ZA	ZA1	ZA2	ZA3	ZA4	ZA5	ZA6
N	276	46	46	46	46	46	46
Manager Type		ENG	ENG	LANG	ENG	ENG	LANG
Productivity (average)	0.854 (0.038)	0.881 (0.029)	0.844 (0.017)	0.880 (0.018)	0.832 (0.025)	0.808 (0.031)	0.876 (0.031)
COMM (average)	0.240 (0.301)	0.442 (0.206)	0.333 (0.147)	0.495 (0.168)	-0.005 (0.335)	0.071 (0.253)	0.106 (0.231)

Standard errors in parenthesis
COMM: An individual worker's evaluation of his/her manager's internal communications skill

3.3 Internal communication skills of managers

The company X required all the assembly line workers to fill a mandatory survey at the end of the year 2017. This year-end survey used a five-point Likert scale for all the questions. I picked up five relevant questions from the survey to measure the internal communication skills of frontline managers. The five questions are as follows. 1. Did your team leader (the frontline manager) give you clear instructions on job planning? 2. Did your team leader do a good job communicating internally to employees? 3. Did your team leader assist actively and positively when malfunction or faults happened in the assembly line? 4. Did your team leader respond to your questions (regarding the operations or malfunction/faults) efficiently? 5. Did your team leader do a good job keeping you motivated and engaged at work? Each of the five individual-level measures of the manager's internal communication skill has a value of 5, 4, 3, 2, or 1 if an individual assembly line worker strongly agreed, agreed, did not know, disagreed, or strongly disagreed with each question, respectively.

The five individual-level measures correlated with each other strongly (the Pearson correlation coefficients = 0.779—0.918), thus implying problems of multicollinearity. A principal component score of the five measures was used instead of the five measures. In the principal component analysis of the five measures, a single component emerged, with an eigenvalue of 6.73, explaining 90.3% of the variance. The component loadings were all over 0.901. The principal component score of the five measures was used as a continuous independent variable "COMM" (descriptive statistics in Table 1), measuring the individual assembly worker's evaluation of the internal communication skill of the frontline manager in his or her working team. A higher score of COMM indicates that a local assembly worker regards his or her Chinese frontline manager as communicating with him or her in a better and more efficient way.

3.4 The educational and professional background of individual assembly line workers

Individual assembly line workers also differ in terms of educational background and working experience. I used two independent variables to differentiate the educational background and working experience of individual assembly line workers. A binary independent variable "EDU" was created, with the value of one when the assembly line worker has a degree or an educational certificate in the field of mechanical engineering or automation engineering and with the value of zero when the worker does not. A continuous independent variable "EXP" was created to indicate the number of years that the worker had worked in the automotive assembly line.

3.5 Models

A multilevel linear regression model was designed, following the equations below. The individual-level (i) was set as the Level 1 and the country-level (j = IR, MX or ZA) was set as the Level 2. The productivity of an individual worker was chosen as the dependent variable. The variable "COMM," the individual evaluation of the internal communication skill of frontline manager was chosen as an independent variable. The binary variable "EDU" and the continuous variable "EXP" were also chosen as independent variables.

$$Productivity_{ij} = \beta_{0j} + \beta_{1j}COMM_{ij} + \beta_{2j}EDU_{ij} + \beta_{3j}EXP_{ij} + e_{ij}$$
$$\beta_{0j} = \gamma_{00} + \gamma_{01}W_j + u_{0j}$$
$$\beta_{1j} = \gamma_{10} + \gamma_{11}W_j + u_{1j}$$
$$\beta_{2j} = \gamma_{20} + \gamma_{21}W_j + u_{2j}$$
$$\beta_{3j} = \gamma_{30} + \gamma_{31}W_j + u_{3j}$$

4. Results and discussion

4.1 The results of the multilevel linear regression

I tested the effects of the manager-level and individual-level predictors in a multilevel linear regression model. The results of the multilevel linear regression are reported in Table 2. The variable COMM measures the individual evaluation of the internal communication skill of the frontline manager in his or her working team. The results indicate that the higher the level of internal communication skills that a frontline manager has, the higher the average productivity that the individual workers in the working team will deliver [$\gamma_{10} = 2.747 > 0$ ($p < 0.001$) in Table 2]. Hypothesis **H1** is thus supported.

Table 2. Results of multilevel linear regression

		γ
Fixed		
	Intercept	-1.092* (0.442)
	COMM	2.747*** (0.230)
	EDU	1.336** (0.231)
	EXP	0.342 (0.299)
	Iran (IR)	2.932*** (0.172)
	Mexico (MX)	1.372*** (0.133)
	South Africa (ZA)	3.588*** (0.208)
Random		
	Country	0.603 (0.448)
	Individual	0.242 (0.168)
Model Fit		
	R^2	0.159

*** $p < 0.001$, ** $p < 0.01$, * $p < 0.05$

Workers who have post-secondary education in the field of mechanical engineering or automation engineering are found to be more productive than those who do not [$\gamma_{20} = 1.336 > 0$ ($p < 0.01$) in Table 2]. Hypothesis **H2** is also supported. Post-secondary education in the field of mechanical engineering or automation engineering can indeed improve the individual assembly line worker's productivity. Workers with relevant post-secondary education may have a shorter response time in case of malfunctions or other mechanical problems in the assembly line. One of the underlying assumptions of the economic model of technology-skill mismatch is that post-secondary education in most less developed countries is not of the same quality as in the developed countries, especially in the field of engineering and technology (Acemoglu & Zilibotti, 2001). One of the sources for the technology-skill mismatch is the mismatch of the quality of technical education. If the manufacturing workers are properly trained in the less developed countries, it can help to fill the gap of technology-skill mismatch between developed countries and less developed countries.

The length of working experience in the assembly line is insignificant in predicting individual productivity. Hypothesis **H3** is rejected. A possible explanation can be that newly hired assembly line workers without previous experience are indeed less productive than the skilled workers with experience are. Once the assembly line workers are properly trained, the additional time that he or she spends working in the assembly line would no longer contribute to increasing his or her productivity.

4.2 Two types of managers and individual productivity of their team members

I have identified two types of managers in the foreign subsidiaries of Chinese SOEs—managers as an engineer (ENG) and managers as a language specialist (LANG). I am interested in whether the two types of managers have different capacity to motivate their team members. The average individual productivity of assembly line workers in each subsidiary and the working teams led by the two types of managers was calculated (Table 3).

Table 3. The average individual productivity across three overseas subsidiaries and across the two types of managers

		Host country			
		IR	MX	ZA	overall
Type of manager	LANG	0.947 (0.033)	0.929 (0.033)	0.878 (0.025)	0.920 (0.041)
	ENG	0.948 (0.032)	0.913 (0.027)	0.841 (0.037)	0.891 (0.061)
	Total	0.948 (0.033)	0.918 (0.032)	0.854 (0.038)	0.905 (0.054)

Standard errors in parenthesis

An independent-sample t-test was also performed to compare the individual productivity in the working teams led by managers ENG with the individual productivity in the working teams led by managers LANG, disregarding the host country. There is a significant difference in the individual productivity in the working teams led by the managers ENG and that in the working teams led by the managers LANG [$t(743) = 7.61, p < 0.001$]. The managers

LANG (the average individual productivity = 0.920) surpass the managers ENG (the average individual productivity = 0.891) in terms of the individual productivity of the team members. I was then curious about the reasons behind the difference in individual productivity. Both types of managers have their own advantage in terms of improving the individual productivity of their team members. One of the possible explanations is that on-site technical skills training indeed can improve the productivity of individual workers and the managers as an engineer can provide better first-hand technical skills training. However, there is an upper limit for the above-mentioned training-based productivity improvement. Similarly, regarding the rejected hypothesis H3, I believe the productivity improvement by the accumulation of working experience in the assembly line has a similar upper limit.

On the other hand, the internal communication skills of the manager can also predict the individual productivity of his or her team members, as good internal communications can help to build trust between managers and workers, encourage teamwork, and finally contribute to improving productivity (Minssen, 2006). I calculated the average score of COMM in each subsidiary, and the working teams led each type of manager (Table 4). I also performed an independent-sample t-test to compare the individual score of COMM in the working teams led by managers ENG with the individual score of COMM in the working teams led by managers LANG, disregarding the host country. There is a significant difference in the individual score of COMM in the working teams led by the managers as an engineer and that in the working teams led by the managers as a language specialist [t(744) = 11.70, $p < 0.001$]. The managers LANG (the average score of COMM = 0.432) surpass the managers ENG (the average score of COMM = 0.165) in terms of internal communication skills.

Table 4. The individual evaluation of the manager's internal communication skills across three overseas operations centers and across the two types of manager

		Host country			
		IR	MX	ZA	overall
Type of manager	LANG	0.162 (0.105)	0.789 (0.181)	0.301 (0.280)	0.432 (0.340)
	ENG	0.047 (0.145)	0.339 (0.334)	0.210 (0.306)	0.165 (0.281)
	Total	0.104 (0.139)	0.672 (0.304)	0.240 (0.301)	0.298 (0.339)

Standard errors in parenthesis

4.3 Limitations

The major limitation of this study is that the case company only has subsidiaries in three host countries. The small number of host country makes it impossible to generate any statistically significant conclusion regarding the relationship between the cross-country differences in individual productivity and the difference in the institutional context between the home and host country. Second, the study compared individual productivity in the three foreign subsidiaries in the year 2017 with the individual productivity of the company's home operations in China in the year 2014—2016. Third, I primarily adopted quantitative methods in this chapter. The results do not reveal information, such as how the management styles of managers ENG and managers LANG differ from each other. Finally, the study did not consider the cross-country differences in how people evaluate others in a higher rank (for example, how assembly line workers evaluated their line managers). In the countries where the power distance is high, such as China and Mexico, people could give a higher evaluation than their real perception towards others in a higher rank.

5. Conclusion

Chinese SOEs play a critical role in the global economy and investment landscape. But people know little about the internal management of Chinese SOEs, as the management culture in China lacks an efficient information-sharing mechanism either between the internal departments or with external stakeholders. Unlike most of the extant studies that focus on how Chinese SOEs interact with other social actors in the home and host country institutional context, this chapter analysed internally collected data in three foreign subsidiaries of a Chinese manufacturing SOEs and studied the relationship between the Chinese expatriate managers and the local assembly line workers. In the chapter, I have identified two types of Chinese expatriate managers—managers as an engineer and managers as a language specialist. Internal communications between Chinese expatriate managers and local workers is one of the obstacles for individual productivity improvement. Chinese expatriate managers with a language specialist background usually handle internal communication issues and motivate local workers more efficiently in foreign subsidiaries. The results can guide the Chinese SOEs to improve subsidiary performance or deal with the potential xenophobia issues towards Chinese SOEs in the post-COVID-19 era by selecting the suitable expatriate managers in their foreign subsidiaries.

References

Acemoglu, D., & Zilibotti, F. (2001). Productivity differences. *The Quarterly Journal of Economics*, *116*(2), 563-606. doi:10.1162/00335530151144104

Barney, J. B., & Zhang, S. (2009). The future of Chinese management research: A theory of Chinese management versus a Chinese theory of management. *Management and Organization Review*, *5*(1), 15-28. doi:10.1111/j.1740-8784.2008.00102.x

Buckley, P. J., Clegg, L. J., Cross, A. R., Liu, X., Voss, H., & Zheng, P. (2009). The determinants of Chinese outward foreign direct investment. *Journal of International Business Studies*, *40*(2), 353. doi:10.1057/s41267-017-0129-1

Brubaker, R. (2020). Populism and nationalism. *Nations and Nationalism*, *26*(1), 44-66. doi:10.1111/nana.12522

Bryan, L. L., Lyhons, T. G., & Rosenthal, J. (1998). Corporate strategy in a globalizing world: The market capitalization imperative. *McKinsey Quarterly*, *1*(3), 6.

Cui, L., & Jiang, F. (2012). State ownership effect on firms' FDI ownership decisions under institutional pressure: A study of Chinese outward-investing firms. *Journal of International Business Studies*, *43*(3), 264-284. doi:10.1057/jibs.2012.1

Ding, D. Z., & Warner, M. (2001). China's labour-management system reforms: Breaking the “Three Old Irons” (1978–1999). *Asia Pacific Journal of Management*, *18*(3), 315-334. doi:10.1023/A:1010697711514

Du, J., & Zhang, Y. (2018). Does one belt one road initiative promote Chinese overseas direct investment? *China Economic Review*, *47*, 189-205. doi:10.1016/j.chieco.2017.05.010

Gaur, A. S., Ma, X., & Ding, Z. (2018). Home country supportiveness/unfavorableness and outward foreign direct investment from China. *Journal of International Business Studies*, *49*(3), 324-345. doi:10.1057/s41267-017-0136-2

Guo, W., & Clougherty, J. A. (2015). The effectiveness of the state in Chinese outward foreign direct investment: The “Go Global” policy and state-owned enterprises. In *Emerging Economies and Multinational Enterprises* (pp. 141-159). Bingley: Emerald Group Publishing Limited. doi:10.1108/S1571-502720150000028009

Harzing, A. W., & Feely, A. J. (2008). The language barrier and its implications for HQ-subsidiary relationships. *Cross Cultural Management: An International Journal*, *15*(1), 49-61. doi:10.1108/13527600810848827

Hofstede, G. (1993). Cultural constraints in management theories. *Academy of Management Perspectives*, *7*(1), 81-94. doi:10.5465/AME.1993.9409142061

Katzenbach, J. R. (1996). Real change leaders. *The McKinsey Quarterly*, (1), 148.

Kuckertz, A., Brändle, L., Gaudig, A., & et al. (2020). Startups in times of crisis–A rapid response to the COVID-19 pandemic. *Journal of Business Venturing Insights*. doi:10.1016/j.jbvi.2020.e00169

Lester, S., & Manak, I. (2018). The rise of populist nationalism and the renegotiation of NAFTA. *Journal of International Economic Law*, *21*(1), 151-169. doi:10.1093/jiel/jgy005

Leutert, W. (2016). Challenges ahead in China's reform of state-owned enterprises. *Asia Policy*, *21*, 83-100.

Minssen, H. (2006). Challenges of teamwork in production: Demands of communication. *Organization Studies*, *27*(1), 103-124.
doi:10.1177/0170840605056400

Miller, P. (2020). Yes, blame China for the virus. *Foreign Policy*. March 25, 2020.
https://foreignpolicy.com/2020/03/25/blame-china-and-xi-jinping-for-coronavirus-pandemic/

Ngo, H. Y., Lau, C. M., & Foley, S. (2008). Strategic human resource management, firm performance, and employee relations climate in China. *Human Resource Management*, *47*(1), 73-90. doi:10.1002/hrm.20198

Ozyurt, S. (2009). Total factor productivity growth in Chinese industry: 1952–2005. *Oxford Development Studies*, *37*(1), 1-17. doi:10.1080/13600810802660836

Ralston, D. A., Wong, Y. Y., Egri, C. P., Lo, C. W., Li, Y., Dutton, X., & Yang, J. (2018). East vis-a-vis West: The evolution of work values within China regions. *Thunderbird International Business Review*, *60*(4), 605-618. doi:10.1002/tie.21926

Ruck, K., & Welch, M. (2012). Valuing internal communication: management and employee perspectives. *Public Relations Review*, *38*(2), 294-302. doi:10.1016/j.pubrev.2011.12.016

Taylor, A., Taylor, M., & McSweeney, A. (2013). Towards greater understanding of success and survival of lean systems. *International Journal of Production Research*, *51*(22), 6607-6630.

doi:10.1080/00207543.2013.825382
UNCTAD. (2017). *World Investment Report 2017: Investment and the Digital Economy*. New York and Geneva: United Nations Publications.
UNCTAD. (2019). *World Investment Report 2019: Special Economic Zones*. New York and Geneva: United Nations Publications.
Zhao, H., & Zou, S. (2002). The impact of industry concentration and firm location on export propensity and intensity: An empirical analysis of Chinese manufacturing firms. *Journal of International Marketing*, *10*(1), 52-71. doi:10.1509/jimk.10.1.52.19527
Zhou, K. Z., Gao, G. Y., & Zhao, H. (2017). State ownership and firm innovation in China: An integrated view of institutional and efficiency logics. *Administrative Science Quarterly*, *62*(2), 375-404. doi:10.1177/0001839216674457

CULTURE FRAME SWITCHING IN INTERNATIONAL ENTREPRENEURSHIP: SENSEMAKING NARRATIVES OF RUSSIAN IMMIGRANT ENTREPRENEURS IN FINLAND

MARIA IVANOVA-GONGNE[1] AND OLGA DZIUBANIUK[2]

[1]Assistant Professor at Åbo Akademi

[2] Teacher, PhD Student at Åbo Akademi

1. Introduction

Constantly increasing migration has led to a greater number of businesses being managed by individuals with backgrounds in several cultures. This may be particularly beneficial for small entrepreneurial firms, in which an entrepreneur is the core representative of the firm. For instance, the multicultural identity of migrant entrepreneurs may result in them having better skills at developing and maintaining business relationships with partners across cultures (see Lowe et al., 2011). Therefore, the increasing amount of migrant entrepreneurs creates the need to consider multiculturality and its consequences for the current and future international business environments.

Previous studies on individuals with several cultural and/or linguistic backgrounds have been carried out predominantly within multinational corporations, focusing on intra-organisational employee relationships and/or expatriates (Fitzsimmons, 2013; Kane & Levina, 2017). However, even in intra-organisational contexts, multicultural individuals and their contributions have not been well researched (Fitzsimmons, 2013; Kane & Levina, 2017), and the notion of bicultural and multicultural individuals has been largely neglected in the literature on inter-organisational relationships. Furthermore, the cultural aspects of entrepreneurship in particular and international business in general have mostly been studied using the Hofstede (1980) model (Leung & Morris, 2015; Dabić et al., 2020). Adopting a social constructivist perspective, we regard culture as "a flexible network of specific and situational knowledge," with individuals possessing a repertoire of cultural schemas that constitute cultural knowledge, assist in the process of sensemaking and are reflected in their actions (Ivanova-Gongne, 2015, p. 610). The more exposure and interactions that individuals have with other cultures, the more varied cultural schemas they might possess. Given a certain level of integration, migrants can possess the cultural schemas of both their host and home countries. Consequently, migrants may engage in cultural frame switching – that is, applying appropriate cultural schemas in different cultural contexts.

In this study, we focus on first-generation migrant entrepreneurs – that is, those who have migrated to the host country and have started a business there. In other words, we consider migrant entrepreneurs who were not born in the host country. First-generation migrants are more likely to retain their traditional culture, whereas second-generation migrants acculturate more to the host country (see Zhou, 1997). Furthermore, first-generation migrants score lower in Bicultural Identity Integration (BII) (Cheng et al., 2006), which implies a preference for keeping the two cultural identities separate and "supress[ing] one identity depending on the context" (Brannen & Thomas, 2010, p. 8). Therefore, first-generation migrants may be better at cultural frame switching than, for instance, second-generation migrants, which means they fit the aims of the current study better. However, the ability to switch cultural frames is achieved over time and is "a complex, contextual dynamic experience" that "is accomplished through cultivation of multi-narrative capabilities that allow switching from one culture/narrative style to the other when the cultural context requires" (Lowe et al., 2011, p. 43). As a result, not all first-generation migrant entrepreneurs may possess the same level of bicultural competence.

The aim of the current chapter was to deepen the understanding of how the bicultural identity of migrant entrepreneurs affects their business practices in host countries and countries of origin. More specifically, we investigated migrant entrepreneurs' cultural frame switching by analysing their sensemaking practices when doing business in host and home countries. To achieve our objectives, we conducted interview-based qualitative research and collected narrative stories from several first-generation Russian entrepreneurs in Finland.

The chapter is structured as follows: First, we provide a brief literature overview of the migrant entrepreneurship field and cultural frame switching. Second, we describe the methods applied in the study. Third, we present the findings from the empirical study of eight Russian migrants in Finland. Finally, we discuss the findings and provide conclusions and implications.

2. Migrant entrepreneurship

Globalisation has dramatically intensified migration processes around the world. The integration of migrants shifts countries' demographic and economic structures and influences business practices and patterns of consumption (Adebayo et al., 2017) as well as ethnic marketing approaches (e.g. Jamal et al., 2015). International migration can be defined as a person's change of residence by moving abroad, irrespective of the reason, for the short term (3–12 months) or the long term (more than a year or permanent residence) (e.g. de Haas et al., 2020). Migration can be caused by various reasons, including forced displacements, such as military conflicts increasing the number of refugees (Shultz et al., 2020), labour migration (or economic migration) in search of better income or business opportunities (Devitt, 2011), and other reasons, such as family or family reunion and study (de Haas et al., 2020). Naturally, the global movement of people leads to increased migrant entrepreneurship.

Migrant entrepreneurship involves all types of entrepreneurial activities performed by immigrants (Dabić et al., 2020). Conventionally, migrant entrepreneurship was said to consist primarily of small businesses, such as ethnic shops or restaurants targeting customers with similar cultural and ethnic identities. Nowadays, migrants' participation is gradually becoming commonplace in knowledge-intensive industries and economies, such as research and development, health care or the information technology industry, and migrants are internationalising their businesses (Nazareno et al., 2019). International migrants' businesses are frequently characterised by transnational business operations that involve family networks or other types of social ties (e.g. Mustafa & Chen, 2010). This process can be illustrated by Chinese businessmen, who develop broad networks of international business relationships via the international Chinese community and family ties, which can be scattered around the world instead of being located only in the country of origin (Wong & Ng, 2002). Social networks and kinship may serve as valuable sources of information about market opportunities and may support market expansion, as shown, for example, by studies on Italian migrants (Smans et al., 2013). Migrants are apt to maintain business relationships with individuals who share their ethnic origin and cultural background. By contrast, social networks may play a small role in the internationalisation of Russian companies, as Russian migrants do not seem willing to support their countrymen and prefer to search for international contacts on their own (Shirokova & McDougall-Covin, 2012). At the same time, Russian migrant entrepreneurs with diverse social networks have the advantage of accessing ex-Soviet countries and establishing partnerships or supply chains with local companies (Shvarts, 2013). Migrant entrepreneurs face fewer difficulties in initiating transnational partnerships with their country of origin because they know the specifics of business conduct, the language, the legislation and the cultural frames.

Internationalising businesses is not only challenging in terms of geographic distance but is also mentally challenging for the entrepreneurs themselves (e.g. Van Houtum, 1999). Even when the countries are located in close proximity, entrepreneurs still may experience uncertainty to do with business expansion due to low trust in other nationalities. Such uncertainty relates to cultural distance that, despite globalisation, is still a major concern for companies' internationalisation efforts, especially when such efforts involve partnerships between developed and developing countries (Beugelsdijk et al., 2018). For example, business interactions between Finland and Russia, neighbouring countries with a common history (e.g. Koskimies 1981), may involve certain differences in culture and ways of doing business despite the geographical proximity. As countries' political and economic developments shape their business environments, entrepreneurs have to adapt and develop strategies accordingly. For instance, studies on small and medium enterprises (SMEs) in Finland and Russia have shown that while Finnish managers may enjoy business growth due to their entrepreneurial capabilities, Russian entrepreneurs have to constantly innovate while struggling with a highly dynamic and hostile business environment (Bogatyreva et al., 2017). Therefore, Russian migrants operating in Finland, equipped with all their knowledge and social networks, can serve as conduits to business internationalisation between the Russian and Finnish markets. However, according to previous research, Russian migrants in Finland frequently experience prejudice as being untrustworthy due to common stereotypes about Russians (Nshom, 2015), which may constrain their business relationships with native Finnish entrepreneurs.

Although the understanding of migrant entrepreneurship has advanced over the past few decades (Kloosterman & Rath, 2001), the demand for empirical studies is growing as the context of migration is changing due to constantly evolving ideas, resources, social ties and connections of migrants to their host and home countries (Nazareno et al., 2018; Dabić et al., 2020; Yang et al., 2020). Some studies on Russian migrants have focused on their business activities in host countries (e.g. Mesch & Czamanski, 1997; Jumpponen et al., 2007; Vinogradov & Gabelko, 2010; Vershinina, 2013), but an international approach to migrant entrepreneurship is still missing, especially in relation to business-to-business interactions (Yang et al., 2020). Among the numerous capabilities of migrant entrepreneurs, researchers distinguish their international entrepreneurial and cultural capabilities (Xu et al., 2019). However, "extant research of migrant entrepreneurship has focused more on national culture impact rather than individuals' cultural adaptation" (ibid., p. 525) and the ability to switch between cultures.

3. Cultural frame switching and acculturation strategies

The amount of research on the cultural aspects of entrepreneurship has grown steadily over the past two decades (Dabić et al., 2020). However, studies of the cultural aspects of entrepreneurship mostly focus on national culture and are based on Hofstede's (1980) model (Xu et al., 2019; Dabić et al., 2020). Hofstede's model (1980) fails to consider the complexity and the multifaceted nature of culture (e.g. Cannon et al., 2010; McGrath & O'Toole, 2014), especially when it comes to the individual level. Several researchers in international business have advocated for a more constructivist approach when looking at culture in the international business context (e.g. Leung & Morris, 2015). The constructivist approach regards culture as a "flexible network of specific and situational knowledge" (Ivanova-Gongne, 2015, p. 610). Thus, individuals are considered to possess a repertoire of cultural schemas that constitute their knowledge of, for example, national, professional, organisational and other cultures and assist in the process of sensemaking, consequently informing the individuals' actions (Ivanova-Gongne, 2015). The application of specific cultural schemas is highly situational and depends on whether an individual is primed with the culture in question (Leung & Morris, 2015) – for example, when needing to interact with a partner from a specific culture. Individuals with backgrounds in several cultures may possess many cultural schemas and may thus be able to engage in cultural frame switching, which implies moving "between different cultural meaning systems in response to situational cues" (Benet-Martinez et al., 2002, p. 493).

In sociology and psychology studies, cultural frame switching is predominantly studied in relation to bicultural individuals (e.g. Nguyen & Benet-Martínez, 2007) and cross-cultural management (e.g. Brannen & Thomas, 2010) and is often linked to bilingualism and the level of acculturation. The level of acculturation depends on "whether to maintain or reject own cultural values" and on "whether to accept and reject the host culture's cultural values" (Pham & Harris, 2001, p. 281). In his seminal work, Berry (1997) outlined several acculturation strategies, namely integration, assimilation, separation and marginalisation. Integrated individuals retain their own cultural values and incorporate those of the host culture. Assimilation implies that an individual is fully integrated into the host culture and rejects native cultural values. When it comes to separation, one's own values are maintained and the host's cultural values are rejected. Finally, when marginalisation occurs, individuals reject both their own and the host country's values.

In the case of cultural frame-switching, the individuals following the integration acculturation strategy are most likely to succeed in effective switching between different cultural schemas and to have a high level of BII (Fitzsimmons, 2013). BII can be defined as the extent to which individuals with multiple cultures "perceive their mainstream and ethnic cultural identities as compatible and integrated versus oppositional and difficult to integrate" (Benet-Martínez et al., 2002, p. 9). Individuals with positive acculturation experiences are frequently better integrated in the host country's culture (Berry, 2011). Furthermore, the absence of prejudices and negative perceptions and the existence of trust towards the foreign culture improve the chances of individuals integrating new cultural schemas into their repertoires (Ivanova-Gongne, 2015). Consequently, individuals with a high level of BII "tend to assimilate to cultural cues and behave in the direction of the cues" (van Oudenhoven & Benet-Martínez, 2015, p. 49), contrary to individuals with a low level of integration.

Few studies have investigated how migrant entrepreneurs' identification with two (or more) cultures affects their activities (Dheer & Lenartowicz, 2018). A recent study by Dheer and Lenartowicz (2018) has shown that a higher level of integration and, as a result, better capabilities at switching between different cultural contexts positively impact migrant entrepreneurs' intentions of establishing a business. Al-Shammari and Al Shammari (2018) have claimed that bicultural skills allow immigrant entrepreneurs to recognise opportunities better and faster. The two studies show that migrant entrepreneurs' cultural skills have a high potential to improve the entrepreneurs' business activities, thus improving their economic contribution to the host countries. However, the aforementioned studies examined migrant entrepreneurship activities solely in the host-country context. More research is needed on the cultural frame switching capabilities of migrant entrepreneurs in the international, cross-border context. In particular, on the benefits that migrant entrepreneurs' identification with multiple cultures has for developing international business relationships with partners from different cultural contexts, a topic that has received scarce scholarly attention (see Yang et al., 2020). This study aims to contribute towards filling this research gap.

4. Methods

To achieve our study aims, we deemed the qualitative approach to be the most appropriate because it allows obtaining more in-depth knowledge on the issues that we are focusing on (Eisenhardt, 1989; Yin, 1989). We conducted eight in-depth semi-structured interviews with Russian migrant entrepreneurs in Finland who have business partners in both Finland and Russia. Russian-speaking immigrants form one of the largest permanently living migrant groups in Finland (Statistics Finland, 2018). Russian migrants are extensively engaged in entrepreneurship and are involved in foreign trade to a higher extent than most migrant entrepreneurs (Joronen, 2012), which may indicate skilful use of cultural frame switching. Finally, despite close geographical proximity and a long mutual history (Tanner & Söderling 2016), cultural differences and misunderstandings still characterise the Russian-Finnish interactions (Ivanova & Torkkeli, 2013; Ivanova-Gongne & Torkkeli, 2018), which makes our study on Russian migrant entrepreneurs in Finland even more worthwhile.

The interviews were conducted between 2017 and 2018 in the native language of the respondents, Russian. Table 1 presents a more detailed overview of the interviewees' characteristics. It should be noted that, by the time of the interview, Interviewee 6 had been living in Finland only for approximately two years; however, being of Russian origin and having previously resided in Israel, he still can be categorised as possessing bicultural skills. We focused on the interviewees' sensemaking stories about developing business relationships with Finnish and Russian business counterparts. To decipher the specifics of cultural sensemaking and cultural frame switching, we used a narrative approach (Brown et al.,

2008) to the collected managerial stories. In particular, we applied the holistic-content approach to the collected narratives and looked to interpret the meaning of the different parts of the interviews in relation to the whole (Lieblich et al., 1998). We divided the results into three sections according to the respondents' levels of integration.

Table 1. Interviewees' Characteristics

Interviewee No.	Entrepreneurial expertise in the industry	Residence in Finland, years	Experience of entrepreneurship in Finland, years	Experience of entrepreneurship in Russia/work with Russian business partners, years
1	Business consulting	22	8	8
2	High-tech industry	14	3	3
3	Reseller	9	3	2
4	Reseller	12	12	> 12
5	Retailer in the fashion industry	5	3	5
6	Dental services	2	2	2
7	IT services, consulting	9	5	12
8	R&D of medical devices	9	4	7

5. Findings

5.1. The assimilated entrepreneurs

The entrepreneurs in the first group came to Finland either to improve their life or for family reasons and had studied in the country. Interviewee 1 had Finnish roots and had gone to high school and university in Finland; Interviewee 2 had gone to a Finnish language school in Russia and then moved to Finland to study in college and later in a university; Interviewee 8 had studied for her PhD in Finland. Studies in the host country might have helped these entrepreneurs to integrate into Finnish society, making them more knowledgeable about how to do business in Finland when initiating their ventures. Almost all of them were fluent in Finnish, with only Interviewee 8 claiming that her knowledge of Finnish was sometimes not enough for her to use the language in a professional business situation. However, her lack of language skills was often resolved by having a native Finnish partner in the company.

Due to high integration, all the interviewees in this group felt much more comfortable in the Finnish business environment than in the Russian one. They were also critical of how business was done in Russia. In particular, they mentioned that Russians are often opportunistic, do not know how to listen to other people, often promise many things without fulfilling all the promises, do not respect others' time and are irresponsible:

> *People [Russians] react very critically to every word, they do not know how to listen, do not dig deeper, rush things and, because of that, quickly draw wrong conclusions and very often, because of that, negotiations end bad very quickly.* (Interviewee 1)

> *Russian business partners are unreliable, they do not care about you. Very often they act disrespectfully towards your time and to their promises to you. They do not feel any responsibility for what is going to happen. How to say it . . . they promise too much and do too little.* (Interviewee 8)

All the interviewees in this group praised the Finnish business environment and the ease of doing business in the country. They felt that it was much faster and easier to reach an agreement in Finland with Finnish companies. In contrast to the other interviewees, all the entrepreneurs in this group claimed to have received immense support for their businesses from the Finnish government and native entrepreneurs:

> *In Finland, there is this phenomenon, I would say, of older people being ready to act as some sort of mentors . . . I had about 3–4 like that, who truly sincerely, with a great, not fake interest observe my business and are ready to help at any second, at any opportunity, and are always ready to advise! . . . Despite the nationality or any other factors.* (Interviewee 1)

> *They provide good support of small business here. If you have a good idea and it is based on some innovation, a unique proposition, then you can receive governmental support . . . I finished my PhD studies and am commercialising the ideas developed in my research. I've developed an innovation, we have applied for patents and started to receive governmental support, which we receive until now . . . Where have you seen such support in Russia? Business is not being supported [in Russia]!* (Interviewee 8)

However, the interviewees in this group also brought up the issue of prejudices based on national identity. Interviewee 8 preferred not to accentuate her origin when dealing with partners. Interviewee 1, at some point in his career, felt like an outsider when doing business, both in Russia and Finland: "In Russia, they told me that you are not Russian, you are a traitor, left our country . . . and in Finland, something like, 'What you Russians can do that does not break?'" However, the interviewees did not perceive the prejudices as being highly negative and claimed that the prejudices did not significantly impact them in their business. In general, the interviewees felt that they should act like a "Western European firm" when doing business in Russia, without switching cultural frames to the Russian ones: "No matter what's the situation, you behave like you become a Finnish company, whether you like it or not, you are a Finnish company, and you live by these principles, they suit you, and you would like to implement them everywhere" (Interviewee 2). Consequently, such an important cultural trait of Russian business as friendship was deemed unnecessary by the interviewees in this group.

5.2. The "ethnic" entrepreneurs

The two entrepreneurs in the second group were female and had moved to Finland with their husbands, who had found jobs in Finland. Thus, they can be partially labelled as "'passive immigrants' pushed by others to leave Russia" (Säävälä, 2010). Both interviewees had learned Finnish to the extent that they could express themselves in common life situations but not at the professional level. They both established their businesses due to a lack of job opportunities. Both female entrepreneurs in this group essentially ran an ethnic business aimed at Russians living in Finland or abroad. At first, Interviewee 5 had a garment shop selling Russian-made clothes to the mainstream Finnish market; however, she mentioned that the shop rarely had Finnish buyers, with most customers being international. The clothing shop eventually went bankrupt after a few years, and Interviewee 5 established a "Russian club" organisation, which organises various workshops, social events and the like for Helsinki's Russian-speaking community. Interviewee 7 had a consulting company that helped mostly Russian-speaking migrants to establish their businesses in Finland or assisted Russian companies located in Russia to internationalise to Finland. While both interviewees experienced some difficulties in conducting business in Finland, they felt that the Finnish environment was safer for starting a business than the Russian environment and good for raising children.

Both entrepreneurs had experienced some level of prejudice from their Finnish customers, but, being integrated in the Finnish society and accustomed to Finnish cultural schemas in everyday life, they did not feel isolated from the overall society. Thus, when framing their understandings of how Finnish customers and partners perceived them, they were kind in their descriptions and tried to reason in a positive way. However, both interviewees admitted that their language level restricted them from doing business to the fullest of their abilities:

> *Sometimes in the shop we heard, "Putin, clothes of Putin!" Well, that's understandable that people still relate it to this, and there is a certain fear, on the level of respect, or somewhere on the level of something else that I don't know.* (Interviewee 5)

> *No, they don't trust [my company] because I cannot fully explain [because of limited language] what I can offer to them. And this is right, you need to sell things in the language of the customer . . .* (Interviewee 7)

Following the Russian cultural schema of close interpersonal interaction in a business context (see Ivanova & Torkkeli, 2013; Ivanova-Gongne & Torkkeli, 2018), social networking with co-natives was important for both interviewees. They often maintained friendships or close relationships with their partners. Social networking with co-natives, both in Russia and Finland, helped them in their businesses, and Interviewee 5 even established a Russian-speaking entrepreneurship society in the Helsinki area to share information about the best business practices, legislation, business opportunities and so on:

> *. . . I decided to create a Russian-speaking entrepreneurship society and did it so that people could network . . . So, at least there is a circle of people with which we discussed things, and we helped each other a lot. Really, we told each other some things [about entrepreneurship] that you won't even be able to read anywhere. You can only experience it first-hand.* (Interviewee 5)

> *I find myself a partner, we work together for quite a long time and then we become friends. We often have it that way, I have several friends with which I started off our friendship from working together.* (Interviewee 7)

In terms of trust between business partners, both women became accustomed to the Finnish cultural schemas of openness and transparency and used them in their everyday life. Even though they knew that if they did business with Russian partners, they should be careful in terms of trusting their partners, they still preferred to act according to the Finnish cultural schema:

> *What is good is that Finland is a small country, everything is transparent and open. You issued an invoice, everything is as it should be and in two weeks it will be paid. There is trust that is based on the fact that everything is open and transparent. In Russia, you cannot trust in such a way.* (Interviewee 5)

> *If we got used in Finland that it is enough to have a verbal agreement or a short letter, in Russia, I think, there is still a need to sign some contract. It is not like they are trying to lie to someone in that way, they [Russians] are simply trying to prove to you that they don't lie . . . But here I calm down people and always say that everything is ok, just come, I believe that you will order, I do not need any proof, I understand it all. . . . We have learned to trust each other.* (Interviewee 7)

5.3. The less integrated entrepreneurs

The three entrepreneurs in the third group considered themselves less integrated in Finnish society. All of them moved to Finland primarily due to work reasons (i.e. they either had their own business or planned to establish one). Interviewee 6 described Finland as "a land of opportunities" and, at the time of the interview, had lived in Finland for about two years, having previously lived in Israel. Interviewees 3 and 4 were a married couple, had lived in Finland for nine years and were in business together. Despite the significant difference in the length of their stays in Finland, all the interviewees in this group had negative feelings towards the Finnish business environment. The entrepreneurs described misunderstandings with local partners or other business and government actors. All the interviewees in this group thought that entrepreneurs should, first of all, seek more profit and expand their businesses. Honesty and timely performance were essential for them. However, the interviewees in this group had encountered cases of Finns being less honest than they are normally assumed to be.

Similar to the previous group (the ethnic entrepreneurs), Interviewees 3, 4 and 6 had experienced problems due to a lack of language skills. However, while Interviewees 5 and 7 knew the language quite well for the purposes of daily life, Interviewees 3, 4 and 6 either resisted learning Finnish or had not managed to learn it:

> *When I came to Finland, I thought that everything here is done accurately and honestly. I was very much wrong. I came like a blind kitten, even*

though I knew how to do business. Of course, language hit me like a hammer, I did not know the language. I signed contracts here, from which I suffered a lot in the end, both financially and business-wise. That's due to lack of language knowledge and the way they translate it here . . . I have not found a person who would properly translate a contract for me. (Interviewee 6)

Difficulties were due to the fact that we speak only English. We don't know Finnish. My husband does not want to learn it on principle because he does not like it . . . So, we spoke English, and companies called us about the products, and we offered them in English. They saw that we are not Finns and no one agreed to buy . . . (Interviewee 3)

All the entrepreneurs in this group stated that they had experienced prejudice due to their ethnicity, which made it harder to do business in Finland. Besides their lack of language skills, the entrepreneurs' names often indicated their origin, and they felt that this made it harder for Finns to trust them. Difficulties due to prejudice ranged from the length of time needed to establish a firm to problems in hiring local personnel and selling the products to local firms. Interviewee 6 stated that only foreigners replied to the job offers posted by his firm and that it took 2.5 months to register the firm, whereas, for locals, it usually takes 2 weeks. The interviewee also mentioned that it was hard for him to attract Finnish partners. Although Interviewees 3 and 4 had a Finnish business partner, they experienced many misunderstandings with their partners, particularly due to different mentalities and views on what is important in business:

We even had a conflict with this Finn. Me and my husband always aimed at increasing the volume, increasing profit, so that the company develops somehow. And for our partner, it was enough like it is. He did not want to increase the amount of sales and volume of purchases. That is where we had our misunderstandings . . . (Interviewee 3)

Interviewee 6 also perceived Finnish businesspeople as being comfortable with what they have and not having the "desire to grow," which differed from the way he wanted to do business. All the entrepreneurs in this group followed the Russian cultural schema of profit orientation in business (Ivanova & Torkkeli, 2013). Furthermore, the entrepreneurs had a feeling that it is not worth to introduce something new to Finnish customers because the latter prefer traditional things:

They do now have a willingness to grow. They don't want to improve themselves. They are happy with what they have, with what they know and they believe in it. And, nowadays, we are thinking with my partner that maybe there is no need to introduce new things here. We should emphasise those things that Finns are already used to. Because they are cautious about new things. They do not want to grow or understand something new . . . they do not need it. (Interviewee 6)

In general, although they felt that doing business in Russia was easier due to similar mentalities, they considered business in Finland to be safer and more predictable.

6. Discussion and conclusions

The results show that despite clearly knowing both countries' cultural schemas, the interviewees mostly refrained from switching between cultural frames in their international business activities, preferring to comply with Finnish business customs. Similar to previous literature on the acculturation of migrants (Berry, 1997), more assimilated entrepreneurs were more prone to use Finnish cultural schemas than the Russian ones. However, it should be noted that all the more assimilated entrepreneurs came to Finland without having proper work experience in Russia. As a result, they might not have had the chance to be exposed to the Russian cultural schemas of doing business and had to base their knowledge of how to operate in the business environment mostly on the Finnish cultural schemas. The less integrated interviewees had already worked as active entrepreneurs before coming to Finland and, as a consequence, referred to the Russian cultural schemas more when discussing how business should be run. They also reported a larger number of challenges, and, consequently, their negative acculturation experiences might have influenced their overall low levels of integration. This was contrary to the assimilated entrepreneurs, who had had a positive acculturation experience and felt like they had received enough support from Finnish entrepreneurs and government. The ethnic entrepreneurs followed an integration strategy and managed to retain their own values while also integrating the host country's values, despite their businesses being aimed at fellow citizens.

In line with previous literature, prejudices on a national basis and lack of language skills were among the main challenges that the entrepreneurs faced when doing business in the host country (Sui et al., 2015; Razin, 1993). However, different groups of entrepreneurs faced different challenges. The assimilated entrepreneurs were fluent or had good language skills and, for the most part, did not perceive the prejudices to affect their businesses. Moreover, some of the assimilated entrepreneurs felt prejudices towards themselves when doing business in Russia. While the ethnic entrepreneurs perceived the prejudices directed at them more intensely, including in business life, they justified such prejudices by referring to their own lack of language skills and insufficient integration. Such an attitude might be explained by their businesses being aimed at fellow citizens and by the lack of need to seek Finnish customers or partners. Furthermore, both ethnic entrepreneurs were female, which might have contributed to a kinder description of Finnish nationals. The less integrated entrepreneurs sensed more prejudices towards them than the other groups, lacked language skills and perceived more the differences in mentalities, which also affected their businesses.

This study contributes to scholarship on international business and entrepreneurship literature in several ways. First, it adds to the growing literature on migrant entrepreneurship by specifically investigating how individuals' identification with two cultures affects their activities (see Dheer & Lenartowicz, 2018). Second, while the current study looks mostly at the host-country context, it also touches on the entrepreneurs' perceptions of doing business in their home-country context. Thus, the study contributes to the scarce literature on migrant entrepreneurs' business activities in an international, cross-border context (e.g. Sui et al., 2015). Third, this is one of the few studies to examine business relationships from a bicultural individual perspective while also adopting a constructivist approach to culture (see Dabić et al., 2020). We posit that multiculturality is an important contemporary issue in entrepreneurship that deserves more attention, both in future research and in practice, and whose analysis may contribute to understanding international business relationships in the context of the ever-increasing global movement of people. This applies not only to companies being multicultural entities but also to individuals masterfully applying different cultural schemas in their business interactions across cultures.

This study carries several managerial implications. Migrant entrepreneurs can benefit from this study by obtaining insights into how to apply their bicultural and multicultural competences when interacting with partners in the host and home countries. The results also provide up-to-date knowledge on the challenges that migrants may face when establishing and leading businesses in Finland. Finally, although the interviewed individuals are entrepreneurs, the results can also be useful for multinational corporations by providing more knowledge on bicultural individuals and how they could potentially be an asset as boundary spanners in international business relationships.

The number of interviews in this study was limited due to the small number of Russian entrepreneurs conducting international business, especially in their country of origin. Thus, further research on bigger samples is required to generalise the findings. We encourage more researchers to focus on the cultural aspects of migrant entrepreneurship, particularly by adopting a constructivist perspective on culture.

References

Adebayo, F. A., Itkonen, S. T., Koponen, P., Prättälä, R., Härkänen, T., Lamberg-Allardt, C., & Erkkola, M. (2017). Consumption of healthy foods and associated socio-demographic factors among Russian, Somali and Kurdish immigrants in Finland. *Scandinavian Journal of Public Health*, *45*(3), 277–287.

Al-Shammari, M., & Al Shammari, H. (2018). The impact of bicultural knowledge, skills, abilities and other experiences (KSAOs) on individual entrepreneurial behavior: The context of entrepreneurial discovery, evaluation and implementation. *International Journal of Entrepreneurship*, *22*(2), 1–18.

Benet-Martinez, V., Leu, J., Lee, F., & Morris, M. W. (2002). Negotiating biculturalism: Cultural frame switching in biculturals with oppositional versus compatible cultural identities. *Journal of Cross-Cultural Psychology*, *33*(5), 492–516.

Berry, J. W. (1997). Immigration, acculturation, and adaptation. *Applied Psychology*, *46*(1), 5–34.

Berry, J. W. (2011). Integration and multiculturalism: Ways towards social solidarity. *Papers on Social Representations*, *20*(1), 2.1–2.21.

Beugelsdijk, S., Kostova, T., Kunst, V. E., Spadafora, E., & Van Essen, M. (2018). Cultural distance and firm internationalization: A meta-analytical review and theoretical implications. *Journal of Management*, *44*(1), 89–130.

Bogatyreva, K., Beliaeva, T., Shirokova, G., & Puffer, S. M. (2017). As different as chalk and cheese? The relationship between entrepreneurial orientation and SMEs' growth: Evidence from Russia and Finland. *Journal of East-West Business*, *23*(4), 337–366.

Brannen, M. Y., & Thomas, D. C. (2010). Bicultural individuals in organizations: Implications and opportunity. *International Journal of Cross-Cultural Management*, *10*(1), 5–16.

Brown, A. D., Stacey, P., & Nandhakumar, J. (2008). Making sense of sensemaking narratives. *Human Relations*, *61*(8), 1035–1062.

Cannon, J. P., Doney, P. M., Mullen, M. R., & Petersen, K. J. (2010). Building long-term orientation in buyer-supplier relationships: The moderating role of culture. *Journal of Operations Management*, *28*(6), 506–521.

Cheng, C.-Y., Lee, F., & Benet-Martinez, V. (2006). Assimilation and contrast effects in cultural frame switching (CFS): Bicultural identity integration (BII) and valence of cultural cues. *Journal of Cross-Cultural Psychology*, *37*, 742–760.

Dabić, M., Vlačić, B., Paul, J., Dana, L. P., Sahasranamam, S., & Glinka, B. (2020). Immigrant entrepreneurship: A review and research agenda. *Journal of Business Research*, *113*, 25–38.

de Haas, H., Miller, M. J., & Castles, S. (2020). *The age of migration: International population movements in the modern world*. Red Globe Press.

Devitt, C. (2011). Varieties of capitalism, variation in labour immigration. *Journal of Ethnic and Migration Studies*, *37*(4), 579–596.

Dheer, R. J., & Lenartowicz, T. (2018). Multiculturalism and entrepreneurial intentions: Understanding the mediating role of cognitions. *Entrepreneurship Theory and Practice*, *42*(3), 426–466.

Eisenhardt, K. M. (1989). Building theories from case study research. *Academy of Management Review*, *14*(4), 532–550.

Fitzsimmons, S. R. (2013). Multicultural employees: A framework for understanding how they contribute to organizations. *Academy of Management Review*, *38*(4), 525–549.

Hofstede, G. (1980). *Culture's consequences: International differences in work-related values*. Sage Publications.

Ivanova, M., & Torkkeli, L. (2013). Managerial sensemaking of interaction within business relationships: A cultural perspective. *European Management Journal*, *31*(6), 717–727.

Ivanova-Gongne, M. (2015). Culture in business relationship interaction: An individual perspective. *Journal of Business and Industrial Marketing*, *30*(5), 608–615.

Ivanova-Gongne, M., & Torkkeli, L. (2018). No manager is an island: Culture in sensemaking of business networking. *Journal of Business & Industrial Marketing*, *33*(5), 638–650.

Jamal, A., Peñaloza, L., & Laroche, M. (Eds.). (2015). *The Routledge companion to ethnic marketing*. Routledge.

Joronen, T. (2012). Maahanmuuttajien yrittäjyys Suomessa [Migrant entrepreneurship in Finland]. *Tutkimuksia* 2012:2. Helsingin kaupungin tietokeskus.

Jumpponen, J., Ikävalko, M., & Karandassov, B. (2007, August 9–11). *Characterizing Russian immigration entrepreneurship in Finland* [Conference presentation]. The 19th Nordic Academy of Management, Bergen, Norway.

Kane, A. A., & Levina, N. (2017). 'Am I still one of them?': Bicultural immigrant managers navigating social identity threats when spanning global boundaries. *Journal of Management Studies*, *54*(4), 540–577.

Kloosterman, R., & Rath, J. (2001). Immigrant entrepreneurs in advanced economies: Mixed embeddedness further explored. *Journal of Ethnic and Migration Studies*, *27*(2), 189–201.

Koskimies, J. (1981). Finland. In A. A. Blum (Ed.), *International handbook of industrial relations: Contemporary development and research* (pp. 147–167). Aldwych Press.

Leung, K., & Morris, M. W. (2015). Values, schemas, and norms in the culture-behavior nexus: A situated dynamics framework. *Journal of International Business Studies*, *46*, 1028–1050.

Lieblich, A., Tuval-Mashiach, R., & Zilber, T. (1998). *Narrative research: Reading, analysis, and interpretation* (Vol. 47). Sage.

Lowe, S., Hwang K. S., & Moore, F. (2011). Sensemaking and sojourner adjustment among Korean entrepreneurs in London (UK). *Culture and Organization*, *17*(1), 31–46,

McGrath, H., & O'Toole, T. (2014). A cross-cultural comparison of the network capability development of entrepreneurial firms. *Industrial Marketing Management*, *43*(6), 897–910.

Mesch, G. S., & Czamanski, D. (1997). Occupational closure and immigrant entrepreneurship: Russian Jews in Israel. *The Journal of Socio-Economics*, *26*(6), 597–610.

Mustafa, M., & Chen, S. (2010). The strength of family networks in transnational immigrant entrepreneurship. *Thunderbird International Business Review*, *52*(2), 97–106.

Nazareno, J., Zhou, M., & You, T. (2019). Global dynamics of immigrant entrepreneurship: Changing trends, ethnonational variations, and reconceptualizations. *International Journal of Entrepreneurial Behaviour and Research*, *25*(5), 780–800.

Nguyen, A. M. D., & Benet-Martínez, V. (2007). Biculturalism unpacked: Components, measurement, individual differences, and outcomes. *Social and Personality Psychology Compass*, *1*(1), 101–114.

Nshome, E. (2016). Predictors of Finnish adolescent's prejudice towards Russian immigrants and the effect of intergroup contact. *Journal of Intercultural Communication Research*, *45*(1), 31–44.

Pham, T. B., & Harris, R. J. (2001). Acculturation strategies among Vietnamese-Americans. *International Journal of Intercultural Relations*, *25*(3), 279–300.

Razin, E. (1993). Immigrant entrepreneurs in Israel, Canada, and California. In P. Bhachu (Ed.), *Immigration and Entrepreneurship: Culture, Capital, and Ethnic Networks* (pp. 97–124). Routledge, New York, NY.

Salaff, J., Greve, A., & Wong, S. L. (2006). Business social networks and immigrant entrepreneurs from China. In E. Fong & C. Luk (Eds.), *Chinese ethnic economy: Global and local perspectives* (pp. 99–119). Routledge.

Shirokova, G., & McDougall-Covin, P. (2012). The role of social networks and institutions in the internationalization of Russian entrepreneurial firms: Do they matter? *Journal of International Entrepreneurship*, *10*(3), 177–199.

Shultz, C., Barrios, A., Krasnikov, A. V., Becker, I., Bennett, A. M., Emile, R., Hokkinen, M., Pennington, J. R., Santos, M., & Sierra, J. (2020). The global refugee crisis: Pathway for a more humanitarian solution. *Journal of Macromarketing*, *40*(1), 128–143.

Shvarts, A. (2013). Russian transnational entrepreneurs in Toronto: How the global capitalist economy influenced entrepreneurship. *International Journal of Sociology and Anthropology*, *5*(8), 269–284.

Smans, M., Freeman, S., & Thomas, J. (2014). Immigrant entrepreneurs: The identification of foreign market opportunities. *International Migration*, *52*(4), 144–156.

Statistics Finland. (2018). *Foreign citizens*. https://www.stat.fi/tup/maahanmuutto/maahanmuuttajat-vaestossa/ulkomaan-kansalaiset_en.html

Sui, S., Morgan, H. M., & Baum, M. (2015). Internationalization of immigrant-owned SMEs: The role of language. *Journal of World Business*, *50*(4), 804–814.

Säävälä, M. (2010). Forced migrants, active mothers or desired wives: Migratory motivation and self-representation in Kosovo Albanian and Russian women's biographies. *Journal of Ethnic and Migration Studies*, *36*(7), 1139–1155.

Tanner, A., & Söderling, I. (2016). *Venäjänkieliset Suomessa. Huomisen suomalaiset [Russian-speaking people in Finland. Finns of tomorrow].* Siirtolaisuus-instituuti, Julkaisuja 3.

van Houtum, H. (1999). Internationalisation and mental borders. *Tijdschrift voor economische en sociale geografie*, *90*(3), 329–335.

van Oudenhoven, J. P., & Benet-Martínez, V. (2015). In search of a cultural home: From acculturation to frame-switching and intercultural competencies. *International Journal of Intercultural Relations*, *46*, 47–54.

Vershinina, N. (2013). *Russian entrepreneurs in London: Are they flying business class?* British Academy of Management Conference, 10–11 September 2013 in Entrepreneurship Track, Liverpool, UK.

Vinogradov, E., & Gabelko, M. (2010). Entrepreneurship among Russian immigrants in Norway and their stay-at-home peers. *Journal of Developmental Entrepreneurship*, *15*(4), 461–479.

Wong, L., & Ng, M. (2002). The emergence of small transnational enterprise in Vancouver: The case of Chinese entrepreneur immigrants. *International Journal of Urban and Regional Research*, 26, 508–530.

Xu, K., Drennan, J., & Mathews, S. (2019). Immigrant entrepreneurs and their cross-cultural capabilities: A study of Chinese immigrant entrepreneurs in Australia. *Journal of International Entrepreneurship*, *17*(4), 520–557.

Yang, Z., Jamal, A., & Zhou, L. (2020). Recent advances in identifying and theorizing the role of immigrant entrepreneurs, ethnicity, and culture in industrial marketing. *Industrial Marketing Management*, *91*, 521-522.

Yin, R. K. (1989). *Case study research—Design and methods* (2nd ed.). Sage Publications.

Zhou, M. (1997). Segmented Assimilation: Issues, Controversies, and Recent Research on the New Second Generation. *International Migration Review*, 31(4), 975–1008.

Future of International Entrepreneurship

Lasse Torkkeli

Adjunct Professor of International Business at Turku School of Economics at University of Turku

Conclusions

The contributions from researchers included in this book paint a picture of a dynamic, highly interesting future for both practitioners and scholars engaged in international business and entrepreneurship. It is a timely contribution: The COVID-19 pandemic has for the last year had a major impact, resulting in a fall of global FDI by over 40% in 2020 (UNCTAD, 2021). Recent studies have started to outline the impact of the pandemic on international business and entrepreneurship (Caligiuri et al., 2020; Kano & Oh, 2020; Verbeke & Yuan, 2021; Zahra, 2020a). However, such crises also mean that new entrepreneurial opportunities are opening to those enterprises that seek out proactive, innovative responses to them (Martiz et al., 2020; Wenzel et al., 2020).

The proclivity towards risk-taking innovativeness and proactiveness is often operationalized as *entrepreneurial orientation* (Lumpkin & Dess, 1996), which is at the heart of some of the main definitions on international entrepreneurship - the combination of innovative, proactive, and risk-seeking behavior *that crosses national borders and is intended to create value in organizations* (McDougall & Oviatt, 2000). International entrepreneurship developed in the intersection of international business and entrepreneurship fields and, during these first two decades of the 21st century, has developed into a field of research on its own (Servantie et al., 2016; Zucchella, 2021). As such, it is at the core of this book and serves as the foundation on which most of the contributions in this book also are founded. Therefore, we conclude with an assessment on the future of the field, with potential trajectories and research paths.

Future opportunities for international entrepreneurship research and practice

What will international entrepreneurship look like in 2030, 2050, or in 2070? We can only present our informed opinions on the long-term development at this point, opinions that are based on the contemporary currents and developments. We are currently living through a time of high volatilities and uncertainties globally. In entrepreneurship, the role of resiliency (Bullogh & Renko, 2013; Bullough et al., 2014) and capabilities (Battisti & Deakins, 2017) in such times is more important than before. A pandemic is also likely to result in disruptions to existing global networks, ecosystems and platforms (Zahra, 2020b). The ongoing COVID-19 is forcing firms to reconsider their business models (Akpan et al., 2020; Ritter & Pedersen, 2020), yet research on international entrepreneurship has only recently started to shed light on the dynamics of business model change and innovation in internationalizing enterprises (Rask, 2014; Abrahamsson et al., 2019; Asemokha et al., 2020; Asemokha et al., 2021). The chapter by Asemokha and Vesin in this book is a welcome contribution to this effect, but the field of international entrepreneurship will continue to benefit from more research helping us understand how and where the business model matters in internationalization of SMEs (Child et al., 2017) and for rapidly internationalizing small enterprises in particular (see Hennart, 2014).

The importance of entrepreneurial self-efficacy, the belief of an individual on his or her capability in performing tasks and roles aimed at entrepreneurial outcomes (Chen et al., 1998), is heightened during volatile times (Bullough et al., 2014). The role of entrepreneurial self-efficacy, well-established in entrepreneurship literature (e.g., Chen et al., 1998; Forbes, 2006; Newman et al., 2019), has received very little attention in international entrepreneurship research. A recent study by Yang et al. (2020) confirmed its relevance for the field, as they linked entrepreneurial self-efficacy to increased degree of internationalization, and future studies could shed light on the role of self-efficacy in, for instance, survival through pandemic-induced business restrictions in internationally operating enterprises around the world. Since entrepreneurial self-efficacy and business model development appears to be interlinked (Keane et al., 2018), international entrepreneurship scholars could look to clarify whether self-efficacy is linked to the kind of business model development that results in the enterprise internationalizing "accidentally" (see Hennart, 2014). Based on the extant research, it may be possible that entrepreneurial self-efficacy both underlies entrepreneurial internationalization in general, as well as the ability to remain successful international operations during recessionary periods and similar challenging times that the world is currently living through with the pandemic. With advances in neuroscience and cognition research, in the coming decades we may well develop an accurate model of international entrepreneurship from the cognitive perspective, the importance of which was already noted in the past (Zahra et al., 2005).

Another phenomenon that is important for both the present-day situation and as a long-term trajectory in international entrepreneurship is the phenomenon of digitalization. Although the foundation and development of international entrepreneurship as a field rests on rapidly internationalizing, often in some way digital enterprises such as born globals (Rennie, 1993; Knight & Cavusgil, 2004) and international new ventures (McDougall et al., 1994), researchers have struggled to develop coherent unifying frameworks under which *digital international entrepreneurship* could be placed. Recently, several studies (Vadana et al., 2019; Monaghan et al., 2020; Vadana et al., 2020) have sought to develop conceptual frameworks and propositions via which that could be achieved under the umbrella term of *born digitals.* The contributions of Kaartemo, Treves and Yadav & Iqbal in this book enrich this discussion, highlighting some of the main technologies and mechanisms of global trade that will come to determine an increasingly digital international entrepreneurship and business world. It is likely that born digitals and other international enterprises with international digital competence (Cahen & Borini, 2020) will not only survive but also thrive in a post-COVID-19 pandemic world, since digitalizing their operations allows exporting small enterprises in particular to overcome such crises (Jaklič & Burger, 2020). The future is also likely to see an increasing number of gig-economy freelancers (e.g., Burtch et al., 2018) engage in entrepreneurship through digital platforms (e.g., Srinivasan & Venkatraman, 2018), and to the extent that the platform they engage in is international - as an increasing number of digital platforms are – then we will be dealing with a large number of new types of digital international entrepreneurs. In sum, the role of born digitals and digital international entrepreneurs is likely to grow in global trade in the long term, and international entrepreneurship scholars will have no choice but to try and keep up.

It is also likely that the presently pronounced role of institutional support for international business and entrepreneurship in trying to cope with the pandemic will continue to be at the core of international entrepreneurs and people who research them. As El Guili et al. note in this book, since each country has tended to favor its own measures to manage export assistance during the COVID-19 crisis, it is important to keep shedding light on different country contexts and the institutional support on international entrepreneurship in them. Governments and regional policy makers are called to take long-term measures to strengthen their local regional entrepreneurial ecosystems in order to help SMEs survive the COVID-19 pandemic (Kuckertz et al., 2020). Regional entrepreneurial ecosystems are key in nurturing born globals (Velt et al., 2018) and should be able to provide significant support to internationalization of firms (Theodoraki & Catanzaro, forthcoming). The international entrepreneurship field of research has at times been criticized for its lack of unifying theoretical frameworks and models (e.g., Baier-Fuentes et al., 2019). The ecosystem framework (Stam & van de Ven; Velt et al., 2020) provides a coherent structural basis which can be used to examine the phenomenon of international entrepreneurship both across different units of analysis as well as in a way that makes comparing results across studies more accurate. Thus, in addition to the entrepreneurial ecosystemic perspective supporting the institutional view of international entrepreneurship (Sadeghi et al., 2019) – several of the ecosystemic framework elements being linked to local and regional institutions after all – international entrepreneurship from the entrepreneurial exosystemic perspective is a highly potential future area of research. It can also help link theory and practice, in that mapping the strengths and weaknesses of different entrepreneurial ecosystems will provide benchmarks and guidelines for policymakers on developing their local and regional ecosystems for best possible support for growth and international entrepreneurship.

Finally, future of international entrepreneurship looks to be *sustainable*. In the midst of the current pandemic, one should keep in mind that there are global challenges that will remain in need of solutions also post-pandemic, and that international entrepreneurship stands at the forefront of helping humanity to answer those challenges. New globally scalable innovations arising from sustainable technologies such as cleantech (Saarenketo et al., 2018), and the international implications of social entrepreneurship around the world (Zahra et al., 2014) mean that international entrepreneurship will be among the key phenomena helping global trade recover from the pandemic in continue in its re-orientation to responding the long-term global challenges such as the climate change and social inequalities between and within countries. Sustainability is not just "nice to have", but can also reduce the cost of equity capital (El Ghoul et al., 2011), mitigate stakeholder reactions in case of negative event (Godfrey et al., 2009), facilitate emergence of innovations, offer new business opportunities and create shared value in a supply chain, for example (McWilliams & Siegel, 2000; Porter & Kramer, 2011). In international entrepreneurship, only very recently have studies (Uzhegova et al., 2018; Uzhegova et al., 2020) started to shed light on the role of corporate social responsibility and responsible business practices in the field. The role of digital, sustainable and ecosystemic perspectives in international entrepreneurship is thus likely to be emphasized even more in the next years and decades. In the light of these notions and the contributions from promising scholars in international entrepreneurship and business in this book, the future of international entrepreneurship research and practice looks as bright as ever.

References

Abrahamsson, J., Boter, H., & Vanyushyn, V. (2019). Business model innovation of international new ventures: An empirical study in a Swedish context. *Journal of International Entrepreneurship*, *17*(1), 75-102.

Akpan, I. J., Soopramanien, D., & Kwak, D. H. (2020). Cutting-edge technologies for small business and innovation in the era of COVID-19 global health pandemic. *Journal of Small Business & Entrepreneurship*, 1-11.

Asemokha, A., Musona, J., Ahi, A., Torkkeli, L., & Sareenketo, S. (2021, January). Business Model Innovation in the Internationalization of SMEs: The Role of Causation and Effectuation. In *Proceedings of the 54th Hawaii International Conference on System Sciences* (p. 5059).

Asemokha, A., Musona, J., Torkkeli, L., & Saarenketo, S. (2019). Business model innovation and entrepreneurial orientation relationships in SMEs: Implications for international performance. *Journal of International Entrepreneurship*, *17*(3), 425-453.

Baier-Fuentes, H., Hormiga, E., Miravitlles, P., & Blanco-Mesa, F. (2019). International entrepreneurship: a critical review of the research field. *European Journal of International Management*, *13*(3), 381-412.

Battisti, M. and Deakins, D. (2017). The relationship between dynamic capabilities, the firm's resource base and performance in a post-disaster environment, *International Small Business Journal*, 35(1): 78-98.

Bullough, A., & Renko, M. 2013. Entrepreneurial resilience during challenging times. Business Horizons, 56(3): 343-350.

Bullough, A., Renko, M. and Myatt, T. (2014). Danger Zone: The importance of resilience and self-efficacy for entrepreneurial intentions, Entrepreneurship Theory & Practice, 38(3): 473-499.

Burtch, G., Carnahan, S., & Greenwood, B. N. (2018). Can you gig it? An empirical examination of the gig economy and entrepreneurial activity. *Management Science*, *64*(12), 5497-5520.

Cahen, F., & Borini, F. M. (2020). International digital competence. *Journal of International Management*, *26*(1), 100691.

Caligiuri, P., De Cieri, H., Minbaeva, D., Verbeke, A., & Zimmermann, A. (2020). International HRM insights for navigating the COVID-19 pandemic: Implications for future re-search and practice. *Journal of International Business Studies,* Jun 2, 1–17.

Chen, C. C., Greene, P. G., & Crick, A. (1998). Does entrepreneurial self-efficacy distinguish entrepreneurs from managers?. *Journal of Business Venturing*, *13*(4), 295-316.

Child, J., Hsieh, L., Elbanna, S., Karmowska, J., Marinova, S., Puthusserry, P., ... & Zhang, Y. (2017). SME international business models: The role of context and experience. *Journal of World Business*, *52*(5), 664-679.

El Ghoul, S., Guedhami, O., Kwok, C. C., & Mishra, D. R. (2011). Does corporate social responsibility affect the cost of capital?. *Journal of Banking & Finance*, *35*(9), 2388-2406.

Forbes, D. P. (2005). The effects of strategic decision making on entrepreneurial self–efficacy. *Entrepreneurship theory and practice*, *29*(5), 599-626.

Godfrey, P. C., Merrill, C. B., & Hansen, J. M. (2009). The relationship between corporate social responsibility and shareholder value: An empirical test of the risk management hypothesis. *Strategic management journal*, *30*(4), 425-445.

Greene, F. J., & Rosiello, A. (2020). A commentary on the impacts of 'Great Lockdown'and its aftermath on scaling firms: What are the implications for entrepreneurial research?. *International Small Business Journal*

Hennart, J. F. (2014). The accidental internationalists: a theory of born globals. *Entrepreneurship Theory and Practice, 38*(1), 117-135.

Jaklič, A., & Burger, A. (2020). Complex internationalisation strategies during crises: The case of Slovenian exporters during the great recession and COVID-19 pandemic 1. *Teorija in Praksa*, *57*(4), 1018-1041.

Kano, L., & Oh, C. H. (2020). Global value chains in the post-COVID world: Governance for reliability. *Journal of Management Studies*, *57*(8), 1773-1777.

Keane, S. F., Cormican, K. T., & Sheahan, J. N. (2018). Comparing how entrepreneurs and managers represent the elements of the business model canvas. *Journal of Business Venturing Insights*, *9*, 65-74.

Knight, G. & Cavusgil, S. T. (2004). the Born-global Firm. *Journal of International Business Studies*, *35*(2), 124-141.

Kuckertz, A., Brändle, L., Gaudig, A., Hinderer, S., Reyes, C. A. M., Prochotta, A., ... & Berger, E. S. (2020). Startups in times of crisis–A rapid response to the COVID-19 pandemic. *Journal of Business Venturing Insights*, e00169.

Lumpkin, G. T., & Dess, G. G. (1996). Clarifying the entrepreneurial orientation construct and linking it to performance. *Academy of Management Review*, *21*(1), 135-172.

Maritz, A., Perenyi, A., de Waal, G., & Buck, C. (2020). Entrepreneurship as the unsung hero during the current COVID-19 economic crisis: Australian perspectives. *Sustainability*, *12*(11), 4612.

McDougall, P. P., & Oviatt, B. M. (2000). International entrepreneurship: the intersection of two research paths. *Academy of management Journal*, *43*(5), 902-906.

McWilliams, A., & Siegel, D. (2000). Corporate social responsibility and financial performance: correlation or misspecification?. *Strategic management journal*, *21*(5), 603-609.

Newman, A., Obschonka, M., Schwarz, S., Cohen, M., & Nielsen, I. (2019). Entrepreneurial self-efficacy: A systematic review of the literature on its theoretical foundations, measurement, antecedents, and outcomes, and an agenda for future research. *Journal of Vocational Behavior*, *110*, 403-419.

Porter, M. E., & Kramer, M. R. (2019). Creating shared value. In *Managing sustainable business* (pp. 323-346). Springer, Dordrecht.

Rask, M. (2014). Internationalization through business model innovation: In search of relevant design dimensions and elements. *Journal of International Entrepreneurship*, *12*(2), 146-161.

Rennie, M. W. (1993). Born global. *The McKinsey Quarterly,* (4), 45-53.

Ritter, T., & Pedersen, C. L. (2020). Analyzing the impact of the coronavirus crisis on business models. *Industrial Marketing Management*, *88*, 214-224.

Sadeghi, V. J., Nkongolo-Bakenda, J. M., Anderson, R. B., & Dana, L. P. (2019). An institution-based view of international entrepreneurship: A comparison of context-based and universal determinants in developing and economically advanced countries. *International Business Review*, *28*(6), 101588.

Servantie, V., Cabrol, M., Guieu, G., & Boissin, J. P. (2016). Is international entrepreneurship a field? A bibliometric analysis of the literature (1989–2015). *Journal of International Entrepreneurship*, *14*(2), 168-212.

Srinivasan, A., & Venkatraman, N. (2018). Entrepreneurship in digital platforms: A network-centric view. *Strategic Entrepreneurship Journal*, *12*(1), 54-71.

Stam, E., & van de Ven, A. (2019). Entrepreneurial ecosystem elements. *Small Business Economics*, 1-24.

Tedeschi, R.G. and Calhoun, L.G. (2004). Posttraumatic growth: Conceptual foundations and empirical evidence, *Psychological Inquiry*, 15(1): 1-18.

Theodoraki, C., & Catanzaro, A. (forthcoming). Widening the borders of entrepreneurial ecosystem through the international lens, Journal of Technology Transfer. https://doi.org/10.1007/s10961-021-09852-7

Theodoraki, C., Messeghem, K., & Rice, M. P. (2018). A social capital approach to the development of sustainable entrepreneurial ecosystems: An explorative study. Small Business Economics, 51(1), 153–170.

UNCTAD (2021). Global Investment Trend Monitor, No. 38. Available: https://unctad.org/system/files/official-document/diaeiainf2021d1_en.pdf

Uzhegova, M., Torkkeli, L., & Saarenketo, S. (2019). Corporate Social Responsibility in SMEs: Implications on Competitive Performance. *Management revue*, *30*(2-3), 232-267.

Uzhegova, M., Torkkeli, L., & Ivanova-Gongne, M. (2020). The Role of Responsible Business Practices in International Business Relationships Between SMEs from Developed and Emerging Economies. In *International Business and Emerging Economy Firms* (pp. 17-59). Palgrave Macmillan, Cham.

Yang, M. M., Li, T., & Wang, Y. (2020). What explains the degree of internationalization of early-stage entrepreneurial firms? A multilevel study on the joint effects of entrepreneurial self-efficacy, opportunity-motivated entrepreneurship, and home-country institutions. *Journal of World Business*, *55*(6), 101114.

Velt, H., Torkkeli, L., & Saarenketo, S. (2018). Uncovering new value frontiers: the role of the entrepreneurial ecosystem in nurturing born globals. *International Journal of Export Marketing*, *2*(4), 316-342.

Velt, H., Torkkeli, L., & Saarenketo, S. (2020). Transnational entrepreneurial ecosystems: The perspectives of Finnish and Estonian born-global start-ups. In *Research Handbook on Start-Up Incubation Ecosystems*. Edward Elgar Publishing.

Verbeke, A., & Yuan, W. (2021). A Few Implications of the COVID-19 Pandemic for International Business Strategy Research. *Journal of Management Studies*.

Wenzel, M., Stanske, S., & Lieberman, M. B. (2020). Strategic responses to crisis. *Strategic Management Journal*.

Zahra, S. A., Korri, J. S., & Yu, J. (2005). Cognition and international entrepreneurship: implications for research on international opportunity recognition and exploitation. *International business review*, *14*(2), 129-146.

Zahra, S. A., Newey, L. R., & Li, Y. (2014). On the frontiers: The implications of social entrepreneurship for international entrepreneurship. *Entrepreneurship theory and practice*, *38*(1), 137-158.

Zahra, S. A. (2020a). International entrepreneurship in the post Covid world. *Journal of World Business*, 101143.

Zahra, S. A. (2020b). International Entrepreneurship (IE) in the Age of Political Turbulence. *Academy of Management Discoveries*, *6*(2), 172-175.

Zucchella, A. (2021). International entrepreneurship and the internationalization phenomenon: taking stock, looking ahead. *International Business Review*, 101800.